God and the Natural Law

Other St. Augustine's Press titles of interest

Thomas Aquinas, *Commentary on the Epistle to the Hebrews*

Thomas Aquinas, *Disputed Questions on Virtue*

Aristotle, *Aristotle – On Poetics*

Averroes, *Averroes' Middle Commentaries on Aristotle's Categories and De Interpretatione*

Averroes, *Averroes' Middle Commentary on Aristotle's Poetics*

Roger Bacon, *Roger Bacon's Philosophy of Nature*

Joseph Bobik, *Veritas Divina: Aquinas on Divine Truth*

Rémi Brague, *Eccentric Culture: A Theory of Western Civilization*

Peter Geach, *God and the Soul*

Zbigniew Janowski, *Augustinian-Cartesian Index*

John of St. Thomas, *Introduction to the* Summa Theologiae *of Thomas Aquinas*

Jacques Maritain, *Natural Law: Reflections on Theory and Practice*

Josef Pieper, *Scholasticism*

Josef Pieper, *The Silence of St. Thomas*

William of Ockham, *Ockham's Theory of Propositions*

William of Ockham, *Ockham's Theory of Terms*

Roger Pouivet, *After Wittgenstein, St. Thomas*

Francisco Suarez, *On Creation, Conservation, and Concurrence:* Metaphysical Disputations 20–22

Francisco Suarez, *Metaphysical Demonstration of the Existence of God:* Metaphysical Disputations 28–29

Henrik Syse, *Natural Law, Religion, and Rights*

Titles from Dumb Ox Books

Thomas Aquinas, *Commentary on Aristotle's De Anima*

Thomas Aquinas, *Commentary on Aristotle's Metaphysics*

Thomas Aquinas, *Commentary on Aristotle's Nicomachean Ethics*

Thomas Aquinas, *Commentary on Aristotle's Physics*

God and the Natural Law

A Rereading of Thomas Aquinas

Fulvio Di Blasi

Translated by David Thunder

Foreword to the American Edition by Ralph McInerny

Foreword to the Italian Edition by Mario A. Cattaneo

ST. AUGUSTINE'S PRESS
South Bend, Indiana

Manufactured in the United States of America.

2 3 4 5 6 28 27 26 25 24 23

Library of Congress Cataloging in Publication Data
Di Blasi, Fulvio.
[Dio e la legge naturale. English]
God and the natural law : a rereading of Thomas Aquinas / Fulvio di Blasi ; translated by David Thunder ; foreword to the American edition by Ralph McInerny. – 1st English ed.
p. cm.
Includes bibliographical references and index.
ISBN 1-58731-351-0 (alk. paper)
1. Thomas, Aquinas, Saint, 1225?–1274 – Contributions in natural law doctine. 2. Thomas, Aquinas, Saint, 1225?–1274 – Contributions in the theology of God. 3. Natural law – Religious aspects. I. Title.
K447.T45D53 2003
340'.112 – dc22
2003015944

∞ *The paper used in this publication meets the minimum requirements of the American National Standard for Information Sciences – Permanence of Paper for Printed Materials, ANSI Z39.48-1984.*

ST. AUGUSTINE'S PRESS
www.staugustine.net

Martha, Martha, you worry and fret about many things,
but only one thing is necessary.

– *Luke* 10: 41

Contents

Foreword to the English Edition

Ralph McInerny

Natural Law, in one definition of it, consists of the first inescapable judgments human persons make as to what is good or evil in their actions. Natural-law precepts are likened to the self-evident judgments anyone must make perforce if he is to reason at all. How then can it be that the subject is so controversial? Books and articles on natural law multiply, attacks and defenses of it abound. The book you are about to read is an excellent contribution to the ongoing controversy. But how can there be controversy over something allegedly so basic?

Perhaps it is helpful to distinguish between the fundamental practical thinking natural law is taken to be and theories about it. While it is difficult to imagine anyone saying that something both is and is not the case, say, that he is at once standing and sitting (save in some Pickwickian sense), it is not at all difficult to recognize that few get around to discussing what a self-evident proposition is or become skilled in discussing the nature of that which is *per se notum quoad omnes*. Theories of natural law presuppose what they are theories of and do not themselves produce it, just as the logic of self-evident propositions presupposes them and does not produce them. Of course, the two, the theory and what it is a theory of, are related, but what the theory is about comes first and is fundamental. Fulvio Di Blasi's book operates on the level of theory and, while it clarifies what is meant by natural law, those judgments no human agent can fail to make, it is not a first-order establishing of them.

St. Augustine said that, while he had met men who wished to deceive others, he had not met anyone who wished to be deceived himself. Of course he did not mean that an account of why this is so goes hand in hand with the realization. Cardinal Newman said that although all men have a reason when they act, not all can give a reason. So too the content of the Golden Rule did not await the Scriptural formulation for its acceptance. Do unto others as you would have them do unto you. When we hear the formulation we recognize that it expresses something we already knew. That the lives of the innocent cannot be taken, that what belongs to others cannot be borrowed without permission, that the spouses of others are not legitimate prey—these and other home truths are rightly thought to be part of the moral outlook of everyone, however they might actually behave. Fulvio Di Blasi's book raises the question whether acknowledgment of the existence of God is present among the things everyone can be expected already to acknowledge.

An affirmative answer to that question would be difficult to defend, as it is not difficult to defend the givenness of judgments about wives and property and innocent human lives. There may be a pre-philosophical knowledge of God's existence—many have argued for it, among them St. Thomas Aquinas and Jacques Maritain—but we are likely to be more struck by the difficulties involved in formulating philosophical proofs of His existence. Religious faith provides conviction on the matter from our mother's knee, of course, but then natural law would seem to be independent of faith. How can God be crucial for natural law?

The distinction between theory and what it is a theory of is crucial here. It would be odd for anyone to say that everyone's grasp of fundamental guides for moral action involves explicit recognition of the existence of God. But it is not odd to say that any adequate account or theory of such fundamental guides must make appeal to God's existence. No wonder another definition of natural law is that it is the peculiarly human participation in the eternal law, that is, in God's providential ordering of things.

If there is a God and we are his creatures, obviously such truths must affect our understanding of what we ought and ought not do. Any adequate theory of basic moral judgments would have to recognize God as the author of the moral law. Fulvio di Blasi has written a book that shows the inevitably theistic character of any adequate account of natural law. You will read it to your profit.

Foreword to the Italian Edition

MARIO A. CATTANEO

The originality of the methodological approach of this book lies in the fact that its author—the young scholar Fulvio Di Blasi—undertakes a rethinking of natural law theory while simultaneously confronting several trends in modern philosophy of law. Di Blasi has in recent years investigated in depth the thinking of philosopher and legal theorist John Mitchell Finnis, whose book *Natural Law and Natural Rights* he translated into Italian in 1996. Finnis, in turn, had carried on a critical "discussion" with the thought of H.L.A. Hart a legal theorist working in the analytic tradition who was certainly open both to substantial values and to natural law theory.

Di Blasi's current research is in a certain sense the offspring of his work on Finnis and of his translation of *Natural Law and Natural Rights*, since in this research he critically engages the "neoclassical theory of natural law," of which Finnis, along with Germain Grisez and Joseph Boyle, is among the principal exponents. His evaluation of this theory leads him to undertake a "rereading" of Thomistic thought and a reevaluation of natural law theory from a metaphysical perspective, calling into question the analytic dogma of the great separation between "is" and "ought," and taking a strong stand against certain interpretive trends that are committed to excluding the religious viewpoint from natural law theory—almost to the point of presenting a "Thomistic" doctrine without reference to God. With respect to this last point, an especially noteworthy feature of the present book is the relationship it establishes between the concept of *lex naturalis* and the proofs for the existence of God. As he considers the scholastic tradition, Di Blasi underlines the perennial centrality of God as a moral problem for man.

This book thus has the merit of showing how modern philosophical approaches to law are still capable of confronting authentic values and truly ethical themes (indeed, metaphysical principles), thereby avoiding the risk of ending up nowhere that threatens all too many contemporary studies. Fulvio Di Blasi's study reminds us that the true task of the philosopher is that of "leaving the cave" and ascending once more to the light of ideas.

Translator's Note

In translating *Dio e la legge naturale* (*God and the Natural Law*), I had the good fortune to be enrolled as a doctoral student in the university at which the author was a visiting Professor (University of Notre Dame, Indiana). Consequently, this translation has benefited from extensive consultation and discussions between the author and the translator, which, under ordinary circumstances, would not have been possible.

The employment of English translations of Aquinas's works was an especially delicate task, which required the author's close collaboration. Where the English translation conflicted with the author's understanding of the Latin text, we did not hesitate to alter it; otherwise, the texts of Aquinas are taken directly from published English translations.

Obviously, wherever an original English text was quoted or referred to in Italian, the English text is restored in this edition. For non-English texts that are referred to (but not quoted) in Italian, either the English translation—where one is available—or the original edition, is cited, in lieu of the Italian edition. For non-English quotations in general, where no English translation was available, I have cited the same edition as the author (whether he used the original, or a published Italian translation) and translated the quotations (from Italian) exactly as they occur in this book. In short, except in cases where an English translation or title is explicitly referred to, quotations of non-English origin have been translated from the Italian version, exactly as they occur in *Dio e la legge naturale*.

There is a saying in Italian, *il traduttore tradice, not traduce*—"the translator betrays, he does not translate." While I believe we must reconcile ourselves to the inevitability of a certain semantic loss in all translations, I hope to have confined this loss as much as possible to the side of style rather than content. This seems appropriate for a philosophical work, whereas it would be much more questionable for a work of literature or art.

Finally, I have kept translator's notes to a minimum, to avoid unnecessarily cluttering or expanding the scholarly apparatus of the book. I have included all of the works in the original Bibliography, except Italian translations of English works; I have also added several English editions used by this translation, especially the editions of primary sources such as Aquinas's works.

Preface to the English Edition

I finished writing *Dio e la Legge Naturale* in 1998—a long time ago for a young scholar! It goes without saying that today I would write it very differently.

While working with the translator, I did not hesitate to change the original text, whether to correct mistakes or to clarify certain points or to add comments and bibliographical references. At the end of the project, the translation became a revised edition. Still, the book is far from doing justice either to the last five years of scholarly debate or or to the developments of my own thought and of my interpretation of Aquinas. This is not to say that I have changed my mind concerning the main theses of the book or its conclusion. Moreover, I still like the book as a whole; especially because it was written with the idea not of giving a complete account of the issues involved but of offering to the reader, from beginning to end, a long, continuous, *personal* train of thought. Many friends and colleagues have assured me that the book is not boring and that, whatever one's personal opinion on the issue, it is very helpful in seriously reconsidering the question of the relevance of God for moral life. This was a tremendous compliment; I trust that it was not just due to politeness.

These are excellent years for Thomistic studies. The debate on Aquinas and his natural law theory is rich and fruitful. Nonetheless, we are still in a moment of *rediscovery*, in which many Thomistic concepts and theses are confused or even unknown. Many students of Aquinas, for example, do not understand the difference between knowledge of the good and practical knowledge, or the connection between the concept of law and the concept of inclination, or in what sense law is an external principle of action. Key concepts like the good, ultimate end, practical reason, and participation often receive such a narrow and limited consideration that Aquinas's genuine thought ends up being seriously distorted and misrepresented. There are even scholars who think that, for Aquinas, "love of God" is not the first precept of natural law and the ultimate end of moral life. In the last five years I have been working on the concepts I just mentioned in a way that goes well beyond the limits of this book. However, recent publications and scholarly discussions have convinced me that the book is still a useful contribution to the *Rereading of Aquinas*.

Acknowledgments

In this moment, my thought goes first of all to my parents, from whose exemplary lives I first received the ethics that I now study, and who have always guided my choices and given me both material and moral support. "With your whole heart honor your father; your mother's birth pangs forget not. Remember, of these parents you were born; what can you give them for all they gave you?" (Sirach 7: 27–28). Then to my brothers Riccardo, Alberto, and Giulio, of whom I like to say—with Aristotle—that we are "in a sense the same thing, though in separate individuals" (*Nic. Eth.*, VIII, 1161b32–3).

I wrote the original version of the book in Palermo while working for the *Collegio Universitario ARCES*, especially as Secretary and Tutor of the *Residenza Universitaria Segesta*. My research in those years owes much to the friends, colleagues and students I met in these institutions. Moreover, the *Collegio Universitario ARCES* gave to me the much-needed financial support for getting the book done.

My greatest debt is to Vittorio Villa, who read the whole manuscript more than once, and to Francesco Viola, who has always supported my graduate and post-doctoral studies. Mario A. Cattaneo strongly promoted the publication of the book. I am grateful for his show of esteem and appreciation for my scholarship in his foreword to the Italian edition. I want to thank him with special affection. I want also to thank the staff of Edizioni ETS's staff and Domenico Corradini Broussard, director of the series "Pubblicazioni di Scienze Filosofiche e Giuridiche" in which the Italian book was published.

I received many useful corrections and suggestions from friends and colleagues at the Department of Politics, Law, and Society of the University of Palermo. I would like to remember particularly Bruno Celano, Isabel Trujillo Perez, Aldo Schiavello, and Lucia Triolo; but also Alessandro Argiroffi, Guido Corso, and Mirella Urso. I am also very grateful for the insightful discussions, suggestions, and support I have received from Miguel Acosta Lòpez, Fortunato Tito Arecchi, Serenella Armellini, Vicente Bellver Capella, Roberto Bin, Gaetano Carcaterra, Pierpaolo Donati, Armando Fumagalli, Robert A. Gahl, Giuseppe Girgenti, Antonio Livi, Vittorio Possenti, and Gianfrancesco Zanetti.

The English version of the book is a story in itself. After I began working with Ralph McInerny as research associate at the Jacques Maritain Center of the University of Notre Dame, he read the original Italian book. Ralph commented that the book should have been published in English, and, fortunately for me, Bruce Fingerhut—director of the St. Augustine's Press—fully agreed with Ralph over a dinner that we were all enjoying together at the Notre Dame University Club. I do not remember what I ate, or even what (red) wine I drank, but it was definitely one of my best dinners ever. Since that memorable moment in the University Club, I have continued to learn a great deal from Ralph and have been able to incorporate many of his suggestions into this English-language edition. While I am in great debt to Ralph for his scholarship, I owe him even more for his example of virtue. Working with him at the Jacques Maritain Center has been for me an important stimulus to be a better person, and this is my greatest debt to him.

I should mention that as work progressed, Bruce Fingerhut and David Thunder became much more than my "publisher" and my "translator." They became very good friends. David and I worked so hard together, even during a period in Sicily, that one could might it a miracle that we have remained close friends even now that we have concluded our work on the last chapter. I am very grateful to both of them. I'm also very grateful to Christopher Mirus, whose help was priceless. He has read most of the essays I have written in the past three years, helping me to improve my English and offering challenging discussion of nearly every concept dealt with in my book. Finally, he proofread the whole translation, making many important corrections *ad mentem auctoris*. I would also like to mention Stephen Brock, who noticed a mistake I made regarding Aquinas's concept of *quidditas rei materialis*; Jeffrey Langan, who helped me in editing and revising the introductory chapter; and Robert A. Gahl, who helped me in editing the acknowledgments and the Preface.

My gratitude to God appears in the dedication of the book: a line from the Gospel that came again and again to my mind while writing, and that reflects in several ways the content and meaning of my thought and my choices.

Introduction

1. Natural Law and Analytical Philosophy

Historically, the term "natural law" acquires its deepest philosophical meaning in Aquinas's famous synthesis. Natural law is nature revealing itself to human reason as willed by God. The existence of such a law is made manifest, in the words of St. Thomas, as "a dictate of reason commanding something (*rationis dictamen per modum praecipiendi*)."[1] The concept of natural law encompasses not only legal theory in the strict sense, but the entire ethical order. It points to God as the axiological foundation of the ethical order, and entails a moral view in which human action ultimately takes its meaning from an *act of obedience*, out of love, to the order placed in things by God. From these few considerations alone, it is clear that the two key notions supporting the concept of natural law, around which this book revolves, are the notions of *nature* and of the *will of God*: natural law implies not only that the human intellect can know the order of nature objectively, but also that, through this order, it can come to know and to love God.

The richest and best known definition of natural law is that of Thomas Aquinas, who is universally considered the greatest and most eminent exponent of this tradition of thought. For him, natural law is a "participation in the eternal law by a rational creature," where participation (as we

1 St. Thomas Aquinas, *Summa theologiae*, I-II, q. 92, a. 2 c. [Translator's note: Quotations of the Summa theologiae generally reproduce the translation of the Fathers of the English Dominican Province, except where the Italian translation differs significantly, in which case I follow the Italian translation of the Domenicani italiani (Florence: Salani, 1967) used by the author.]

will see in chapter two) refers to created beings' relationship of similarity with and essential dependence on the first cause that produced them from nothing. The eternal law is the act of "divine wisdom" that wills things in view of an end, this end being God himself, and governs them in view of that end, imprinting in their being a movement that is necessary in non-rational beings, and normative in man. The "dictate of reason commanding something" of which the eternal law consists, exists, then, in the divine intellect "as in that which rules and measures" and in created beings "as in that which is ruled and measured." More specifically, the eternal law exists in non-human beings as the rationality of the inclination that regulates their movement by necessity (laws of nature), and in man as the rational inclination—or normative knowledge—of his practical reason, which regulates his free action in view of the ultimate end (natural law).[2]

St. Thomas's thought, both theoretical and practical, is currently attracting a surprising degree of interest, especially on account of the attention it has received from contemporary analytic philosophers. Just a few of the more distinguished names are Elizabeth Anscombe and Peter Geach, Alasdair MacIntyre, Anthony Kenny, Ralph McInerny, and John Finnis. Aquinas has become so popular among analytic thinkers that John Haldane has spoken of an "analytical Thomism," which he discussed in the *Oxford Companion to Philosophy* (1995), and to which the entire fourth issue (1997) of *The Monist*, edited by Haldane, was dedicated, with contributions from Hilary Putnam and Brian Davies among others.

For Haldane, analytic philosophy is "the most developed form of critical analysis and rigorous argumentation in history," but it has for long falsely maintained that "clarifying philosophical problems was all there was to do." Analytic philosophy has maintained, for example, that the "mind-body problem" is not that of knowing whether the mind is "something physical or immaterial," but that of understanding that the word "mind" indicates "certain capacities (to think, to feel, to decide, etc.)" and that "which types of things can have such capacities is another question." By this tendency, Haldane says, analytic philosophy has shown a "characteristic negligence towards the history of philosophy." The idea, for example, that "having a mind does not imply having an object other than one's body, but rather having a collection of capacities, is at least as old as Aristotle," and "it is a mistake to suppose that arriving" at consciousness about the meaning of the term "puts an end to the metaphysical question

2 *ST*, I-II, q. 91, aa. 1–2.

of materialism." "It is interesting to note," he points out in this regard, "that Aristotle, towards the end of his *De anima*, appears to argue" that the nature of intellectual capacities is such "that they cannot belong to something purely material."

"A constant defect of analytical philosophy," continues Haldane, "is the lack of a sense of the metaphysical dimension of the majority of traditional philosophical problems. Clarity is necessary in order to adequately bring to light the important questions, but it is not sufficient in order to respond to them." The "genius" of St. Thomas has created an "interesting, complete and coherent" body of thought, that "synthesizes brilliantly Aristotelian philosophy and Christian theology," and can do "much to complement the methodological approach emphasized by analytical philosophy." Analytical Thomism, however, is not interested in any "particular set of doctrines" of Aquinas; neither is it a "movement of pious exegesis." "Instead, it seeks to deploy the methods and ideas of twentieth-century philosophy—of the sort dominant within the English-speaking world—in connection with the broad framework of ideas introduced and developed by Aquinas." "The possibility of a synthesis of analytical form and Thomistic content," Haldane concludes, "is a fascinating prospect."[3]

In general, besides Haldane's observations, one could say that the analytic revival of St. Thomas has meant, in the theoretical field, that metaphysical thought is enjoying more attention and credibility than it previously had; while in the practical field, the same can be said of the objectivity of moral judgments, virtue and natural law. In both cases, the Thomistic renewal has eroded the traditional, and long-undisputed, positivistic presuppositions of analytic philosophy.

The present work, however, was inspired neither by St. Thomas nor directly by natural law, but by a study begun in my Master's thesis of the meaning and implications of the current revival of natural law theory, specifically in Anglo-American analytic philosophy. During the course of this research I discovered, first through the Thomistically inspired "neo-classical" school of thought, the idea of a natural law that is both *atheistic* (that is, not "law" properly speaking, since it does not depend on the will of God, and so is not produced by a Legislator) and *without nature*

3 See both the *Oxford Companion to Philosophy* and no. 4 (1997) of *The Monist*; see also J. Haldane, "Tomismo Analitico," *Il Sole-24 Ore*, 2 August 1998. For a recent critical response to the idea of analytical Thomism, see B.J. Shanley, O.P., "Analytical Thomism," *The Thomist* 1 (1999).

(that is, not properly speaking "natural" because dissociated from the facts knowable by theoretical reason). Then, through the observations of neo-Thomist Henry Veatch, I discovered the concept of a natural law that was atheistic, but truly "natural," since it was founded on the experiential knowledge of *human nature*. And finally, through St. Thomas himself, I discovered the full concept of a law that is both natural and *promulgated* by God in the very being of things. Within this concept, contrary to common belief, reference to God does not depend on religious belief, and it turns out to be essential to the very idea of a philosophical ethics of natural law.

The present book will follow the outline set out below:

In the first chapter, the main objective will be to bring to light, by comparing the "neoclassical" and the so-called "conventional" schools of thought, the way in which the dialectical interplay of "order of nature" and "will of God" is characteristic of natural law theory. Interpretations of Aquinas have often been determined by different approaches to this interplay, which is expressed in the language of contemporary philosophical discourse in terms of ethical autonomy and heteronomy. In this context, the challenge frequently facing contemporary interpretations of Thomistic moral philosophy is to rediscover, in the face of a robust voluntaristic and legalistic tradition termed "conventional" or "neoscholastic," an accurate concept of ethical autonomy.

Generally, the conventional position is thought to have originated with Francisco Suárez. However, in reality Suárez was searching in his work for a mediation between the nominalists on the one hand—who traced the natural law back to the will of God *alone*—and the antinominalists on the other—who, removing all value from God's will, traced natural law back to human nature *alone*. The antinominalist or autonomist tends both to adopt the idea of an ethics without God (or a double ethic, one philosophical and one theological), and to depreciate the *law-like* character of natural law. The historical backdrop provided by the nominalist-antinominalist dispute enables us to frame the current trend of contemporary interpreters of St. Thomas, such as the neoclassicists, in terms of a new antinominalism.

In the second chapter, "The Presupposition of *Lex Naturalis:* Man as *Capax Dei*," having noted the current interpretive tendency, I will begin by clarifying how Aquinas understood the ethical relevance of the will of God. This relevance is radical—absolute—because, according to the Angelic Doctor, man is good only when he wants something *because God wants it.* Now if the term "natural law" indicates a philosophical view in which morality ultimately means obedience to God, this approach is entirely consistent. But it can only be justified if St. Thomas's philosophy is capable not only of reaching knowledge of God, but also of giving an account of such knowledge that encompasses and explains the entire ethical horizon of human beings. The overall purpose of the second chapter, accordingly, will be to do justice to both of these concerns.

Having dealt with what is now the most delicate and controversial philosophical presupposition of natural law, and perhaps of Thomistic thought more generally, we can finally move on in the third chapter to address directly the concepts of *lex* and *lex naturalis*. Law is introduced into Aquinas's system as the extrinsic principle of human acts that, in the natural order, directs them toward the good (in the supernatural order, law is supplemented by the extrinsic principle of grace). It is thus that the *heteronomy* essential to the Thomistic concept of law originates. The law always presupposes at least two subjects: one (the legislator) in whom it resides "as in that which rules and measures;" and one in which it resides "as in that which is ruled and measured." For St. Thomas, obligation always arises from the heteronomy of the command, but the relationship of obedience between the two subjects can depend either on love (obligation in a moral sense) or on fear (obligation in a merely legal sense), and obedience out of love implies a *sharing of the end.*

"Eternal law" (of which natural law is a part) means God—as "that which rules and measures"—directing all created things to Himself as to their ultimate end. The *efficacy* of eternal law lies in the necessary movement imposed on everything with respect to its specific and proper end: this is the origin of the doctrine of natural inclinations and ends. The natural inclinations are the mode in which the eternal law exists in things "as in that which is ruled and measured," and are therefore the source of *autonomy* in the Thomistic concept of law. In the case of the natural law, such autonomy implies that man—"as that which is ruled and measured," and is called to obey the law freely, out of love—necessarily knows his ultimate end and wants it more than anything else. The intrinsic openness and natural inclination of the human intellect and will to God as the Fullness of Truth and Goodness are at the root of the doctrine of natural law (the intrinsic openness of human knowledge to God is treated in particular in section 3.8, "The Metaphysical Experience of Being," while all of section 4, "The Inclination To God," is an explanation of the openness and inclination to God of the human will).

Love of God as one's ultimate end is the foundation of the morality of human acts, and it depends on respect for the natural order willed by God. Therefore, after explaining that the essential character of natural law is the ordering of man to his ultimate end, I will dedicate most of chapter three to showing the harmony, within Thomistic ethics, between the order of nature and the will of God. In that chapter I will point out the different elements that constitute the natural order and address in detail a specific moral case discussed by Aquinas: fornication. A shortcoming of many general explanations of Thomistic ethics is their failure (or reluctance) to pursue thoroughly the application of this ethics to concrete cases.

A final point: in order to deal with the typology of laws delineated by St. Thomas, and to develop the more interesting aspects of it, I have chosen to follow, for the most part, the thematic and expository order of the *Summa contra gentiles*, indicating as I proceed its relationship with the *Summa theologiae*. This strategy is fitting for several reasons, which I will explain in the third chapter. Not least among them, however, is that the clarity and completeness of the *Summa theologiae* have often led scholars to neglect St. Thomas's other works, or even to mistakenly perceive elements of discontinuity between these and the *Summa theologiae*. The *Summa contra gentiles* does not yet achieve the breadth and systematicity of the *Summa theologiae*, but precisely for this reason, read in the light of developments found in Aquinas's more mature work, it does permit a more flexible treatment of his concept of *lex*, and one more directly linked to the other aspects of his theoretical and practical thought.

In the remainder of this introduction I will briefly outline the developments, especially those in Finnis, Hart, the neoclassical school, and Veatch, that have led me to reread the original Thomistic concept of natural law, and to open up my research to the wider field of ethics. Only by coming to this broader perspective is it possible to address the special spheres of justice and rights.

2. John Finnis

My research was originally stimulated by the theory of natural law advanced by John Finnis in his *Natural Law and Natural Rights* (Oxford: Clarendon Press, 1980).[4] Indeed, this book, from its first appearance, attracted the attention of scholars of ethics, law and politics as the most

4 I subsequently had the opportunity to translate this book into Italian (J. Finnis, *Legge naturale e diritti naturali*, trans. F. Di Blasi [Turin: Giappichelli, 1996]).

impressive and original attempt to provide a critical defense of the classical themes of natural law and of natural rights, which, in contemporary philosophy of law, especially in the analytic tradition, had by then fallen into total discredit.[5]

Scholars spanning a range of backgrounds immediately took up Finnis's book with a certain enthusiasm. According to Neil MacCormick, one of its greatest merits is to have drawn fresh attention to the problematic nature of the terms "natural law" and "positivism," which do not indicate two unitary and contrasting conceptions of law, but whole families of theories so diversified that "there are at least as many ways of being a natural lawyer as there are of being a positivist," and the problem is to see whether one of them is defensible.[6] Henry Veatch opines that before Finnis's book all scholars who were "of [any] note or standing" would have considered natural law doctrines to be "entitled to survival only as historical curiosities."[7] A few years later Lloyd Weinreb wrote in *Natural Law and Justice* that "in his book [...] John Finnis has developed the most substantial and serious contemporary theory to which the label 'natural law' attaches."[8] Around the same time, Russell Hittinger published *A Critique of the New Natural Law Theory*, which is still considered by many to be one of the most significant texts in which the theory is

5 A typical example would be the following words of Ronald Dworkin: "Everyone likes categories, and legal philosophers like them very much. So we spend a good deal of time, not all of it profitably, labeling ourselves and the theories of law we defend. One label, however, is particularly dreaded: no one wants to be called a natural lawyer. Natural law insists that what the law is depends in some way on what the law should be. This seems metaphysical or at least vaguely religious. In any case it seems plainly wrong. If some theory of law is shown to be a natural law theory, therefore, people can be excused if they do not attend to it much further." R. Dworkin, "Natural Law Revisited," *University of Florida Law Review*, 34 (1982), p. 165.

6 N. MacCormick, "Natural Law Reconsidered," *Oxford Journal of Legal Studies*, 1 (1981), p. 99. See also MacCormick's "The Ideal and the Actual of Law and Society," in J. Tasioulas (ed.), *Law, Values and Social Practices* (Aldershot: Dartmouth Publishing Co., 1997).

7 H.B. Veatch, "Natural Law and the 'Is-Ought' Question: Queries to Finnis and Grisez," in H.B. Veatch, *Swimming against the Current in Contemporary Philosophy* (Washington, DC: The Catholic University of America Press, 1981), p. 293.

8 L.L. Weinreb, *Natural Law and Justice* (Harvard: Harvard University Press, 1987), p. 108.

expounded and criticized.[9] Robert George offered a response to the criticisms advanced by Weinreb and Hittinger in one of his earliest works, *Recent Criticism of Natural Law Theory.*[10] Today the credibility of Finnis's natural law theory is undisputed, and an ever-increasing body of writings touches upon his thought, directly or indirectly.[11]

3. Finnis and Hart

As Finnis himself has pointed out, Anglo-American analytic jurisprudence—most notably the work of Herbert Hart—played a significant role in the genesis of his natural law theory.[12] This notable relationship, however, does not hold with respect to the "minimum content of natural law" which Hart speaks of in Chapter IX of *The Concept of Law* (Oxford: Oxford University Press, 1961).[13] Regarding the "minimum content," Finnis would certainly agree with Mario A. Cattaneo that such a concept cannot solve the problem of obligation, or indeed the naturalistic fallacy, since it confines itself to a simple descriptive analysis of the minimal conditions for the existence of a legal system.[14] The connection between

9 R. Hittinger, *A Critique of the New Natural Law Theory* (Notre Dame: University of Notre Dame Press, 1987).

10 R.P. George, "Recent Criticism of Natural Law Theory," *University of Chicago Law Review*, 55 (1988).

11 Among the more recent works, see C. Covell, *The Defence of Natural Law* (New York: St. Martin's Press, 1992); A. J. Lisska, *Aquinas's Theory of Natural Law: An Analytic Reconstruction* (Oxford: Clarendon Press, 1996). As a general introduction to Finnis's thought, see G. Zanetti, *John M. Finnis e la nuova dottrina del diritto naturale*, in G. Zanetti (ed.), *Filosofi del diritto contemporanei* (Milan: Cortina, 1999).

12 Hart supervised Finnis's doctoral studies, and a year after their completion, when Finnis returned to Hart's college as a colleague, he asked Finnis to write a book for the Clarendon Law Series (of which Hart was founder and editor), suggesting that it be entitled *Natural Law and Natural Rights.*

13 See also H.L.A. Hart, "Are there Any Natural Rights?," *Philosophical Review*, 64 (1955) (also published in A. Quinton, ed., *Political Philosophy* [Oxford: Oxford University Press, 1967]); "Positivism and the Separation of Law and Morals," *Harvard Law Review*, 71 (1958). The Italian edition of *The Concept of Law* includes a very useful introduction to Hart's thought by M.A. Cattaneo: see H.L.A. Hart, *Il concetto di diritto*, trans. M.A. Cattaneo (Turin: Einaudi, 1965).

14 See M.A. Cattaneo, "Il diritto naturale nel pensiero di H.L.A. Hart," Rivista internazionale di filosofia del diritto 4 (1965), 690–92: "This natural law cannot support a general ethical theory, to the extent that it cannot found an obligation of obe-

Finnis's and Hart's thought lies rather in the so-called "internal point of view," which is at the core of Hart's doctrine. The "internal point of view," according to Finnis, opens the possibility of a critical reflection on the agent's values (understood as practical principles); and this reflection, through the analysis of "the central case and focal meaning," leads to the identification of a series of basic and objective human values.

In a 1977 article dedicated to an explanation and defense, in a dispute with Hart, of the basic value of truth, Finnis ascribed to Hart the notable merit of having restored the "theoretical vigour of jurisprudence," opening it up to the possibility of an *analysis* of the values which guide human conduct. "By inviting and inciting us to reflect on the implications of our own dispositions to act, *The Concept of Law* restores the theoretical vigour of jurisprudence and its openness to all the other philosophy and sciences of human affairs. Throughout that book, we are asked to reflect on 'what we would say when...' But having been coaxed beyond the observation and correlation of external events and behavioral responses, we are asked not merely to relate such patterns of activity with patterns of language use, but also, and more fruitfully, to relate both external activity and use of language with the attitudes, dispositions, desires, interests, acceptances, presuppositions, and, indeed, the reasons, which we either have, or could understand having, in relation to such ways of acting and speaking. Patterns of behaviour and patterns of linguistic activity alike *display* patterns of reason(ing) and will(ingness); jurisprudence advances by going behind the display."[15]

For Finnis, behavioral and more strictly linguistic analyses conceal a deeper explanation of human attitudes and dispositions, which ultimately leads back to what the agent sees as *good reasons* for action. In the introduction to a collection of writings on natural law published in 1991, Finnis even suggests that there is a parallel between this Hartian perspective and

dience which is meaningful for everyone, and different from mere fear, submission to force [...] It seems to me, then, that the most accurate interpretation of Hart's natural law doctrine is that which considers it an essentially descriptive theory, fulfilling at this level a legitimate function." On the other hand, with respect to the concept of "critical morality" which Hart refers to in *Law, Liberty and Morality* (London: Oxford University Press, 1963), Cattaneo argues that such a concept "is not determined with much precision (nor, perhaps, is it possible to do so)."

15 J. Finnis, "Scepticism, Self-Refutation, and the Good of Truth," in P. Hacker and J. Raz (eds.), *Law, Morality and Society: Essays in Honour of H.L.A. Hart* (Oxford: Clarendon Press, 1977), p. 247.

internal ethical reflection on practical knowledge; and that in drawing attention to the various types of justification for human decisions, contemporary jurisprudence is in line with the principal mode of argumentation used by natural law and political theory.[16] The basic criticism Finnis addresses to Hart in *Natural law and Natural Rights* is that he did not develop an adequate range of the possible internal (practical) points of view, and consequently, failed to distinguish secondary or peripheral points of view from the central one. If he had done this, he would have noticed, according to Finnis, that the central internal point of view, which the student of social facts must assume in his analysis in order to describe his subject-matter, is that of the citizen who confers on norms an intrinsic moral value.[17]

4. The Neoclassical Theory of Natural Law

Hart, however, is only a starting point, the source of an intuition. In reality, Finnis elaborates and grounds his theory on a peculiar rereading of Thomas Aquinas's *lex naturalis*. This fact moved me, in a second stage of my investigation, to divert my attention from Hart, Raz and analytical jurisprudence toward the Thomistic concept of natural law and the various interpretations of it offered by contemporary scholars. Finnis is not alone in his interest in Aquinas's thought. On the contrary, since 1963, he, along with Germain Grisez and Joseph Boyle, have sustained an interpretive school that explicitly names itself *neoclassical*, in open opposition to those interpretations commonly described and generically defined as *neoscholastic*, and more specifically *conventional*.

Over successive years, several other authors (such as G.V. Bradley, J. Ford, R.P. George, P. Lee, R. Lawler, W.E. May, R. Shaw, and O. Tollefsen) have joined the neoclassical school of thought. These thinkers, though they have advanced personal (and sometimes conflicting) opinions and claims on a variety of particular questions, have all accepted a single concept of natural law, understood as a particular method of grounding ethics objectively.[18] Neoclassical theory has given rise to a wide-ranging

16 J. Finnis (ed.), *Natural Law*, Vol. I (Aldershot: Dartmouth, 1991), Introduction.

17 See J. Finnis, *Natural Law and Natural Rights*, ch. 1. S. Toddington takes the same line as Finnis on this point, in *Rationality, Social Action and Moral Judgment* (Edinburgh: Edinburgh University Press, 1993).

18 Among the most important texts for understanding the theory correctly, from its first steps to its most complete elaboration, are (in chronological order): G. Grisez, *Contraception and the Natural Law* (Milwaukee: The Bruce Publishing Company,

debate,[19] and is assuming ever greater importance not only within legal philosophy, but also in philosophical ethics more strictly speaking,[20] as well as in moral theology[21] and in the ongoing ethical and political debate between liberals and communitarians. This is due in no small part to Robert George, not only because of his personal interest in political theo-

1964); G. Grisez, "The First Principle of Practical Reason: A Commentary on the *Summa theologiae*, 1–2, Question 94, Article 2," *Natural Law Forum*, 10 (1965); G. Grisez, *Abortion: The Myths, the Realities, and the Arguments* (New York: Corpus Book, 1970); G. Grisez-R. Shaw, *Beyond the New Morality: The Responsibilities of Freedom* (Notre Dame: University of Notre Dame Press, 1974) (also the third revised edition, 1988); J. Finnis, *Natural Law and Natural Rights* (1980); J. Finnis, *Fundamentals of Ethics* (Oxford: Clarendon Press, 1983); G. Grisez, *The Way of the Lord Jesus*, Vol. I, *Christian Moral Principles* (Chicago: Franciscan Herald Press, 1983) (with the help of Joseph M. Boyle, Jr., Basil Cole, O.P., John M. Finnis, John A. Geinzer, Jeannette Grisez, Robert G. Kennedy, Patrick Lee, William E. May, and Russell Shaw); Finnis, Grisez, Boyle, Jr., *Nuclear Deterrence, Morality and Realism* (Oxford: Clarendon Press, 1987); Finnis, Grisez, Boyle, Jr., "Practical Principles, Moral Truth, and Ultimate Ends," *American Journal of Jurisprudence*, 32 (1987); J. Finnis, *Moral Absolutes: Tradition, Revision and Truth* (Washington, D.C.: The Catholic University of America Press, 1991); G. Grisez, *The Way of the Lord Jesus*, Vol. II, *Living a Christian Life*, (Quincy, Illinois: Franciscan Press, 1993) (with the help of Joseph Boyle, Jeannette Grisez, Russell Shaw, and others); J. Finnis, *Aquinas: Moral, Political, and Legal Theory* (Oxford: Oxford University Press, 1998).

19 Criticisms not already cited include R. McInerny, "The Principles of Natural Law," *The American Journal of Jurisprudence*, 25 (1980); R. McInerny, *Ethica Thomistica* (University of Notre Dame Press: Notre Dame, 1982); H.B. Veatch, "Natural Law and the 'Is-Ought' Question: Queries to Finnis and Grisez"; H.B. Veatch, *Human Rights: Fact or Fancy?* (Baton Rouge, Louisiana: Louisiana State University Press, 1985); R.A. McCormick, *Notes on Moral Theology: 1981–1984* (University Press of America: Lanham, Md., 1985); A. Donagan, *The Theory of Morality* (University of Chicago Press: Chicago, 1977); R.A. Gahl Jr., *Practical Reason in the Foundation of Natural Law According to Germain Grisez, John Finnis and Joseph Boyle, Jr.*, Doctoral Dissertation directed by Prof. Gabriel Chalmeta, Roman Atheneum of the Holy Cross, Faculty of Philosophy, Rome 1991.

20 See M. Rhonheimer, *La prospettiva della morale: Fondamenti dell'etica filosofica*, trans. A. Jappe (Rome: Armando, 1994).

21 See, for example, R.G. de Haro, *La vida cristiana: curso de teología moral fundamental* (Pamplona: EUNSA, 1982); L. Melina, *Morale: Tra crisi e rinnovamento* (Milan: Edizioni Ares, 1993); E. Molina, *La moral entre la convicción y la utilidad: La evolución de la moral desde la manualística al proporcionalismo y al pensamiento de Grisez-Finnis* (Pamplona: Ediciones Eunate/Servicio de Publicaciones de la Universidad de Navarra, 1996).

ry, but also because the collections he has recently edited have facilitated a wide-ranging scholarly debate on different elements of the theory.[22]

The neoclassicists, with their background in contemporary analytic philosophy, are deeply affected by the methodological principle that value judgments cannot be logically derived from the knowledge of facts of nature: a principle generally referred to as Hume's law or, after Moore, the naturalistic fallacy.[23] This rigid separation between facts and values is in large part the fruit of modern science's rejection of the concept of natural finality,[24] and has led contemporary ethics to a general attitude of skepticism toward norms or moral principles; these are mostly seen as not ultimately justifiable, but the outcome of arbitrary personal preferences.

It is precisely in this sense that Alasdair MacIntyre has defined contemporary culture as emotivist, meaning by emotivism "the doctrine that all evaluative judgments and more specifically all moral judgments are nothing but expressions of preference, expressions of attitude or feeling, insofar as they are moral or evaluative in character."[25] For MacIntyre, the emotivist culture is the domain of arbitrariness in which there is no rational foundation for objective ethical statements, but only individual preferences of the will. In this domain, the attitude toward the other tends to be manipulative; that is, people attempt to bring the will of the other into conformity with *their own* preferences.[26]

22 See, R.P. George (ed.), *Natural Law Theory: Contemporary Essays* (Oxford University Press: Oxford, 1992); *Making Men Moral: Civil Liberties and Public Morality* (Oxford University Press: Oxford, 1993); (ed), *The Autonomy of Law: Essays on Legal Positivism* (Oxford University Press: Oxford, 1995); (ed), *Natural Law, Liberalism, and Morality: Contemporary Essays* (Clarendon Press: Oxford, 1996); *In Defence of Natural Law* (Clarendon Press: Oxford, 1999).

23 The best text on Hume's law that I am aware of is B. Celano, *Dialettica della giustificazione pratica: Saggio sulla legge di Hume* (Torino: Giappichelli, 1994).

24 On this question, see H.B. Veatch, *Human Rights: Fact or Fancy?*, p. 54: "ever since the advent of modern science, it has tended to be supposed that morals and ethics could not be based on facts of nature."

25 A. MacIntyre, *After Virtue* (Notre Dame: University of Notre Dame Press, 1984) (first edition 1981) pp. 11–12.

26 Carcaterra speaks, in the same sense, of a "philosophy of decisionism," in which "not only would ethical judgments be closed to the predication of truth or falsehood, but it would be impossible to give any justification of them that was not itself derived from a moral choice. In this way, there would always be at the outset a purely subjective decision, not open to any further reasoning and in this sense arbitrary." G. Carcaterra, "Per una fondazione dei valori," in F. D.'Agostino, *Ontologia e fenomenologia del giuridicio: Studi in onore di Sergio Cotta* (Turin: Giappichelli, 1995), p. 67.

In this context, neoclassical thinkers welcome the progress achieved in analytic philosophy in the study of moral reasoning, not only insofar as it highlights the existence of a particular type of rational argument, and so of a certain objectivity in reasoning that leads to action,[27] but also insofar as it brings out the fact that moral reasoning is intrinsically characterized by values in the form of *good reasons* for action.[28] Those values that can no longer be derived by observing the nature of things already exist in moral reasoning itself. This is the insight at the root of the general recovery by analytic philosophers of Aristotle's and Aquinas's concept of practical reason. These two thinkers granted practical reason a certain autonomy from speculative reason precisely with respect to knowledge of the good.

By remaining cognitively in the order of practical reason, the neoclassicists believe they can escape the objection of the naturalistic fallacy, and recover for ethics an adequate objectivity, by showing that every man's practical reason rests on some first premises, in the form of evaluative judgments about what constitutes a good reason for action. Such evaluative judgments, precisely because they are primary, are not known by the agent deductively but with an original intuition, and they cannot be strictly demonstrated, but only identified. These premises therefore reveal the basic values, or the ultimate ends, of human existence, and anyone capable of reflecting with sufficient attention can find them in himself as well as in others. This way of viewing the problem is reflected above all in the distinction between *objectivity* and *nature*: the natural law of the neoclassicists wants to be an objective ethics, but one that does not in any way derive values from the knowledge of human nature.[29]

27 It is interesting, in this context, that Dworkin returns to a kind of natural law framework that proceeds not from nature, but through the analysis of legal reasoning: in particular, he distinguishes the dimension of "fit" (legal reasoning as a technical task) from that of justification (legal reasoning as a moral act). See R.A. Dworkin, *Law's Empire* (London: Fontana Press, 1986). For a recent interpretation of Dworkin's thought, see A. Schiavello, *Diritto come integrità: Incubo o nobile sogno? Saggio su Ronald Dworkin* (Turin: Giappichelli, 1998). For a critique of this aspect of Dworkin's thought see J. Finnis, "Natural Law and Legal Reasoning," in R.P. George (ed.), *Natural Law Theory: Contemporary Essays*, pp. 134–57.

28 See also J. Raz, *Practical Reason and Norms* (London: Hutchinson, 1975).

29 See for example J. Finnis, *Fundamentals of Ethics*, p. 10. Hans Jonas also sees reflection on the objectivity of value as the way to overcome the problem of Hume's law, but unlike the neoclassicists he places such reflection within a meta-

How is all this connected to Thomas Aquinas's *lex naturalis*? The answer to this question turns essentially on *Summa theologiae* I-II, question 94, article 2, in which it is stated that "as 'being' is the first thing that falls under the apprehension simply, so 'good' is the first thing that falls under the apprehension of the practical reason, which is directed to action: since every agent acts for an end under the aspect of good," and that "the precepts of the natural law are to the practical reason, what the first principles of demonstrations are to the speculative reason, because both are self-evident principles."

A rereading of St. Thomas leads us first of all to a concept of practical reason completely different from the technical or instrumental one espoused by Hume.[30] The good that Thomistic practical reason seeks is not extrinsic to practical reason itself. In Grisez's words, practical reason is not "simply knowledge sought for practical purposes," but rather "the mind playing a certain role" in which the ordering to the action and the operative principle are intrinsic to it.[31] The first principle of practical reason laid out by St. Thomas, "*bonum est faciendum et prosequendum et malum vitandum*," should therefore be thought of first and foremost as an internal principle of operation. And the precepts of natural law are thought of as the general premises of action which, precisely by virtue of the orientation determined by the first principle of the practical order, guide moral action in the different spheres of human existence. "So it is," says Finnis, "that the practical principles which enjoin us to participate in those basic forms of good [...] have been called in the Western philosophical tradition the first principles of natural law, because they lay down for us the outline of everything one could reasonably want to do, to have and to be."[32]

In the most developed elaboration of their theory, the neoclassicists identify the following seven categories of basic human goods: (1) life, health and safety; (2) knowledge and aesthetic experience; (3) some degree of excellence in work and play; (4) living at peace with others, neighborliness, friendship; (5) inner peace; (6) peace of conscience and consistency between one's self and its expression; (7) peace with God, or

physical framework. See. H. Jonas, *The Imperative of Responsibility* (Chicago: University of Chicago Press, 1985), p. 46 ff.

30 On this point see also A.R. Luño, *Etica* (Florence: Le Monnier, 1992), pp. 138–40.

31 See G. Grisez, "The First Principle of Practical Reason: A Commentary on the *Summa theologiae*, 1–2, Question 94, Article 2," p. 175.

32 J. Finnis, *Natural Law and Natural Rights*, p. 97

the gods, or some nontheistic but more-than-human source of meaning and value.[33]

When man, either as an individual or in his social interactions with others, pursues with full reasonableness these ultimate values, he fulfills himself and is morally good. However, the basic values or goods, of themselves, do not indicate what is the good or just action to be done: in this sense, they are pre-moral. Morality obtains only in concrete choices, when one pursues the basic values within different contexts in a reasonable manner, that is to say, according to the following first principle of the moral order: "In voluntarily acting for human goods and avoiding what is opposed to them, one ought to choose and otherwise will those and only those possibilities whose willing is compatible with integral human fulfillment."[34] The interaction of this principle with the different contexts of human choice allows one to make some specifications of the principle that can logically be called "intermediate principles," and which correspond to the moral principles of common sense. Examples of an "intermediate principle" are the golden rule (do not do to others what you would not want done to yourself) and the rule whereby one cannot do evil that good may come of it.

Neoclassical theory ends up taking a position that distances it decisively from Aquinas, rejecting two essential elements of his concept and of the entire classical tradition of natural law: the existence of an ultimate end for man, and an objective hierarchy of values. From the point of view of an analysis of practical reasoning, the basic values are those good reasons for action to which any possible reason for action can be analytically traced: *irreducibility*, as an essential feature of ultimate values or ends, not only excludes the possibility of a single further good which would trump all others, but renders all values logically incommensurable, and thus prevents one from situating them in any form of hierarchy.

I have elsewhere dwelled at length on the serious problems of consistency and the argumentative gaps that prevent neoclassicists from reaching their conclusions about basic values, the absence of an ultimate end, and the absence of hierarchy.[35] I can now add that neoclassical theory does not succeed in explaining either duty or moral responsibility, for two basic

33 See Finnis-Grisez-Boyle Jr., *Nuclear Deterrence, Morality and Realism*, pp. 278–80; "Practical Principles, Moral Truth, and Ultimate Ends," pp. 107–8.

34 Finnis-Grisez-Boyle Jr., *Nuclear Deterrence, Morality and Realism*, p. 283.

35 F. Di Blasi, "I valori fondamentali nella teoria neoclassica della legge naturale," *Rivista Internazionale di Filosofia del Diritto*, 2 (1999).

reasons: First of all, failing to establish an intrinsic connection between the *objectivity* of practical reason and the *nature* of man, it lacks any real response to the ultimate "why" of moral life. At the end of the day, in spite of several somewhat convoluted attempts at justification which the neoclassicists have offered in response to this challenge, it could be said that for them, man is obliged to respect values not because it is good to do so, but *simply* because practical reason grasps them as goods. And it should be noted that this is no small difference, because it is the very difference that can cut off the belief that something is good from its being good in reality.

The second reason, no less important than the first, is related to the rejection of both the ultimate end and the possibility of a hierarchy. The neoclassicists, as I have already said, believe that their basic values are so many ultimate ends of human action, and that they are mutually "incommensurable," i.e. there can be no type of measurement that applies to them all. Now I do not think we need a lengthy logical disquisition to state that if man, objectively speaking, has several ultimate and incommensurable ends to pursue, his particular moral choices will depend in the end on a subjective and arbitrary element—just as a ship that simultaneously has two possible routes, one toward Naples and the other toward Palermo (with no other qualification), cannot sail until it chooses one of the options *arbitrarily*. This is exactly what has happened in neoclassical theory, where the rejection of an ultimate end capable of justifying an objective hierarchy guiding individual ethical choices leads to the positing of a "subjective hierarchy" among values (or, we might add, of a *subjective ultimate end*) as the necessary premise of every concrete action.[36]

At this point, it seems more than a coincidence that criticism of Aquinas on the ultimate end is accompanied in "neoclassical" scholarship by an explicit attempt to construct an ethics without God. Ultimately, if indeed man must have an ultimate end, the most natural assumption to make is that the ultimate end would somehow coincide with God. This is certainly true as far as the Doctor of the Catholic Church is concerned. It is also curious that, at least at first glance, the very points on which "neoclassical" thought appears somewhat inconsistent and undeveloped turn out to be the reasons that neoclassicists have subsequently distanced themselves from Thomistic philosophy. As a matter of fact, if one undertakes a close and attentive study of Aquinas's works, one notices that they are

36 J. Finnis, *Natural Law and Natural Rights*, pp. 92–93.

decidedly more complex, consistent and profound than the neoclassical interpretation would suggest. It seems to me that the mistaken neoclassical reading depends, essentially, on an initial approach that is neither broad enough in its approach nor sufficiently disinterested: that is, on an approach driven by the search for a solution to the modern epistemological problem of Hume's law. Obviously, "focusing on our own problems" is not the correct methodology for interpreting another's thought, and it eventually leads to misunderstandings and criticisms. That is why, at this stage in my research, I thought it more correct and more fruitful to approach St. Thomas without any particular, pre-determined objective—whether to better understand the neoclassical theory or to criticize it—but directly and, so to speak, *dispassionately*.

In any case, what is most surprising at this point is that the neoclassical theory of natural law, conceived as an authentic interpretation of Thomas's *lex naturalis*, has in the end managed to deny what are precisely its two essential aspects: that is, its existence as *lex*—i.e., as a command promulgated by a ruler—and its existence as *naturalis*—i.e., as inscribed in the nature of man and knowable through that nature.[37] As I will point out in the first chapter, the depreciation of the law-like character of natural law, combined with a concern to define ethical duties without reference to God, has become a very widespread tendency among contemporary interpreters of Aquinas. This goes hand in hand with another tendency, namely, to undervalue the description of the objective natural order as St. Thomas conceived of it, and instead, to focus almost exclusively on the interiority and intentionality of the moral agent. I believe both of these tendencies result from an impoverished understanding of St. Thomas's thought. Indeed, some of the more interesting aspects of Aquinas' thought have to do with the theological foundation (by this I mean *natural* or *philosophical theology*) of the moral order and the way in which the order of nature and its ethical relevance are understood.

5. Natural law, Natural Rights, and Contemporary Liberalism

Viewed from another perspective, the neoclassical theory of natural law wants to propose an ethical foundation for human rights which is opposed to utilitarianism, to neocontractualism and, in general, to liberal positions. It is now some time since Norberto Bobbio wrote, not without a certain

37 On this last point, Veatch's observations in his "Natural Law and the 'Is-Ought' Question: Queries to Finnis and Grisez," pp. 302–5, are especially apt.

delight, that the consensus created around human rights thanks to the *Universal Declaration* had definitively resolved the theoretical problem of their foundation.[38] In reality, the consensus turned out to be rather fleeting and deceptive, and the need for a more solid theoretical justification is more evident today than ever.

In this context, the alternative on the liberal side is well expressed by the title of a collection of essays edited by Raymond Frey and published in 1985: *Utility and Rights*. "The fundamental point of contrast, and conflict, between utilitarian and right-based views is that the former, at least in their basic theory, aggregate the interests or preferences of all the persons or parties who are being taken into account, whereas the latter insist, to the end, on the separateness of persons."[39] For utilitarianism in general, any right must give way in concrete cases to the calculus of the greatest good of the greatest number. This approach is instantiated today in the jurisprudence of the "Law and Economics School," headed by Richard Posner. For this school of thought, when one is faced with a legal dispute one must adopt, not an "*ex post* approach" in which the positions of the parties are taken as given, and losses and gains are fairly distributed, but an "*ex ante* approach" "in which the court is interested not so much in doing justice in the case in hand, as in creating valid rules to govern the conduct of the world in its complexity."[40]

The "*ex ante* approach" and the "*ex post* approach" correspond to "utilitarian rights" and "autonomy rights," which Meir Dan-Cohen discusses in his book *Rights, Persons, and Organization: A Legal Theory for Bureaucratic Society* (Berkeley: University of California Press, 1986).

38 N. Bobbio, "Presente e avvenire dei diritti dell'uomo" (1967), in Bobbio, *L'età dei diritti* (Turin: Einaudi, 1990), pp. 17–44: "But when I say that the ever more urgent problem confronting us is not the problem of foundation but that of guarantees, I mean that we consider the problem of foundation not nonexistent but, in a certain sense, resolved; that is, we should no longer preoccupy ourselves with its solution. Indeed, one could say that today the problem of the foundation of the rights of man has been solved in the Universal Declaration of Human Rights, approved by the General Assembly of the United Nations on 10 December 1948. The Universal Declaration of Human Rights represents the only proof by which a system of values can be considered humanly founded and thereby recognized, and this proof is general consensus concerning its validity."

39 J.L. Mackie, "Rights, Utility and Universalization," in R.G. Frey (ed), *Utility and Rights* (Oxford: Basil Blackwell, 1985), p. 86.

40 L.H. Tribe, "Constitutional Calculus: Equal Justice or Economic Efficiency?," *Harvard Law Review*, 3 (1985), p. 593.

There, he identifies utilitarian and autonomy rights as types of rights protected by utilitarian and deontological versions of liberal jurisprudence. The protection of utilitarian rights must look to the future, to the consequences for social welfare, that is, to the future behavior even of those who are not party to the present dispute: here the individual can be instrumentalized, yielding to the interests of collective well-being. The protection of deontological rights, on the other hand, looks to the past, to the conduct of the parties in question, and cannot be based on objectives external to the dispute. Dan-Cohen maintains that there is often no clear way to resolve the conflict between the two types of right, but in his effort to offer a valid justification for the role of intermediary organizations, he says that "autonomy rights" must be given greater weight in questions regarding individuals, while organizations can invoke to their advantage only "utilitarian rights," based on the contribution that they make to social welfare.

The strongest reaction against the ethical doctrine of utilitarianism comes from John Rawls's deontological liberalism, whose intention is well expressed by the following words from *A Theory of Justice*: "Each member of society is thought to have an inviolability founded on justice, or, as some say, on natural right, which even the welfare of every one else cannot override. Justice denies that the loss of freedom for some is made right by a greater good shared by others. The reasoning which balances the gains and losses of different persons as if they were one person is excluded. Therefore in a just society the basic liberties are taken for granted and the rights secured by justice are not subject to political bargaining or to the calculus of social interests."[41]

A central feature of the liberal defense of human rights is the tendency toward minimalism concerning the list of rights to be protected. Concerned to avoid the danger of a government intolerant toward the liberty of individuals, liberals have posited the so-called *principle of neutrality* as fundamental to their doctrine. According to this principle, the state must not pronounce upon what is good and what is bad, but only assure in public life those conditions necessary (the right) for everyone to exercise his liberty to a maximum degree without being harmed by others (the *harm principle*).[42]

It is commonplace, particularly after Rawls, for liberal neutrality to be

41 J. Rawls, *A Theory of Justice* (Cambridge, MA: Belknap Press of Harvard University Press, 1971), p. 28.

42 See R. Dworkin, "La fonte di ogni libertà," *Il Sole-24 Ore*, 10 March 1996: "Liberals have an obvious reason for holding this opinion about their political the-

referred to as the requirement of a "priority of the right over the good":[43] where the right is the sphere of social relationships and law, and it is *important*, in order to avoid any form of discrimination, that it not be given an ethical justification but only an instrumental one. The state *ought to* protect justice and rights not because it is good to do so, but only because all individuals maintain that this is always and in all circumstances the best instrument for guaranteeing their autonomy; and it therefore *ought to* guarantee only those rights upon which a real, virtual or merely hypothetical *agreement* can be reached among the parties.

The obvious dialectical criticism that the requirement of neutrality is not itself ethically neutral[44] has led some exponents of deontological liberalism to attempt to supply an explicit ethical justification of "autonomy rights." It is along these lines that Ronald Dworkin recently criticized the typical liberal "strategy of discontinuity." "Liberal philosophers," he wrote, "who adopt the restrictive interpretation according to which liberalism is a theory of the right but not of the good, are faced with the problem of explaining what reasons a person can have to be liberal. They adopt what I shall call a 'strategy of discontinuity': they try to find motives, both in self-interest and in morality, for setting aside their convictions about the good life when they act politically. I maintain that liberals should reject this restrictive interpretation of their theory. On the contrary, they should try to connect ethics and politics by constructing a view about the nature or character of the good life that makes liberal political morality continuous rather than discontinuous with appealing views about the good life."[45]

In deontological liberalism, therefore, whether neocontractualist or perfectionist, there is, sometimes implicitly and other times explicitly, an undeniable drift toward natural law. From this point of view, the real distinction to be drawn is not between liberalism on the one hand and natural law on the other, but between the *minimalist-and-individualist* and

ory. A fundamental, almost defining, principle of liberalism is that the government of a political community should be tolerant with respect to the different and often conflicting convictions of its citizens about the right way to live [...]. It is easier to understand, and perhaps to defend, liberal tolerance, if one accepts the thesis that liberalism is not derived from, and does not depend upon, any particular ethical ideal."

43 See J. Rawls, *A Theory of Justice*, p. 31.

44 See, for example, J. Finnis, *Natural Law and Natural Rights*, pp. 221–23.

45 R. Dworkin, "La fonte di ogni libertà." Another prominent example of this non-neutral, deontological liberalism is J. Raz, *The Morality of Freedom* (Oxford: Clarendon Press, 1986).

non-minimalist-and-non-individualist approaches to identifying and protecting human rights.[46] More traditional natural law theory thus joins with communitarianism in affirming that "autonomy rights" do not exhaustively fulfill the inherent requirements of human rights, and that social relationships have an intrinsic and not a purely instrumental importance. If neutrality is really impossible, and if the human being is not conceivable outside the society in which he lives and develops, then consistent and conscious political action must not only take account of all the essential aspects of man, but also directly protect the moral environment in which he lives and the traditions within which he constitutes and perfects his personal identity.

Finnis's "basic values" conceptually reflect the first precepts of natural law, which St. Thomas speaks of in the *Summa theologiae* according to a three-part order: (a) self-preservation, common to all substances; (b) union of male and female, the nurturing of offspring, and other such things common to all animals; and (c) the search for truth and life in society, which is proper to rational beings.[47] In *Natural Law and Natural Rights*, Finnis explains that these basic values correspond perfectly to human or natural rights. The modern language of rights is, in fact, a way of expressing virtually all the demands of practical reasonableness insofar as they bear on relations of justice; and the language of human rights is a useful way of pointing to all the basic aspects of the human good as the primary objective of the political community. "When we survey" the rights proclaimed in the Universal Declaration, "we realize what the modern 'manifesto' conception of human rights amounts to. It is simply a way of sketching the *outlines of the common good*, the various aspects of individual well-being in the community. What the reference to rights contributes in this sketch is simply a pointed expression of what is implicit in the term '*common* good,' namely, that *each* and everyone's well-being, in each of its basic aspects, must be considered and treated favorably at all times by those responsible for co-ordinating the common life."[48]

Neoclassical theory's fundamental criticism of Rawls's neocontractualism—and of deontological liberalism in general—is that it is arbitrary, "in selecting the principles of justice," to consider as primary only goods

46 On this point, see J. Finnis, "Is Natural Law Theory Compatible with Limited Government?" in R.P. George (ed.), *Natural Law, Liberalism and Morality: Contemporary Essays*, p. 9.

47 Thomas Aquinas, *ST*, I-II, q. 94, a. 2 c.

48 J. Finnis, *Natural Law and Natural Rights*, p. 214.

such as "liberty, opportunity, wealth and self-respect," refusing to confer intrinsic value upon goods "such as truth, or play, or art, or friendship."[49] On the other hand, its fundamental criticism of utilitarianism is that the basic values, which form the basis of individual as well as political action, are mutually incommensurable, and consequently that it is not possible to instrumentalize them and treat them as the object of a calculation for the greatest overall good or the least overall evil.[50] Given that the basic values have this status, they are to be respected in all circumstances, and it is thus possible that there are actions which it is never licit to engage in. In other words, it is possible to speak of absolute human rights, as the *Universal Declaration* does about slavery and torture—which, precisely for this reason, according to a careful exegesis of the text, seem to escape the limitations envisaged in article 29 when it speaks of "securing due recognition and respect for the rights and freedoms of others" and "meeting the just requirements of morality, public order and the general welfare in a democratic society."[51]

Unfortunately, neoclassical theory (like deontological liberalism) remains tied to ethical intuitionism, which besides being theoretically difficult to justify does not lead to a clear identification of human values.[52] From this point of view, the real challenge facing natural law theory is to provide a strong identification and justification of values, human rights, and the common good that are based on *facts*, that is, on human nature: but this is precisely what the neoclassicists refuse to do from the outset.

On the other hand, the idea of incommensurability as a critique of utilitarianism implies the acceptance, at least at the most general level, of incurable ethical conflict. The choice between different values or rights in

49 Ibid., p. 106.

50 After 1977, Grisez, Finnis and Boyle changed their original criticism of proportionalism by focusing no longer on the incommensurability of the basic goods, but on the incommensurability of the "prospective benefits and disadvantages" of each choice we make. See especially G. Grisez, "Choice and Consequentialism," *Proceedings of the American Catholic Philosophical Association*, 51 (1977); and "Against Consequentialism," *American Journal of Jurisprudence*, 23 (1978).

51 J. Finnis, *Natural Law and Natural Rights*, pp. 210–18.

52 For a critique of the intuitionism of neoclassical theory, see J. Porter, "Basic Goods and the Human Good in Recent Catholic Moral Theology," *The Thomist*, 47 (1993). For a response from the neoclassical side see G.V. Bradley and R.P. George, "The New Natural Law Theory: A Reply to Jean Porter," *The American Journal of Jurisprudence*, 39 (1994).

a particular case always remains arbitrary, and the so-called *balancing* can never be part of an attempt to understand ethical reality prudentially, or in accord with an objective practical wisdom. Rather, it involves the mere *ad hoc* creation of a *subjective hierarchy* among values—the same subjective hierarchy that, in neoclassical theory, dominates individual choice in specific cases. The backdrop of an irreducible ethical pluralism in human existence, source of a tragic and conflictual dimension in the moral life, is perfectly described in the virtue ethics of the early MacIntyre[53] and of Martha Nussbaum.[54] From this perspective, virtue pluralism and value pluralism coincide in conceiving moral action as ultimately arbitrary (they coincide, if you will, in their participation in the emotivist culture of which MacIntyre himself complained), and they produce exactly the dramatic effect that prudential choice among different goods, made in view of the ultimate end, was meant to avoid in the Thomistic natural law ethic.[55]

6. Henry Veatch: Objectivity, Nature, and Natural Rights

The refusal of the neoclassicists to base a natural law ethic on the *facts of nature* has received the strongest and most direct criticism from Henry Veatch, one of the most renowned contemporary American natural law theorists. Veatch has devoted the greater part of his efforts to elaborating an original defense of natural law, starting from ethical naturalism in the Aristotelian-Thomistic tradition. In a 1981 article, he takes a sharply defined position on this issue: either one finds a way of moving from facts to norms or one gives up trying to be a *natural law theorist*.[56] He criticizes Finnis and Grisez for creating a disproportionate separation between practical and theoretical reason, and thus misunderstanding the distinction

53 See, A. MacIntyre, *After Virtue*.

54 Cf. M. Nussbaum, *The Fragility of Goodness: Luck and Ethics in Greek Tragedy and Philosophy* (Cambridge: Cambridge University Press, 1986).

55 It is interesting, in this context, that MacIntyre's *telos*—that is, the unique element of his triadic justification of ethical reality (virtues, values, *telos*) capable of conferring unitary value on moral life, and hence, comparable to an ultimate end—has an absolutely subjective value (see *After Virtue*, ch. XV) and that Aquinas is explicitly criticized because he excludes the possibility of a *moral-physiological* conflict, that is, a conflict not arising from any moral fault (ibid., pp. 179–80).

56 Cf. H.B. Veatch, "Natural Law and the 'Is'-'Ought' Question: Queries to Finnis and Grisez," p. 295.

developed by Aristotle and Aquinas.[57] Veatch's thought on natural law, on the distinction between facts and values, and on the theory of Finnis and Grisez is by no means insignificant, and for our purposes deserves a close rereading.

Veatch sees natural law as the ethics which law needs and is "in search of," that is, as the ethical foundation of human rights.[58] The fundamental question, when we are confronted with claims resting on human or fundamental rights[59] (to liberty, property or due process of law, for example), is "Why should they be respected?" The mere prescription of positive law, or obligation in a "merely legal sense," is obviously not a response that can satisfy the "ethical meaning" of the question. On this point, all natural law theorists concur.[60] Yves Simon, for example, explains that the question of the justice or injustice of positive law is, if not the only possible approach, certainly the preferred route to reflection on natural law.[61] What makes Veatch particularly interesting, however, is his keen dialectical engagement with the various currents of modern and contemporary philosophy in their attempts to provide an ethical foundation for human rights.

The first ethical justification that Veatch criticizes is the appeal to natural rights existing in the so-called "state of nature": "as if in such a state of nature," he says, "a human being's natural right to liberty had somehow been established; and given the existence of such a natural right, then no subsequent social contract, or any other social or political arrangement of mere human invention or convention, could justifiably deprive the individual of his natural right to liberty."[62] This attempted grounding, according to Veatch, cannot work in any of its versions, simply because it is

57 McInerny raises the same type of criticism in "The Principles of Natural Law," pp. 7–9.

58 Cf. H.B. Veatch, *Human Rights: Fact or Fancy?*, ch. I, "The Law in Search of an Ethics."

59 For purposes of the present argument, I assume that there is no difference between human rights and fundamental rights. For the most common conventional distinction between the two expressions, see R. Guastini, "Diritti," in P. Comanducci-R. Guastini, eds., *Analisi e diritto: Ricerche di giurisprudenza analitica* (Turin: Giappichelli, 1994), pp. 163–74.

60 See for example J. Finnis, *Natural Law and Natural Rights*, pp. 354–62.

61 Cf. Y. Simon, *The Tradition of Natural Law: A Philosopher's Reflections* (New York: Fordham University Press, 1965), pp. 111–18.

62 H.B. Veatch, *Human Rights: Fact or Fancy?*, p. 4.

based on an absolutely *nonmoral concept* of liberty, understood as the mere possibility of moving at one's ease without being subject to any "moral or legal" prohibition. This is something like saying that in the state of nature, water is free "to seek its own level" because there is "no moral or legal prohibition against its doing so," and it therefore has the "right" to do so.[63] From a fact such as this, clearly no right can be inferred. Indeed, the mere hypothesis of a right (that is, of a duty on the part of others) would, in such a case, contradict the concept of liberty already posited, because it would imply the "moral or legal" impossibility of behaving as one prefers in the state of nature.

The idea of a social contract is no more helpful than the idea of a "state of nature" for grounding a morality of rights. Indeed, given a completely amoral state of nature, such a contract would remain the only possible foundation of rights, and precisely for this reason would deprive them of any intrinsic moral value. "[G]ranted that we do acquire rights and duties by some social convention, then it can be said to be only by social convention that we are morally bound in any way," and "if I have agreed by social contract to respect the liberties of others, then presumably I need have not the slightest moral compunction about violating such liberties."[64] Using similar arguments, Finnis concluded in *Natural Law and Natural Rights* that simple self-interest is not sufficient to ground a moral obligation to respect rights.[65]

Much more interesting, however, than his critiques of natural rights and the social contract, are the objections Veatch raises to the more modern teleological (or utilitarian) and deontological (or Kantian) ethics, which he prefers to call "desire-ethics" and "duty-ethics" respectively. His basic point becomes clear through the manner in which he relates them to each other: "It might be said that both of them represent attempts to found an ethics without having to make appeals to any 'goods' or 'bads' in reality, or to any 'rights' or 'wrongs,' 'oughts' or 'ought nots,' as these might be supposed to exist in the real world, or *in rerum natura*."[66] In other words, both teleological and deontological ethics arise, for Veatch, out of a cultural environment that presupposes the total immanence of value judgments within practical reason, and they therefore claim that ethics

63 Ibid., pp. 8, 157–58.

64 Ibid., pp. 10–11.

65 J. Finnis, *Natural Law and Natural Rights*, pp. 300–303.

66 H.B. Veatch, *Human Rights: Fact or Fancy?*, p. 13.

cannot be grounded on *nature*—on "the way the world is"—but only on the *objectivity* of a certain type of reasoning.[67]

Veatch argues that from the point of view of the ethical foundation of rights, teleological ethics "have at least one initial advantage in their dialectical interchange with" the deontological ones. Indeed, with respect to any moral judgment about what one ought or ought not to do, the most obvious and pertinent question is "Why?" and here teleological ethics can offer an immediate response: "You ought to because it is to your advantage; or if not to your own personal advantage, then at least to mankind's advantage, or to the advantage of the greatest number of human beings." This advantage, however, is also the weak point of the argument, which remains vulnerable to the deontological critique. As with the social contract, here too the mere fact of desiring something (or of deriving some interest or pleasure from it) is not capable of explaining, either psychologically or logically, moral obligation and rights: from the fact that one wants something it does not follow that one ought to do it or respect it.[68]

Deontological ethics, for their part, have difficulty with the initial "why" question. Moral matters in fact "would seem never to be self-evident" and the question about the why of duty "is always relevant with respect to them." But the most "embarrassing" thing, in this regard, is that "there would seem to be no way of answering" such a question except to appeal to the ends or desires of the moral agent. Kant tried to avoid a "total arbitrariness and lack of foundation" of obligation by affirming, through the application of the principle of universalizability, the logical *inconsistency* of the type of reasoning underlying immoral acts. In such reasoning, the agent, thinking that it is right for him to commit a bad action, should also think that it is equally right for anyone else, and his intention is thus no longer the original one of creating an exception, but rather that of inverting an entire moral principle. In such a case, however, continues Veatch, in order to avoid inconsistency it is sufficient to admit an explicit intention of the agent to pursue his own advantage rather than a principle of justice.

Contemporary deontologists, unlike Kant, prefer to appeal to a presumed capacity to *intuit* the moral duties themselves; but this leads even further toward arbitrariness and dogmatism. Two contemporary examples

67 Lisska gives a good explanation of this aspect of Veatch's thought in his *Aquinas's Theory of Natural Law: An Analytic Reconstruction*, esp. pp. 166–87.

68 H.B. Veatch, *Human Rights: Fact or Fancy?*, pp. 16–19.

of intuitionism that Veatch recounts are Alan Donagan's principle, "respect human nature," and Dworkin's principle, "the right to equal consideration and respect."[69]

Veatch thinks it important to dwell further on utilitarianism, in order to bring out "an even more deep-seated weakness" consisting of an "embarrassing compromise" with the deontological ethic. Indeed, having affirmed that individual self-interest is the end that grounds ethical choices, utilitarianism "moves its foundation" to "the greatest happiness or the good of the greatest number." The initial justification for this move is, of course, the "feeling of benevolence." However, faced with someone who does not possess this feeling, the only justification that remains available to the utilitarian is that of "duty." The most elaborate attempt to explain such a duty comes from several recent utilitarians, such as William Frankena, as an application of the principle of universalizability: "If I judge my own pleasure or happiness as being something that it is only right that I should pursue, then I am committed to recognizing" also the pleasure and happiness of others as something to be pursued. Other considerations aside, the central problem of this argument, according to Veatch, is that the premise suffers from the general defect of utilitarianism, that is, the impossibility of justifying the identification of my pleasure with my duty. This defective premise ultimately makes utilitarianism into a "bona fide deontology."[70]

There is nonetheless another recent "desire-ethic," namely "ethical egoism" or "rational individualism," which according to Veatch manages to avoid the two principal defects of utilitarianism: the sacrifice of individual rights to the greatest good of the greatest number, and the compromise with some kind of categorical or deontological duty. The rational egoist effectively attributes a hypothetical character to all the duties arising out of social life. He maintains that one *ought to* respect them only to the extent that this furthers one's personal advantage—insofar as, by maintaining peace with others, one's freedom will be better safeguarded. In this way, he need not attribute any intrinsic moral value to duties towards others, and he remains entirely consistent with his egoistic premises. Furthermore, since he understands that his demands for liberty are mere "desire-words" and not "moral or value-words," it would be fruitless to use the principle of universalizability against him by arguing that in

69 Ibid., pp. 20–25, 213–17.
70 Ibid., pp. 30–33.

conferring value upon his own freedom he ought also, for this very reason, to attribute value to the liberty of others.[71] This type of individualism, therefore, constitutes the most perfect elaboration of the teleological ethic.[72]

What, then, for Veatch, is the defect of "rational egoism?" On the one hand, it does not seem practicable: the idea of convincing people that to respect the life, liberty, property, etc., of others ultimately contributes to their own advantage—and of thus securing their adherence to social rules under all circumstances—seems at best unrealistic. But at a deeper level, the real difficulty with rational egoism is that, as Veatch says, "it is not an ethics at all." A duty that is solely instrumental to one's personal objectives (I must do *a* if I want to obtain *b*) is not a moral duty. If I respect the rights of others only to the extent that this corresponds to my self-interest, and if others do the same for me, then properly speaking, we cannot say that either I or they possess rights. This difficulty can thus be reduced to the fundamental difficulty of all desire-ethics: from the mere fact of wanting or desiring something, one cannot derive a duty or right: desires "are not universalizable."[73]

Finnis's and Grisez's "natural law theory" is, according to Veatch, a correct response to the difficulties that "desire" and "duty" ethics encounter in attempting to justify moral duty. Such a response lies in the notion of "obligatory ends," capable of giving life to "an entirely different sort of teleology" that also incorporates the valid claim of deontological ethics. In brief, according to Finnis and Grisez ethics is effectively based upon the desire for something, but our desire for that thing depends on a prior recognition of "its true excellence or goodness or value"; in this way, "we have to deal with something that is objectively good; and because it is objectively good, it is in the nature of an obligatory end—something that we ought to desire or seek after or value whether or not we actually do."[74]

Veatch accepts this logical solution offered by neoclassical theory but maintains that it is only a partial ethical response. Even if the notion of "obligatory ends" is in itself logically workable, it cannot tell us whether such ends really exist or what they are "specifically and concretely." It is

71 On the analytic difference between descriptive and prescriptive language, see R.M. Hare, *The Language of Morals* (Oxford: Oxford University Press, 1954).

72 H.B. Veatch, *Human Rights: Fact or Fancy?*, pp. 33–34.

73 Ibid., pp. 45–48, 159–60.

74 Ibid., pp. 93–104.

precisely here that Finnis and Grisez, according to Veatch, distance themselves from the classical tradition of natural law, remaining tied to the position typical of modern philosophy—a position that he had already characterized, in his *For an Ontology of Morals* (Evanston, IL: Northwestern University Press, 1971), as a "transcendental turn": that is, the idea that good and evil, right and wrong, or duty and obligation are "completely absent from the natural world." Veatch maintains that this idea radically undermines the possibility of a valid ethical justification precisely because it implies this justification's total "lack of connection with reality." As a matter of fact, the neoclassicists are careful to point out that in ethical questions we must not refer in any way to nature,[75] and for this reason the lists of values that they have produced at different times amount to a form—albeit a rather elaborate one—of ethical intuitionism.[76]

In working out their scheme of basic values, the neoclassicists did not confine themselves to a single path. Initially, they thought of two parallel but necessarily unconnected ways of knowing basic values: one starting from empirical data about our natural inclinations, the other from the intuitions of practical reason.[77] As it has evolved, however, the theory has followed the second path, which is perfectly in line with the concept of obligatory ends criticized by Veatch.

Veatch, while aiming above all to bring out the limits of "transcendental ethics," nonetheless underestimated the consequences of the neoclassical notion of "obligatory ends" when it is combined with the denial of the existence of a single ultimate end. For Veatch—an excellent interpreter of Aristotelian ethics—it goes without saying that the multiple values or human goods that practical reason perceives, even if they differ from each other, are all included in the agent's single intention to pursue his own good, perfection, or happiness (which, given the social nature of man, includes the good of others by participation) "wisely and intelligently."[78] And from this perspective, the ethics of Finnis and Grisez, on the one hand, and that of Veatch on the other, would appear to coincide in their

75 See, for one of many examples, G. Grisez, "A New Formulation of Natural Law against Contraception," *Thomist*, 30 (1966).

76 See H.B. Veatch, *Human Rights: Fact or Fancy?*; see also H.B. Veatch and J. Rautenberg, "Does the Grisez-Finnis-Boyle Moral Philosophy Rest on a Mistake?," *Review of Metaphysics*, 44 (1991).

77 I explain this in my article, "I valori fondamentali nella teoria neoclassica della legge naturale."

78 H.B. Veatch, *Human Rights: Fact or Fancy?*, pp. 77–85.

attempt to explain *how* the various human goods (including sociability and friendship) can be rationally pursued.

In my view, this apparent coincidence is the reason that even the Thomistic philosopher Ralph McInerny, although perplexed when confronted with the lack of hierarchy and the premorality of the basic values, did not immediately develop a critique of the irreducible plurality of ends in neoclassical theory.[79] The gap created by the neoclassicists is nonetheless huge. For them there is not *one* ultimate end but *several.* Any ethical choice, therefore, even if it is the fruit of the wisest man's virtue, or of the perfected art of living well, always conceals the drama of renouncing some good in favor of another. To clarify, we are not dealing here with the ethical drama of being unable, as humans, to attain full certainty concerning the right (or wrong) moral choice in complex circumstances and situations, but with the *logical impossibility* of making a fully good choice, and the admission that one's ethical conduct, through the damage it necessarily inflicts on some goods, is always in some respect bad.[80]

7. From Nature to God

Let us now return to Veatch. The route he takes to avoid the difficulties created by the "transcendental turn" in ethics is what he calls the "ontological turn." He attempts to recover, with Aristotle, the ability of human reason to know the natural finality of things (and especially of man) as the rule, the cause, or the reason for their behaving in a particular way. Indeed, "the very essence of any natural-law ethics is that there should be a true natural end, or natural perfection, or natural *telos*, of human life, discernible empirically and directly in the facts of nature."[81]

Veatch's first step in this direction is to reexamine the concept of "laws of nature as rules of action." Ultimately, he says, there is a completely reasonable (and common) sense in which one can speak of the "nature of things" as the "laws" that regulate their behavior in view of the attainment of a given end. Thus, the "development of the embryo" is subject to certain rules of a biological nature—rules that the scientist seeks to

79 R. McInerny, "The Principles of Natural Law." McInerny explicitly criticized this aspect of neoclassical theory several years later in his "Grisez and Thomism," in N. Biggar-R. Black, eds., *The Revival of Natural Law* (Ashgate: Aldershot, 2000), pp. 53–72.

80 See, for example, Finnis-Grisez-Boyle Jr., *Nuclear Deterrence, Morality and Realism*, p. 281.

81 H.B. Veatch, *Human Rights: Fact or Fancy?*, p. 56.

understand ever more deeply, and that *ought to* be respected so that the embryo can attain its "proper end."[82]

The second step will be to explain how the rules inherent in the human context, whether those of art and technical skills or those of morality, can be understood as natural laws. The artist, in fact, relies upon the laws of nature because art (or technology) "is a knowledge of how to use and exploit natural forces and natural conditions so as to accomplish one's particular end as artist or expert." The artist, in order to attain his end, "seeks to proceed in the way nature would have proceeded" if it had the same end. This is the sense in which, for Aristotle, "art imitates nature," and this is the sense in which the rules of art, also, are in some way "natural laws." To use an analogy with the rules of art, moral rules may be understood as the "laws that govern the art of living well," since they too must, of necessity, base themselves on how man is *made*. For this reason alone, moral rules could be called natural laws, but they have an additional claim to this title because the end to which they are ordered is not chosen by the agent: it is a "natural end." However, they also differ from mere laws of nature because the moral end is of a kind that can only be pursued consciously and deliberately.[83]

Obviously, this discussion does not yet solve the problem of whether the human being has a natural end, and if so, what it is. The Aristotelian concept of nature, however, does not render "queer" (as John Mackie suggests) the idea that each species has a natural perfection or excellence and that such a perfection is the ultimate actuality to which its potentialities are ordered—in other words, the good or the end towards which they naturally tend or that they naturally desire.[84] For man, this tendency to the ultimate end manifests itself to reason in moral terms, and might be expressed through Thomas's first principle of practical reason: *bonum est faciendum et prosequendum*... Thus, "when it is said that we all ought to seek the good, that means that we all ought to seek that which we are naturally disposed toward, as toward an end, and that which we therefore naturally desire and are thus ordered to, insofar as we are human."[85]

82 Ibid., pp. 58–62.

83 Ibid., pp. 63–67.

84 See J.L. Mackie, *Ethics: Inventing Right and Wrong* (London: Penguin, 1977). For a criticism of Mackie's arguments "from relativity" and "from queerness," see also P. Geach, *The Virtues* (Cambridge: Cambridge University Press, 1977), p. 13.

85 H.B. Veatch, *Human Rights: Fact or Fancy?*, pp. 68–70. Unlike the neoclassical authors, for Veatch the first principle of practical reason has an immediate moral significance, not a "pre-moral" one.

With this concept of nature in mind, it would be reasonable, Veatch continues, and more consistent with common sense, to think of our judgments about the good not as *a priori* judgments, but as judgments based on an objective experiential knowledge of the world. Just as it is only through experience that we learn to recognize "a truly healthy or flourishing condition of a fish, or of a live oak," or the condition of a good surgeon as distinct from a bad surgeon, similarly it is only through experience that we arrive at judgments about human beings who, even if in excellent physical condition and rich in talents and material goods, have nonetheless made bad choices, and have not attained the full (moral) flourishing that they could have reached by putting their talents to use differently.[86]

This said, Veatch proposes to directly follow "Aristotle's guidelines," and to seek the ultimate end of human action in that which is most peculiar to man: "the possession of reason." With this task in mind, he underlines four characteristics of the Aristotelian view with which to orient oneself in determining the contours of the concept of ultimate end: activity, practical reason, choice and liberty.

(1) The Aristotelian ultimate end, above all, should not be understood as a specific objective to be attained but as the activity of "living well," i.e., behaving oneself "in a way that best befits a human being." And this way entails managing our various needs and desires, and using the goods that correspond to them, "wisely and intelligently and as they ought to be used and employed."

(2) The ultimate end thus consists "not just of living but in living intelligently," bringing the order of reason to bear upon "our day-by-day decisions and choices." It would be useless here to object that wise decisions, such as not having "another drink of whiskey" are not strictly "questions of knowledge": in fact, practical reason is precisely the capacity to evaluate particular circumstances in light of one's universal knowledge. As the good surgeon "knows," not abstractly but at the moment of acting, how deep the incision should go, and as the good cook knows how much salt should be added to the dish and when, "[i]n the same way, the [morally] good man is one who knows what should be done and whose judgment can therefore be relied upon in the day-by-day circumstances of our lives."

(3) Living well, however, is not just a question of knowing what to do in different circumstances, but also a "question of choice." At the moment

86 Ibid., pp. 71–76.

of choice one must know how to bring one's own "desires," along with the "sentiments, the passions and the emotions," into harmony with the requirements of reason. This task is performed, for Aristotle, by the moral virtues.

(4) Finally, the activity in which humans realize their end or natural perfection is obviously such that nobody else could "do it for them," or help them, so to speak, from the *outside*. Such an activity cannot be understood, in any relevant sense, as *extrinsic* to the agent.[87]

Veatch then goes on to exhibit the intimate relationship between man's good and his social nature (that is, the good of others, realized through the various forms of friendship), and thus the demands of the common good understood as a "necessary means" for the attainment of individual happiness. For now, there is no need to dwell at length upon these issues.[88] It is important, however, to stress that the "natural law ethics" that Veatch elaborates through his rereading of Aristotle is characterized, essentially, by the "*duty*" that the individual perceives himself to be under to pursue his "natural end" (or his happiness): an end that everyone shares and understands through the *experience* of his own *natural* needs and requirements. Man's "every action," then, "and all of his conduct, is ultimately governed in consideration of his duties towards himself."

With this premise, Veatch unfolds an explanation of rights *based on duties*, which is supposed to overcome the limitations of both "*desire-ethics*" and "*duty-ethics*." This explanation, he says, "does not simply beg the question," moving from rights that are claimed against others to duties towards others—that would amount to "little more than a triviality on the order of six of one, half a dozen of the other."[89] Rather, one ought to think of rights as a consequence of "duties that one has towards oneself." Man, in other words, knows (his own and others') natural end as a "*moral word*": in other words, not as a mere desire but as a *duty*. By virtue of the principle of universalizability, he is led to recognize as *rights* all the "means" that prove to be "necessary" for each person, in different circumstances, to "do what he and anyone else recognizes that he must do."

87 Ibid., pp. 77–86.

88 On this point, see ibid., pp. 113–51.

89 From a very similar viewpoint, Finnis concludes his analysis of the term *ius* saying that it is not "appropriate to argue that 'as a matter of juristic logic' duty is logically prior to right (or vice versa)." J. Finnis, *Natural Law and Natural Rights*, p. 210.

If I *recognize* that somebody else has the duty to do a certain thing because anyone in his place would have the duty to do it, I will also *recognize* that the means necessary in order to do it are in some sense *due to him*. In this sense, it is logically possible to say that the "prior duty" towards oneself "generates rights." Moreover, following Aristotle's characterization of the ultimate end, it will not be difficult for Veatch to identify the rights to life, liberty and property—but also political rights, by considering Aristotle's understanding of freedom to "govern and be governed"—as the "means necessary" to fulfill one's duty towards oneself, and hence as "human rights" or as specifications of them.[90]

Oddly, however, Veatch denies the existence of "positive human rights," and this is surely an inconsistency due to a prior personal view on this question. Indeed, he asserts that life, liberty, and property, which compose the nucleus of our negative rights, are things we already possess in our *natural* condition, and for this reason, are to be respected. "In contrast, all of the so-called positive rights are those that human beings who are said to have a right to them do not possess, and therefore it is claimed that they have a right to become possessed of them."[91] After all Veatch's criticisms of natural rights and of the social contract, this appeal to the *state of nature* to discriminate between negative and positive rights is quite surprising.

In reality, on Veatch's original account, the only important thing that everyone has by nature—and that Aristotle's good man is capable of recognizing—is the natural end. Thus neither life, nor liberty, nor property can be thought of as something that is ready-made or prearranged by nature for everyone in the same way. The virtuous man, rather, recognizing everyone's ultimate end in its full meaning, will understand that everyone somehow has the right to those conditions of life, resources, education, etc., without which he cannot become truly free to know and pursue his end. Exactly at this point, through the principle of universalizability, the problem of distribution (and redistribution) becomes a moral problem for him. Seen from this perspective, there clearly cannot be any difference between positive and negative rights.

Furthermore, it is surprising that Veatch, while asserting that many of the benefits connected to the problem of positive rights are secured by just

90 H.B. Veatch, *Human Rights: Fact or Fancy?*, pp. 160–77.
91 Ibid., p. 181.

political action in view of the common good, can speak of "a situation in which there are duties without corresponding rights" on the part of the beneficiaries.[92] If the existence of right, as he has explained, is not linked to the claim of the presumed beneficiary but to the recognition by others of a common end and duty, then recognizing a (universalizable) duty must always be equivalent to recognizing a correlative right.

Finnis is helpful here when he explains that the language of human rights is a language of two terms: man, as the abstract right-holder, and a certain good that belongs to him (right to life, right to work, etc.) insofar as he is a human being. This language, evidently, cannot take on a concrete moral meaning unless someone individually, or the political collectivity as a whole, engages in a *prudent process of specification*. This process involves a careful evaluation of what is possible and suitable in light of the concrete circumstances of the case at hand, of the community's resources, etc.; it concludes with the identification of the specific content and subjects (both active and passive) of a three-term legal relation involving a right-holder, a duty-holder, and an act required.[93] The abstract recognition of any human right (whether positive or negative) does not automatically imply the existence of specific duties and rights on the part of particular individuals.

In any case, an explanation that justifies rights by appealing to the normativity of man's natural end appears to be consistent with the relationship that obtains, in St. Thomas, between "natural law"—understood essentially as an ordering to the ultimate end—and "right" (*ius*)—understood as "that which," according to the circumstances of the case, "is due to each." Otherwise put, it appears to be consistent with the relationship between the treatise on *lex* (*Summa theologiae*, I-II, qq. 90–105), concerning the end and the norm, and the treatise on *iustitia* (*Summa theologiae*, II-II, qq. 57–79), concerning the moral virtue whose object is *the* right (*ius*).

Human reason's ability to know the objective order of natural ends and man's ultimate end in normative terms is one of the essential presuppositions of Thomistic ethics. Moreover, the interpretation that leads Veatch back *from objectivity to nature* recovers for the doctrine of natural law one of the essential features that the neoclassical school had rejected.

92 Ibid., p. 187.
93 J. Finnis, *Natural Law and Natural Rights*, pp. 218–21.

The most important feature, however, without which no natural duty can ever assume the absoluteness required by a properly ethical demand, is still missing.

Especially in light of the clarity achieved by atheism over the past two centuries on the connection between ethics and God, Veatch's account, even if well-grounded, cannot yet be considered sufficient. In the words of Yves Simon: "The connection of the problem of natural law with the problem of God is perhaps more frequently recognized in our times than in any other period. The readers of Jean-Paul Sartre, who have also read Dostoevsky, would dismiss as inconsistent, timid and perhaps hypocritical the philosophy expressed in Grotius's famous words, *etiamsi daremus non esse Deum*."[94] "If there is no God"—today this is clear to everyone—"then everything is permitted." And even if an objective natural order were demonstrated, this would not be enough to make it *important*, and it would, for the contemporary mind, only be an intolerable brake and limit on its demand for absolute freedom.

We are not dealing here with a sentimental reaction to a logical account, but a further refinement of the problem. The "why" of ethical duty not only requires a "principle of universalizability" but also a *principle of absoluteness*, which evidently cannot find an adequate response in the relativity of merely individual existence. If man is to be an absolute (something inviolable) for himself and for another, the basis of ethics must, of necessity, *transcend* both: otherwise the experience of duty would be transformed, sooner or later, into the awareness that one is living a strange *psychological joke*, in the case of the transcendental ethic, or a *joke of nature*, in the case of Veatch's ethics. It would be transformed, in other words, into a crisis of meaning. The ethics of natural law requires, for its very survival, that the order of nature be raised to a transcendent end, i.e., that it be in some sense *willed by God*. In this light it may be utopian, but it is certainly not strange, to think that the only person capable of respecting himself and others, whatever the consequences, and right down to the smallest detail, is somebody who *believes* in God and sees the human person as something sacred. In any case, if there exists a philosophical way to ground the rights of the person absolutely, it is certainly worth attempting to take this path as far as it will go—if for no other reason, then in order to help us *believe* in such rights.

94 Y. Simon, *The Tradition of Natural Law: A Philosopher's Reflections*, p. 62.

Throughout the entire philosophical tradition of natural law, "*natural order*" and "*God's will*" have been at once the two central and the two most delicate and disputed elements.[95] A careful study of Aquinas shows that he is fully aware of these elements, and this awareness goes hand in hand with an extremely refined philosophical explanation separable from his specifically theological vision. The natural order, for St. Thomas, is necessarily and naturally known by man as created—that is, as willed—and the very exercise of his cognitive faculty leads every man necessarily to some kind of knowledge of and search for God. Knowledge and love of God, as we will see, are for Aquinas the most basic philosophical presuppositions of the concept of natural law.

95 On the connection between natural law ethics and God, see also E.M. Anscombe, "Modern Moral Philosophy," *Philosophy*, 33 (1958).

Chapter 1
The Neoclassical Critique of Conventional Natural Law Theory

1. Introduction

The reinterpretation of Aquinas's *lex naturalis* undertaken by those who subscribe to the neoclassical school of natural law was initially prompted by their dissatisfaction with a traditional reading of Thomas's doctrine that they often call the "conventional theory of natural law."[1] The entire essay by Germain Grisez, "The First Principle of Practical Reason: A Commentary on the *Summa theologiae*, 1–2, Question 94, Article 2"—which can be considered the manifesto of the neoclassical school—is designed as a dialectical antithesis to the central claims of the conventional theory, referred to as the "common" and "erroneous" interpretation of Aquinas's thought.

The conventional theory is ultimately faulted for its tendency to separate the ultimate source of moral duty from the concrete requirements and needs of the human being, which are thus disconnected from the moral value of the person. In this way, the ground of obligation remains entirely extrinsic, voluntaristic and disproportionate to man's mode of being. In the language of the ethical autonomy/heteronomy debate, we could say by way of a preliminary approximation that by conventional theory is meant the tendency toward complete heteronomy with respect to the

1 As I pointed out in the introduction, it was only later that exponents of the neoclassical school explicitly distanced themselves from some Thomistic theses. In this regard, see Finnis-Grisez-Boyle Jr., "Practical Principles, Moral Truth, and Ultimate Ends," p. 99; J. Finnis (ed.), *Natural Law*, I, Introduction.

concrete goods of the human being, and that the neoclassical critique, on the contrary, tends toward an autonomy that confers on these concrete goods an intrinsic moral value.

Grisez traces the conventional position back to Francisco Suárez (*Tractatus de legibus ac Deo legislatore*, 1612); Finnis finds traces of it also in the *Commentarium* to Thomas Aquinas's *Summa theologiae* by Gabriel Vazquez (1598–1615).[2] Indeed, the idea that Suárez is merely representative of the beginning of the modern voluntaristic interpretation of natural law is now undisputed among contemporary historians of thought.[3] Nonetheless, the work of the Spanish Jesuit reveals the most fundamental problem in the history of natural law, namely, the problem of identifying the correct relationship between ethical autonomy and heteronomy.

In order to better frame the subject—and the neoclassical point of view, with all its possible consequences—it is therefore appropriate to briefly revisit some aspects of Suárez's position, and of the criticism he levels at Vazquez, in the context in which they emerged and developed. I will do this in section 2, "Suárez's Mediation Between Nominalism and Antinominalism."

In section 3, "Manualistic Morality," I will touch upon the significant impact that, not only according to the neoclassicists, the so-called conventional interpretation has had on the history of Christian moral thought. More especially, and with particular reference to Finnis's and Grisez's observations, I will try to outline in section 4, "The Neoclassical Image of the Conventional Theory," the essential features commonly attributed to the conventional interpretation.

Among these features, the central idea that emerges is that the con-

2 G. Grizez, *Contraception and the Natural Law*, p. 46; J. Finnis, *Natural Law and Natural Rights*, pp. 42–47.

3 Apart from the representatives of the neoclassical school, see the recent historical explanation of G. Abbà, *Quale impostazione per la filosofia morale?*, (Rome: Las, 1996), pp. 83–103. For Villey, on the doctrine of law and the laws "there is," between St. Thomas and Suárez, "a radical opposition, indeed a reversal," in a voluntaristic sense: see M. Villey, *La formazione del pensiero giuridico moderno*, trans. R. D'Ettore, F. D'Agostino (Milan: Jaca Book, 1986), pp. 325–30. For a more balanced position, see J. De Finance, *An Ethical Inquiry*, trans. Michael O'Brien, S.J. (Rome: Editrice Pontificia Università Gregoriana, 1991), pp. 210–27. For a non-voluntaristic interpretation, see L. Recasens Sichez, *La Filosofia del Derecho de Francisco Suárez* (Mexico: Editorial Jus, 1947); and G. Ambrosetti, *Il diritto naturale della riforma cattolica: Una giustificazione storica del sistema di Suárez* (Milan: Giuffrè, 1951), pp. 91–130.

ventional theory, in order to confer normative force on *mere facts* of nature, artificially has recourse to an alleged command of God (or at least to an unjustified absolute ethical principle) that necessarily renders the foundation of the moral order extrinsic and impositional, and falls foul of the naturalistic fallacy. The absence of an intrinsic connection between nature, on the one hand—repository of the content of rules of conduct—and the source of obligation, on the other, gives rise to a rationalistic model of ethical justification based on an unwarranted absolutizing of the so-called natural ends of human acts.

Finnis's and Grisez's critiques expose an objective deficiency in the conventional theory, both in its *extrinsic* recourse to the will of God and in its specific model of justification for norms of conduct. However, as we will see in section 5, "The Transcendental Aspect of the Neoclassical Critique," the school of thought of which Finnis and Grisez are the major exponents, because of its analytic approach, is pushed to the point of denying any relevance, in the justification of moral rules, either to nature or to the ultimate end. Not only, moreover, does it offer an equally deficient model of ethical justification, but it does not even manage to discover the conclusive critique of the conventional model that a proper consideration of St. Thomas's thought would have suggested.

In light of the neoclassical attitude toward God and the ultimate end, I will attempt, in section 6, "The Antinominalism of Neoclassical Theory," to recover a sense in which the will of God can assume ethical relevance without dissolving into a total and arbitrary heteronomy. In this way, I will also leave open the possibility of a non-voluntaristic interpretation of Suárez's approach to natural law theory—or at least of his initial moves—and I will show that the neoclassicists' rejection of the ethical relevance of God's will originates in a metaphysical approach to the problem of knowledge of God that is incompatible with St. Thomas's. The burden of this section, finally, will be to show how the tendency to exclude God from philosophical reflection on moral conduct leads not only the neoclassicists, but other contemporary interpreters of Aquinas as well, to advance what is substantially a doctrine of natural law *without law*—that is, to advance a new ethical "autonomism" similar to that of the fourteenth-century antinominalist reaction.

2. Suárez's Mediation Between Nominalism and Antinominalism

On the theme of natural law, Suárez's reflections aim to achieve a conclusive synthesis of the wide-ranging debate, played out from the fourteenth to the sixteenth century, between nominalists and antinominalists. His conclusions can be summarized in terms of the distinction between preceptive law (*lex praecipiens*) and merely indicative or demonstrative law (*lex indicans*).[4]

In this regard, it must be said that the tradition of philosophical reflection on the moral law—which Christians inherited primarily from the Stoics—had faced two conceptually distinct demands ever since its inception. On the one hand, the goodness of man's behavior depends on his obedience to God, who creates and rules the universe, directing it to an end which is God Himself. Here the famous Augustinian notion of sin in terms of the *lex aeterna* is emblematic: "Ergo peccatum est factum vel dictum vel concupitum aliquid contra aeternam legem. Lex vero aeterna est ratio divina vel voluntas Dei ordinem naturalem conservari iubens, perturbari vetans."[5] On the other hand, the principle of moral action is internal to man himself. It is the dictate (law) of his reason that naturally indicates to him what is good and what is bad. The main source and emblem of this insight is the well-known passage of St. Paul in which, referring to the Pagans who have not received the gift of divine revelation, he asserts that "what the law requires is written on their hearts, while their conscience also bears witness (*testimonium reddente illis conscientia ipsorum*) and their conflicting thoughts accuse or perhaps excuse them" (Rm 2:15).

These two demands are carried to opposite extremes in the positions adopted by the nominalist school, originating with William of Ockham, and by the antinominalist reaction, led by Gregory of Rimini.

The nominalists reduce the source of morality to mere obedience to the will of God (which can be arbitrary but not contradictory). If human

4 On this distinction see especially Frederick Copleston, *History of Philosophy* (London: Burns Oates & Washbourne Ltd., 1953), III, pp. 384–85; and P. Suñer, "Teocentrismo de la ley natural," in Francisco Suárez, *De legibus*, III (Madrid: C.S.I.C., 1974), pp. XXXVIII–XXXLV. The critical bibliography on Suárez is vast; for an introduction to his legal-political thought I recommend especially G. Ambrosetti, *La filosofia delle leggi di Suárez* (Rome: Editrice Studium, 1948); *Il diritto naturale della riforma cattolica: Una giustificazione storica del sistema di Suárez*; Recasens Sichez, *La filosofía del Derecho de Francisco Suárez;* H. Rommen, *Die Staatslehre des F. Suárez* (Munich: M. Gladbach, 1926).

5 Augustine, *Contra Faustum Manichaeum libri triginta tres*, book 22, ch. 27 (PL 42, 418).

nature has a role to play, it is only by the command of God, not on account of its intrinsic goodness.[6] The antinominalists, eager to defend the traditional metaphysics of essences and the natural law from the Ockhamist attack, remove all value from the will of God, and conceive of morality as simply conforming oneself to the intrinsic truth of human nature, witnessed to by the dictates of right reason which judges what is good and what is evil. As is well known, this is the view that prevailed in the modern age, and that probably best defines modern natural law as different from the classical.[7] The so-called "modern school of natural law" of Hobbes, Locke and Rousseau—from which, through the American and French Revolutions, the first declarations of universal human rights stem[8]—builds upon Grotius's famous *etiamsi daremus non esse Deum.*[9] This is why it is common to say that the modern tradition is no longer reli-

6 Such an interpretation, going back, even before Ockham, as far as John Duns Scotus, is usually believed to have initiated the voluntaristic tradition in the history of natural law, a history marked, in this first phase, by the exegetical need to clarify the passages of Sacred Scripture that seem to sanction exceptions to or dispensations from the Ten Commandments. See H. Rommen, *The Natural Law: A Study in Legal and Social History and Philosophy* (St. Louis: B. Herder Book Company, 1947), trans. T.R. Hanley, p. 42 ff.; see also G. Fassò, *Storia della filosofia del diritto, vol. 1: Antichità e Medioevo* (Bologna: Il Mulino, 1966).

7 See for example B. Bix, "Natural Law Theory," in D. Patterson (ed.), *A Companion to Philosophy of Law and Legal Theory* (Oxford: Oxford University Press, 1996), pp. 223–40.

8 Bobbio (*L'età dei diritti*, pp. 21 ff) distinguishes three main moments in the history of human rights. The first is philosophical: it is the moment of modern natural law theory, where rights are already proclaimed as universal but do not have yet legal validity. The second is the moment of the declarations following the American and French Revolutions: here the rights do have legal validity, for the first time in history, but precisely as legal they are no longer universal since they necessarily belong either to France or to the United States. The third moment is, finally, both universal and legal: it is, of course, the moment of the *Universal Declaration* of 1948. On the history of human rights from the beginning to the *Universal Declaration*, a very useful text is Felice Battaglia, *Le carte dei diritti* (Florence: Sansoni, 1946).

9 Hugo Grotius, *De iure belli ac pacis*, Paris 1625, Prolegomena 11. On the importance of Grotius for the history of natural law, see Alessandro Passerin D'Entrèves, *Natural Law: An Introduction to Legal Philosophy* (London: Hutchinson University Library, 1951); and H. Rommen, *The Natural Law: A Study in Legal and Social History and Philosophy.* Passerin D'Entrèves, unlike Rommen, very much emphasizes the role played by Grotius's contribution.

gious but secular; or that it is no longer controlled by a "heteronymous attitude of the spirit"[10] but by an autonomous one, in which it is clear that the moral law is only "given by that 'nature,' that peculiar essence of man, which is his reason."[11]

Francisco Suárez expresses his settled opinion on the question in his renowned *Tractatus de legibus ac Deo legislatore*, and, in particular, in the Second Book, "On the Eternal Law, the Natural Law and the Rights of People," in chapters V ("Whether Natural law is Natural Right Reason Itself") and VI ("Whether Natural Law is Truly a Preceptive Divine Law").

Suárez lived immediately after the Council of Trent, which had condemned the Lutheran doctrine of justification, reaffirming the intrinsic moral value of human acts. For him, it is clear that the natural law must be grounded in the order of essences, which do not depend on the arbitrary will of God. In chapter V of the Second Book, however, he criticizes the thesis, advanced by Vazquez in his *Commentarium* (*in Primam Secundae*, disp. 150, chap. 3), according to which "rational nature, strictly speaking, is natural law itself, insofar as rational nature involves no inconsistency and is the basis in human actions, either of all their righteousness (through their accord with the said rational nature), or else, on the contrary, of their turpitude (through their discord with that nature)."[12] Indeed, Suárez spends all of chapter V attempting to demonstrate that the natural law does not consist properly in rational nature as such, but rather, in the dictate of natural right reason.

According to Suárez, Vazquez adduces as a fundamental argument for

10 G. Del Vecchio, *Storia della filosofia del diritto* (Milan: Giuffrè, 1958), p. 31.

11 G. Fassò, *Storia della filosofia del diritto, vol. II: L'età moderna* (Bologna: Il Mulino, 1968), p. 113.

12 Suárez, *Tractatus de legibus ac Deo legislatore*, II, v, 2: "affirmans naturam rationalem secundum se et ut non implicat contradictionem estque fundamentum omnis honestatis actuum humanorum vel convenientium tali naturae vel contrariae turpitudinis eorum per disconvenientiam ad eandem, esse ipsam legem naturalem." For the Latin text I used the Spanish critical edition in six volumes, Suárez, *De legibus*. For the Italian edition of this book I translated Suárez from Latin, taking into account the Spanish translation. For this English edition, I used James Brown (ed.), *Selections from Three Works of Francisco Suárez, S.J.*, trans. Gladys L. Williams, Ammi Brown and John Waldron, with certain revisions by Henry Davis, S.J. (Oxford: Clarendon Press, 1944). However, I occasionally made minor alterations to the English translation to match my original Italian translation.

his thesis the premise that there are actions "so intrinsically bad of their very nature, that their malice in no way depends upon external prohibition, either of judgment or of the divine will," and similarly, "actions so essentially good and upright, that their possession of these qualities is in no sense dependent upon any external cause."[13] On this point Suárez shows himself to be in agreement: "moral actions have their own intrinsic nature and immutable essence, which in no way depend upon any external cause or will any more than does the essence of other things which in themselves involve no contradiction."[14]

Starting with this common premise, Suárez summarizes the three proofs[15] given in support of Vazquez's thesis. The first is that the rectitude or evil of moral acts "is to be found in their conformity [or lack of conformity] with some law, and not with a judgment pronounced by reason; therefore, the character of the said actions is determined by their conformity with the rational nature itself, and consequently, that rational nature in itself is the natural law, with respect to all those things which are prescribed or forbidden, approved or permitted by the natural law." We are given a significant example of this proof: "Lying," says Suárez, "is not evil because it is adjudged by reason to be evil; rather, the converse is true, that lying is adjudged evil because it is essentially evil; therefore, it is not judgment that measures the evil of this action, and consequently, it is not a prohibitory law on the subject [...] the action in question is evil for this reason, namely, that in its very essence it is out of harmony with rational nature; hence, [that] nature itself is the standard by which this action is measured, and, consequently, that nature is the natural law."[16]

The point of this argument is to call our attention to the experience of the objectivity of moral precepts, as opposed to the experience of the subjectivity of judgments expressed by particular individuals. Law is understood here as the objective measuring stick of morality, as opposed to the subjective measure supplied by judgment. However, nothing in the argument implies that "rational nature," as such, can be known apart from the judgments and interpretations of the agent. It only implies that there must

13 Ibid.

14 Ibid.

15 The use of "proof" is probably more accurate (and classical) in the context of medieval dialectics, but one could also use "argument" without any relevant loss in meaning.

16 Suárez, *Tractatus de legibus ac Deo legislatore*, II, v, 3.

be a constant, objective, measure for those judgments and interpretations.

The second proof is that the precepts of natural law precede all judgments of reason; "hence, with respect to such actions and precepts, a judgment cannot have the nature of law, seeing that prior to every [possible] judgment they possess their good or evil character, and are prescribed or forbidden accordingly."[17] The difference between the first and the second proof seems to be that, while the first focuses on the experience of the objectivity of the ethical criterion, the second looks to the experience of the imperative which presents itself to the conscience of the individual *before* the ethical choice has been made. The imperative, in other words, cannot be generated by the very ethical choice it requires.

The third proof is based on a simple comparison with non-rational beings, whose nature is itself the standard for their behavior: "[the standard in question] dwells in like manner, in rational nature; and in this harmony or discord between a free act and rational nature itself, as such, consists the goodness or turpitude of that act; so that, more properly speaking, that nature falls into the category of law."[18]

For our purposes, the most important thing to note here is that Suárez, in criticizing Vazquez, does not reject the idea that morality depends on conformity or lack of conformity with rational nature; he simply affirms that nature, albeit a "measure" of human actions, is not "law" properly speaking, whose function is to command and prohibit: "Not everything which forms the basis of the goodness or rectitude of an act prescribed by law, and not everything which is the ground for the turpitude of an act forbidden by law, may [in themselves] be called law; and, consequently, although the rational nature is the foundation of the objective goodness of the moral actions of human beings, it may not for that reason be termed law; and, by the same token, that nature may be spoken of as a measure, yet it is not therefore correct to conclude that it is 'law,' because 'measure' is broader than 'law'."[19]

According to Suárez, we must distinguish "two aspects of rational

17 Ibid., II, v. 4.

18 Ibid.

19 Ibid., II, v, 6: "quia non omne id quod est fundamentum honestatis seu rectitudinis actus lege praecepti vel quod est fundamentum turpitudinis actus lege prohibiti, potest dici lex. Ergo licet natura rationalis sit fundamentum honestatis obiectivae actuum moralium humanorum, non ideo dici potest lex. Et eadem ratione, quamvis dicatur mensura, non ideo recte concluditur quod sit lex, quia mensura latius patet quam lex."

nature: one being that nature itself, insofar as it is (so to speak) the basis of the conformity or non-conformity of human acts with itself; the other consisting in a certain power which this nature possesses of discriminating between the actions in harmony with it and those discordant with it, a power to which we give the name of natural reason. With regard to this first aspect, rational nature is said to be the basis of natural rectitude; but with regard to the second, it is said to be natural law itself (*lex ipsa naturalis*) which lays commands or prohibitions upon the human will regarding what must be done [or left undone], according to natural right (*ex naturali iure*)."[20]

It seems that Suárez here wants to express the requirement that practical reason, in the process that leads it to an ethical judgment concerning a particular act to be carried out in a particular situation, must have a starting point (a measure or standard) that is both objective and universal: the term "nature" in and of itself points to the *universal*. Judgment, however, as an act of the intellect which presents itself to one's conscience as a precept, is not a universal judgment; rather, it is a particular judgment about the goodness or badness of a particular act that is about to be done. Law, from this perspective, is strictly speaking the proximate rule of action expressed by practical reason at the end of the deliberative process. Let us return to Suárez's words: "the exercise of dominion and the function of ruling are characteristic of law; and in man, these functions are to be attributed to right reason, that he may be rightly governed in accordance with nature; therefore, the natural law must be constituted in reason as in the immediate and intrinsic rule of human actions."[21]

In this explanation of the natural law, the (proximate) basis of obligation is right reason, which commands and prohibits, while its content and objective measure are given by the rational nature, whose ends reason

20 Ibid., II, v, 9: "in natura rationali duo distinguit: unum est natura ipsa, quatenus est veluti fundamentum convenientiae vel disconvenientiae actionum humanarum ad ipsam; aliud est vis quaedam illius naturae, quam habet ad discernendum inter operationes convenientes et disconvenientes illi naturae, quam rationem naturalem appellamus. Priori modo dicitur haec natura esse fundamentum honestatis naturalis. Posteriori autem modo dicitur lex ipsa naturalis, quae humanae voluntati praecipit vel prohibet quod agendum est ex naturali iure."

21 Ibid., II, v, 12: "proprium est legis dominari et regere. Sed hoc tribuendum est rectae rationi in homine ut secundum naturam recte gubernetur. Ergo in ratione est lex naturalis constituenda tanquam in proxima regula intrinseca humanarum actionum."

itself is capable of discerning. Thus far, good and evil have been rooted in man himself, and we remain within the confines of a completely autonomous morality, along the lines of the antinominalist school. It is at this point, however, that Suárez feels the need to go further, and begins his work of mediation between the schools that had preceded him: for there cannot be a true law unless the will of somebody who commands intervenes. If the natural law consists solely in the dictates of natural reason, it follows that it is not really law at all: it is only indicative (*indicans*) and not preceptive or binding (*praecipiens*).

The argument Suárez adduces in favor of a source of moral obligation external to man is the most classical one for the existence of a natural law;[22] an argument that Kierkegaard would also take up.[23] According to this argument, the natural law cannot be a precept that man gives to himself, "since a command of this kind either does not exist save as an act of judgment manifesting the truth of the matter in hand, or else, if it be an expression of the will or of a choice already made, it is not in itself necessary to action, nor does it impose an obligation, but [merely] leads to the actual execution of the act in question, so that it neither suffices for, nor contributes anything to, the true or proper character of law."[24] The problem of reconciling human nature as the source of morality with the need for an external source of moral obligation (and thus of morality itself) is the subject-matter of the whole sixth chapter of the second book. And it is not a matter, according to Suárez, of simply pointing to the source of creation in God as its efficient cause, because what is at stake is not the created nature of man and his reason, but the actual role played by knowledge

22 See for example J. Hervada, *Introduzione critica al diritto naturale* (Milan: Giuffrè, 1990), pp. 137–38. A similar argument in support of the heteronomy of moral obligation is made by H.P. Owen, *The Moral Argument for Christian Theism* (London: Allen and Unwin, 1965).

23 See G. Modica, *Fede libertà peccato: Figure ed esiti della "prova" in Kierkegaard* (Palermo: Palumbo, 1992). Heteronomy appears in Kierkegaard as the foundation of liberty: "if in giving oneself the law, 'what binds is not something higher than the 'I' itself, and it is up to me to bind myself, where then as A (the one who binds) should I find the severity that I lack as B (the one who is bound), given that A and B are the same 'I'?'" (p. 69). This view, of course, is directly opposed to Rousseau's concept of moral liberty as "obedience to the law one has prescribed for oneself" (*On the Social Contract*, trans. by D.A. Cress [Indianapolis: Hackett, 1987], p. 27), which is the immediate forerunner of Kant's concept of autonomy. Rousseau, for Kant, had been the Newton of ethics.

24 Suárez, *Tractatus de legibus ac Deo legislatore*, II, vi, 1.

of God as Legislator in the human conscience's perception of moral obligation.

Suárez explicitly contrasts the antinominalist thesis, attributing it mainly to Gregory of Rimini, with the nominalist one, which he attributes mainly to William of Ockham. The former, distinguishing between indicative, or demonstrative, law and preceptive law, holds that the natural law—precisely because it is not the expression of the will of a superior—only indicates what must be done or not done in conformity with the rational nature of man: natural law does not proceed, then, from God as Legislator. In saying this, Gregory of Rimini, who died in 1358, enunciated for the first time in history and with surprising lucidity the "*etiamsi daremus*" hypothesis—significantly, three centuries before Grotius. "Indeed, if, *per impossibile*, divine reason and God Himself did not exist, or His reason were erroneous, even so, whoever were to act against angelic or human right reason, or the right reason of any being whatsoever, would nonetheless sin."[25] Suárez himself, during the first phase of his studies (*De bonitate et malitia actuum humanorum*, 1582), had adhered wholly to this thesis,[26] and the idea of a *merely philosophical* sin can still be found in *De legibus*.[27]

At the opposite extreme, Ockham (*Super quatuor libros Sententiarum*, 1318–1323) reduces the natural law to the character of a mere precept. Considered in God it is nothing but the eternal law, which, residing in the divine will, commands and prohibits various actions. In man, on the other hand, it is the judgment of reason revealing the will of God concerning what must be done or avoided regarding those things that are in conformity with natural reason. Acts are good or bad simply because God has commanded them or prohibited them, "and there is no

25 Gregory of Rimini, *In librum secundum Sententiarum*, d. 34, q. 1, a. 2, l. H: "Nam si per impossibile ratio divina sive Deus ipse non esset, aut ratio illa esset errans, adhuc, si quis ageret contra rectam rationem angelicam vel humanam aut aliam aliquam si qua esset, peccare." Cf. also Suárez, op. cit., II, VI, 3: "Immo ait Gregorius [...] licet Deus non esset vel non uteretur ratione vel non recte de rebus iudicaret, si in homine esset idem dictamen rectae rationis dictantis v. g. malum esse mentiri, illud habiturum eandem rationem legis quam nunc habet, quia esset lex ostensiva malitiae, quae in obiecto ab intrinseco existit"; Grotius, *De iure belli ac pacis*, Prolegomena 11.

26 On the evolution of Suárez's thought on the natural law, see Suñer, "Teocentrismo de la ley natural."

27 See, for example, Suárez, *Tractatus de legibus ac Deo legislatore*, II, vi, 17.

act incapable of becoming a good act if commanded by God; and conversely."[28]

"I hold," says Suárez, "that a middle course should be taken, this middle course being, in my judgment, the opinion held by St. Thomas and common to the theologians."[29] Such a position is based on the conviction that the natural law, even if it manifests (or indicates) the intrinsic rationality of human nature, should not be considered law in a diluted sense of the term, but in the strictest sense, which entails a command capable of imposing obligations: "so that the natural law, as existing in man, points out a given thing not only as it is in itself, but also as being forbidden or prescribed by some superior."[30] This conviction is all the more interesting because, as I mentioned earlier, it is the fruit of a re-thinking of the issue on the part of the author.

More specifically, however, chapter VI is based on three basic claims. The first is that the natural law, as already explained, is not only *indicative* of good and evil, but also includes the command of one and the prohibition of the other. Besides what has already been said concerning the perception of obligation and its external basis, it might be useful to point out that—contrary to what some might believe—Suárez's reasoning is based on the idea of the primacy of intellect over will in rational action. It cannot be one's own will that binds one's judgment, because the will can only desire what the intellect knows. But because the intellect cannot bind itself, the presence of obligation in the moral conscience, even in the absence of any command on the part of other men, requires the presence of a will that is prior and external to man himself.

Suárez draws a comparison between the acts prescribed by the natural law and those acts whose evil derives merely from the prohibition of human law. In the latter case, the subject's judgment concerning the goodness or evil of an act has the function of making known what the law prescribes; it is not, however, the source of obligation, which is the existence (external to the acting subject) of human law. In the same way, when there is no human law (or when there is more than just human law), the judgment of the subject presupposes a law external to and prior to himself, which is the source of the binding moral character of human acts. Suárez concludes that if judgment alone were the norm of good and evil, even

28 Ibid., II, vi, 4.
29 Ibid., II, vi, 5.
30 Ibid., II, vi, 7.

God would be subject to a natural law, because "even in God an intellectual act of judgment logically precedes an act of His will."[31]

Suárez's second claim is that prohibition or command is not the only reason for the goodness or badness of an act: rather, they presuppose another reason, to which they *add* a special obligation of divine law. Here too, the discussion flows from the primacy of the intellect over the will, in the context of the metaphysics of essences. Human willing cannot be empty; rather, it is always the willing of something known previously by the intellect (*nihil volitum nisi precognitum*). Intellectual cognition, on the other hand, is always conceptual or *essential* knowledge of something. Obligation, then, is not indifferent to content because it always presents itself to conscience in relation to the intellectual knowledge of a certain essence. In this way, it can be said that acts are not evil simply because they are prohibited, but they are prohibited because they are evil.[32]

The third claim, finally, is that the natural law is a true and proper law whose legislator is God. This assertion complements the preceding two in that it considers the natural law *as it exists in man* in light of *how it exists in God*. In God, it presupposes a judgment about the morality of human acts, to which is *added* the will to obligate men to do whatever right reason dictates. It cannot be admitted that "the divine will, whereby the natural law is sanctioned, does not presuppose the existence of a dictate of the divine reason" concerning what is good and what is evil because even in God, as already noted, intellect precedes will. Natural law, then, involves both the reason and the will of God. And this is why, in the last analysis, natural law, "as it exists in man, does not merely indicate what is evil, but actually obliges us to avoid the same; and it consequently does not merely point out the natural disharmony of a particular act or object with rational nature, but is also a manifestation of the divine will prohibiting that act or object."[33]

There is no need for our purposes to dwell any further upon Suárez's arguments. It is important, however, to stress that his definitive explana-

31 Ibid., II, vi, 6. This argument, of course, is taken from Aquinas. See, esp., *ST*, I–II, q. 93, a. 4 ("Whether Necessary and Eternal Things are Subject to the Eternal Law?").

32 Suárez, *Tractatus de legibus ac Deo legislatore*, II, vi, 11–12.

33 Ibid., II, vi, 13: "Unde tandem fit legem naturalem, prout in nobis est, non tantum esse indicantem malum, sed etiam obligantem ad cavendum illud, ac subinde non solum repraesentare naturalem disconvenentiam talis actus vel obiecti cum rationali natura, sed etiam esse signum divinae voluntatis vetantis illud."

tion of natural law is heteronymous to the extent that, as for the nominalists, moral obligation rests (outside of man) on the will of God. But it is also autonomous, since morality consists essentially in following the dictates of right reason, which, by knowing the rational nature of man and what accords with it, knows it also as willed by God—and therefore as ultimately good and binding. Ockham is different in that for him, the human knowledge of essences serves only to manifest to man the way in which the will of God is channeled concretely, while for Suárez the knowledge of essences manifests to man above all divine reason itself, and thus reveals the existence of moral value inherent in nature.

3. Manualistic Morality

Let us now leave Francisco Suárez, at least for the moment, to focus on the contemporary theory of natural law that the neoclassicists have defined as "conventional." What is it exactly and who advances it? Germain Grisez, writing in 1964, remarked that it is "commonly considered the only traditional explanation of the moral law accepted by Catholic philosophers," and probably for this reason he decided to call it "conventional."[34] Additionally, both Finnis and Grisez have characterized this approach as the method of natural-law reasoning proper to "manualistic" morality.[35]

These two simple statements are sufficient to understand the scope of the critique that the neoclassicists intend to undertake. Basically, they connect the conventional theory of natural law with an entire historical period of Catholic morality; a period that begins in the middle of the sixteenth century and that has, in recent years, undergone a profound re-thinking. This period, it is said, generated an approach to ethical problems that has become so pervasive in doctrine and in common understanding that it is universally considered the classical one, but that in fact has lost some of the elements essential to classical morality. In recent years this approach has been defined pejoratively as "manualistic." With regard to this term it may be useful to keep in mind a broad historical overview.

In the history of moral theology it is now usual to distinguish—after the Patristic, the Great Scholastic, and the late Medieval periods—a long era reaching from the Council of Trent to the second Vatican Council and

34 G. Grisez, *Contraception and the Natural Law*, p. 46.

35 Ibid. See also, by the same author, *The Way of the Lord Jesus*, ch. I, "Christian Moral Principles," p. 6 ff; and J. Finnis, *Natural Law and Natural Rights*, pp. 43–44.

characterized by the use of manuals that, despite their differences, reveal a common approach to ethical problems. "Regardless of the differences between schools, nearly all moral manuals from the seventeenth to the twentieth century adopted the same base and structure that appeared in fundamental moral theology. There were four treatises—on human acts, conscience, laws, and sins. These were always included, with minor variations. Some manuals changed their order. Others, in fidelity to St. Thomas, added a treatise on the virtues, attempting to make room for it in the division of moral theology. Some even began with a treatise on man's final end. Most of these addictions and reactions have cropped up in our own century. But however praiseworthy, they have effected no essential change in the structure and logic of the moral system which has become classic"[36]

I do not intend to investigate the merits of this historical categorization. I will simply stress that the negative trait chiefly attributed to the manuals is to have over-emphasized the legalistic and casuistic aspects of ethics, to the point of producing an unfortunate theoretical and practical tension that is commonly identified today in terms of a conflict between the requirements of law and the requirements of freedom. In reaction against such a view, the current renewal in moral theology is directed toward a more personalistic ethics, one closer to modern man and more capable of grasping the richness of real-life situations. This is the context within which the reflections of Finnis and Grisez, as well as the recent phenomenological and proportionalist approaches, should be evaluated.[37]

By connecting the conventional theory with the moral theology known until Vatican II as "classical,"[38] the "neoclassicists" join, even terminologically, the current effort to recover—especially through an attentive rereading of Thomas Aquinas—the ethical view that preceded the

36 S. Pinckaers, *The Sources of Christian Morality* [1985] (Washington, D.C.: Catholic University of America Press, 1995), trans. Sr. Mary Thomas Noble, O.P., p. 267. On this subject see also Melina, *Morale: tra crisi e rinnovamento*.

37 On this subject see, most recently, E. Molina, *La moral entre la convicción y la utilidad: La evolución de la moral desde la manualística al proporcionalismo y al pensamiento de Grisez-Finnis*. This author, judging the thought of Finnis and Grisez favorably, associates it with proportionalism with respect to the common desire to overcome the scholastic manualistic morality. Among the major exponents of the other approaches I have just mentioned, think, for example, of P. Knauer, L. Janssens, J. Fuchs, R. McCormick, G. Hallett and B. Schueller.

38 On this connection see also R. Hittinger, *A Critique of the New Natural Law Theory*, p. 14.

Protestant crisis and the Council of Trent. At a philosophically level, in particular, they try to do this by offering a renewed version of the traditional doctrine of natural law, which they understand first and foremost as a "method" used in Catholic ethics to derive moral norms: the method of the natural law.

4. The Neoclassical Image of the Conventional Theory

Let us see how, exactly, the neoclassical thinkers reconstruct the theory they set out to criticize. First, however, we must acknowledge that the detailed description they offer of conventional natural law theory "does not intend to reflect the position of any particular author." Indeed, given the characterization of an entire historical epoch (and not a short one at that) as "manualistic," we are clearly dealing here with a term of convenience. To my knowledge, the only contemporary author to whom they occasionally refer as a typical example of the conventional view is Thomas J. Higgins (*Man as Man: The Science and Art of Ethics*, revised edition [Milwaukee: The Bruce Publishing Co., 1958]).[39]

In *Contraception and the Natural Law*, Grisez lays out one by one the basic features that, in his view, characterize the conventional theory. We can reduce them, for the sake of simplicity, to five: (1) a factualistic concept of human nature, assumed as the source of moral norms; (2) the need for an absolute and extrinsic moral principle, founded, in the last analysis, on the arbitrary will of God; (3) a secondary role assigned to practical reason; (4) an excessive attention to casuistry and the negativity of precepts; and (5) a lack of proportion between man's moral acts and his ultimate end, which in turn leads to an undervaluing of intention in the evaluation of the objective morality of human acts. This detailed explanation is followed by four main points of criticism: the conventional theory is said to suffer from (a) the naturalistic fallacy; (b) a voluntaristic notion of obligation; (c) a negative emphasis in ethics; and (d) the absence of a link to man's ultimate end.[40]

The scheme just outlined is substantially reflected in the five characteristics that Grisez, in *Christian Moral Principles*, attributes to classical (manualistic) moral theology: (1) rationalism; (2) voluntarism; (3) legal-

39 See (also for the quotation at the beginning of the paragraph) Grisez's *Contraception and the Natural Law*, p. 72; and "The First Principle of Practical Reason: A Commentary on the *Summa theologiae*, 1–2, Question 94, Article 2," p. 168.

40 G. Grisez, *Contraception and the Natural Law*, pp. 46–53.

ism; (4) otherworldliness (that is, reference to a supernatural end that deprives the goods of this world of their value); and (5) minimalism.[41]

Rationalism, which the neoclassical critics attribute to the conventional theory, is the key element of their reconstruction, upon which all the other aspects depend. Moreover, it is precisely the element to which their main criticism, concerning the naturalistic fallacy, is connected. It is, therefore, the element on which an adequate explanation of the neoclassical reconstruction must focus.

According to the neoclassicists, the conventional theory's rationalism is a result not so much of employing a particular deductive method as of a tendency to separate reasoning directed to the elaboration of moral norms from practical reflection centered on the proper and genuine good of man. This tendency is well illustrated by the following triadic explanation offered by Grisez:

> Many proponents and critics of Thomas Aquinas's theory of natural law have understood it roughly as follows. The first principle of practical reason is a command: Do good and avoid evil. Man discovers this imperative in his conscience; it is like an inscription written there by the hand of God. Having become aware of this basic commandment, man consults his nature to see what is good and what is evil. He examines an action in comparison with his essence to see whether the action fits human nature or does not fit it. If the action fits, it is seen to be good; if it does not fit, it is seen to be bad. Once we know that a certain kind of action—for instance, stealing—is bad, we have two premises, 'Avoid evil' and 'Stealing is evil,' from whose conjunction is deduced: 'Avoid stealing.' All specific commandments of natural law are derived in this way.[42]

From this chain of reasoning there clearly emerges a dissociation of the ultimate source of duty and goodness (represented by a first principle, in itself empty) from human nature, the knowledge of which does not in itself reveal what is good and what is due. We are thus confronted with a separation through which the basic ethical norm is located outside of nature: ethical heteronomy.

It is easy to derive two immediate consequences from this position. The first is that, the problem of duty and the good having been resolved

41 G. Grisez, *The Way of the Lord Jesus, Vol. I, Christian Moral Principles*, p. 12 ff. See also R. Hittinger, *A Critique of the New Natural Law Theory*.

42 G. Grisez, "The First Principle of Practical Reason: A Commentary on the *Summa theologiae*, 1–2, Question 94, Article 2," p. 168.

once and for all by positing an absolute and extrinsic first principle ("*Avoid morally bad acts*" or "*Act in conformity with nature*" or "*Follow reason*"),[43] the moralist's attention will tend to shift entirely toward the observation of nature so as to grasp the content of specific moral norms. The second consequence is that nature itself, once separated from the source of goodness, will tend to be understood in a factualistic way. That is, the moralist will concentrate on the physical and biological finality of human beings, attempting to deduce from this the norms of morality, or what amounts to the same thing, the content of the natural law.

On this view, clearly, "the moral norm simply is human nature" as it presents itself to rational knowledge; and the appropriate method in ethics involves a purely speculative judgment of conformity between possible actions and the intelligible structure of nature.[44]

More specifically, this sort of rationalistic methodology—or so the neoclassicists say—stems largely from an excessive focus on the human being's natural ends, which leads either to an absolutizing of individual human goods—transforming them into morally obligatory ends—or to an unjustified transformation of the ends of organic functions into morally obligatory ends. Grisez, addressing the case of contraception, sets out these two possibilities as variants of what he calls the "typical syllogism" of the conventional theory:

> Major premise: To prevent any human act from attaining its natural end is intrinsically immoral.
>
> Minor premise: Contraception prevents sexual intercourse from attaining its natural end.
>
> Conclusion: Contraception is intrinsically immoral.[45]

After excluding an equivocal, banal, interpretation in which the meaning of "natural end" is different in the major and minor premises, Grisez

43 G. Grisez, *Contraception and the Natural Law*, p. 47.

44 Cf. ibid.: "What is most characteristic of conventional natural-law theory is its notion of the objectivity of moral norms. The moral norm simply is human nature as it is given – given, of course, not to sense experience but to rational understanding. Moral goodness and badness can be discerned simply by comparing the essential patterns of possible human actions with the intelligible structure of human nature considered both in its inner complexity and in its extrinsic relationships."

45 For his complete explanation of the typical syllogism, see ibid., pp. 20–33.

tests the consistency of the syllogism on two possible interpretations of "natural end."

First, in a broad sense, "natural end" can mean a morally obligatory good (procreation) that (in sexual relations) one must, to the extent possible, seek to realize.

Understood in this light, the good of procreation creates numerous difficulties with regard to exactly the normality of sexual behavior that the conventional theory, in attacking contraception, meant to preserve. At the individual level, for example, it calls into question the use of natural methods intended precisely for the enjoyment of sexual intercourse when conception is least likely. From a broader perspective, considering the duty of procreation in relation to the common good, one might even question the practice of periodic abstinence, or indeed of celibacy. Moreover, the syllogism cannot be defended by referring to the possible consequences—for the marital relationship, the education of children or the population of the planet—of a generalized use of contraception. By focusing on these consequences, one can at most justify a condemnation of the "generalized use" of contraception, but not of the "marginal or isolated case"; and here again, sufficiently reliable natural methods of birth control would have to be condemned as well. Neither, as Grisez concludes, can one mount a defense of the syllogism by deriving the absolute obligation of procreation from "a more general principle of sexual ethics" according to which "*any sexual activity apart from the conditions necessary for it to be suited of itself to the procreation and proper education of children is intrinsically immoral.*"[46] This principle, as a support for the syllogism, cannot by itself explain, for example, the licitness of incomplete sexual intercourse realized within marriage, or of intercourse realized when procreation is physically impossible. In any case, its absoluteness, not being self-evident, would require further justification.

In a more restricted and perhaps its most immediate sense, "natural end" can mean the purpose of the organic functions of human beings. It is this interpretation that gives rise to the well-known "perverted faculty" argument, which is so discredited today that Finnis does not hesitate to say that "as a general premise, in any form strong enough to yield the moral conclusions it has been used to defend," it is "ridiculous."[47]

The most obvious question that the perverted faculty argument raises is: why should the natural teleology of the human functions require

46 Ibid., p. 26.

47 J. Finnis, *Natural Law and Natural Rights*, p. 48.

absolute moral respect? And the most obvious objection is that if this is the case, it is not clear why it should not be so for all of the human functions. Trivial examples might come from comparing contraception to the use of ear plugs or to walking on one's hands. More serious examples might be the artificial draining, for medical reasons, of breast milk (which would conflict with the natural end of the nutrition of the child), or causing a patient to vomit for similar reasons (thus preventing the digestive system from reaching the natural end of nutrition). An example especially pertinent today might be smoking: ultimately, many are easily convinced that smoking, even if not particularly grave in every case, is intrinsically wrong because it does harm to the natural function of the respiratory system. Finally, it is clear that interpreted in this way, the syllogism cannot be defended by arguing that in the aforementioned examples, moral licitness derives from the absence of an irreversible harm. This is precisely because even contraception (unlike sterilization) does not bring about an irreversible harm—not to mention that in various cases where the patient's health is in grave danger, irreversible harm to human functions (including sterilization) is generally held to be licit.

It is not my intention here to examine in detail the examples, arguments and peculiarities of the two alternative interpretations of the conventional theory's typical syllogism, which Grisez has presented in *Contraception and the Natural Law*: for this I refer the reader to that book. Rather, what matters here is to highlight the logical formulation of the criticism that Grisez addresses to both interpretations, alleging an unwarranted move from the "is" to the "ought."

In the first case: from the fact that procreation is a good for man, one cannot derive an absolute obligation to pursue it. In the second: from the mere fact that natural functions have certain ends (e.g. sexual activity has the end of procreation; the intellect has the end of truth), it does not follow that we have an obligation to pursue these ends.[48]

It goes without saying that Grisez's objective here is not simply to split hairs, but to encourage a reflection on human duties that is based not on hasty abstractions and generalizations, but on a constant attentiveness to what is really good for man. It may therefore be helpful to determine more precisely where Grisez, whose words on this point are not particularly clear, locates the naturalistic fallacy in the first of the two interpretations we have examined. As the argument stands, one might object that in the premise there is not a mere fact but rather a good (procreation). Upon

48 G. Grisez, *Contraception and the Natural Law*, pp. 22, 27.

closer consideration, however, one realizes that the expression "procreation is a good," on its own, might be an ethically useless abstraction: it might express the simple fact that many men in history have appreciated procreation and sought it, and continue to appreciate it and seek it; or even the fact that anyone fully aware of what it is cannot fail to consider procreation something to be valued. But the expression does not say whether, when, and under what conditions procreation is a duty: it does not say, in other words, whether and when anyone is obliged to pursue it. All the difficulties mentioned above in relation to the first interpretation of the syllogism arise from this deficiency, which we can summarize as *the absence of duty in the premise of the argument*, i.e., the fallacy of a duty turning up in the conclusion.[49] Only a more probing understanding of the human good can lead to a valid explanation of its correlative duty, both positive (the good is to be pursued) and negative (it is not to be impeded).

We will now move on to consider briefly to the other features that the neoclassicists ascribe to the conventional theory of natural law. Let us begin with the second feature listed above, namely the need for an absolute and extrinsic moral principle.

It becomes necessary to posit an absolute and extrinsic moral principle, which corresponds to the first step in Grisez's triadic scheme, precisely in order to fill the gaps in the syllogism just examined. In other words, such a principle must supply the foundation of obligation and thus avoid the naturalistic fallacy. "The conventional arguments begin from an equivocation on 'natural end' and then proceed by one way or another to try to reunite the facts with a strong premise—i.e., one expressing obligation."[50]

Problems arise with this solution as soon as one attempts to justify the first principle. Since there is no intrinsic, content-based, connection with nature—the source of the concrete good and the first premise of the syllo-

49 In the different context of a critique of Alan Gewirth's natural law, Russell Hittinger expresses a similar concept, saying that even an eventual consensus on a certain set of basic necessary goods would not resolve the problem of morality, for which, in his view, ordering principles would inevitably be required: "Moral questions arise once the goods are put in relation, according to concrete issues of means and ends, contexts, and judgments concerning how they are to be balanced when they conflict. Consensus about basic goods is not the same thing as consensus about morality". This idea coincides substantially with the premoral character ascribed by the neoclassicists to the basic goods. Cf. R. Hittinger, "Natural Law and Virtue," in R.P. George (ed.), *Natural Law Theory: Contemporary Essays*, 54.

50 G. Grisez, *Contraception and the Natural Law*, p. 51.

gism—one inevitably falls into arbitrariness and voluntarism. More specifically, either (1) one stops at that first principle without any further explanation, or (2) one connects it to a sovereign will of God, which nonetheless remains impenetrable and arbitrary. This second solution is more closely associated with the legalistic tone that Grisez encounters in the history of manualistic moral theology, which obfuscates the intrinsic reasons for the moral norms, making them appear as a mere contingent product of the will of the legislator.

It is important to underline that according to the neoclassicists, even with these additional features the schema of the conventional theory does not escape the naturalistic fallacy, since the voluntarism inherent in the first principle, or in the arbitrary will of God, is ultimately nothing but another *mere fact*, incapable of yielding normativity.[51]

Let us next consider the characteristic that we have defined as the *lack of proportion between man's moral acts and his ultimate end (other-worldiness)*. This is brought about directly by the heteronomy of the first principle. In fact, the ultimate end of following such a principle—i.e., following God, by obeying His will—does not have any intrinsic connection with the goods, or ends, of human nature that it imposes as obligatory. Man's ultimate fulfillment (eternal happiness) depends on the goods of his nature only on account of obedience to God which, by respecting them, he can exercise every time he acts: "human life in itself and the actual attainments and failures which constitute it are of no real account in the long run."[52] One of the natural consequences of all of this is the union of an ever greater attention to the formal respect for norms, and a loss of interest in the relationship between the intentionality of man's will and the goods that form the object of his acts. The only intentionality that counts, for the evaluation of the objective morality of behavior, is the one that aims at respect for the first principle.

It is easy to understand, at this point, the aspect of the conventional theory that I have called the *secondary or instrumental role of practical reason*. In fact, on the conventional theory nothing remains for practical reason to do but to unite the two theoretical premises, that is (1) the ultimate principle that makes the natural ends obligatory, and (2) the opposition of a particular act to one or more natural ends, in order to deduce

51 Ibid., pp. 47, 50; see also *The Way of the Lord Jesus*, I, "Christian Moral Principles," p. 105; and Hittinger, *A Critique of the New Natural Law Theory*, p. 19.

52 Grisez, *Contraception and the Natural Law*, p. 50.

mechanically (3) the intrinsic immorality of that act.[53] In other words, reason is practical simply because it is concerned with human acts and because it involves the application of universal precepts to particular cases, but *not* because it intervenes directly in the knowledge of the good and duty. The role that remains for practical reason could be loosely compared to that reserved for a judge by the rationalist ideology of codification: the mere subsumption of the particular case under the general and abstract legal "fact," without any creativity or innovation as regards the normative element.[54]

Let me finally comment briefly on the criticism, already sufficiently clear in the preceding considerations, of the conventional theory's negative or minimalist attitude in ethics. Heteronomy, voluntarism, the secondary role assigned to practical reason—all these elements lead not to an inquiry about the meaning of the human good, but to the mere prohibition of immoral actions; moreover, they nourish an excessive growth in the casuistic study aimed at understanding which actions fall under the prohibition and which remain free (or ethically neutral). The conventional theory's syllogism, according to Grisez, gives it only a "veto power"[55] over actions, but does not make it capable of positively directing them toward the fullness of the human good.

Having reached this point, we can sum up how all this relates to the natural law tradition, and in particular to the Thomistic teaching, simply by recalling that in his treatise on *lex naturalis* Aquinas speaks of (a) a first principle of practical reason, "*bonum est faciendum et prosequendum, et malum vitandum*," and (b) the first principles of natural law, which are connected to the natural inclinations of the human being.[56]

From here, the next step for the conventional theorist is easy: (a) the first principle provides the remote legitimation of moral duty; and (b) the various inclinations become the starting point of the search for particular precepts of the natural law.

5. The Transcendental Aspect of the Neoclassical Critique

The analysis undertaken by Finnis and Grisez of the various features of conventional theory and their defects is very well done, especially where

53 Ibid., p. 48.

54 See, for example, F. Viola-M. Urso, *Scienza giuridica e diritto codificato* (Turin: Giappichelli, 1989); and A. Cavanna, *Storia del diritto moderno in Europa: Le fonti e il pensiero giuridico 1*, (Milan: Giuffrè, 1979).

55 G. Grisez, *Contraception and the Natural Law*, p. 52.

56 Aquinas, *ST*, I–II, q. 94, a. 2 c.

it brings into relief both the crisis of meaning in moral action caused by the lack of any intrinsic connection between particular actions and the ultimate end, and the consequent tendency to absolutize the various natural ends in evaluating the morality or immorality of acts. In these respects the accusations leveled at the so-called "typical" approach of manualistic morality are certainly justified, and the need to reevaluate the rational and interior character of the moral law and of its norms is entirely understandable and deserving of attention.

Here, however, the neoclassicists go well beyond a criticism of conventional theory. Convinced of the analytical principle that one cannot derive any value from the knowledge of nature, they go so far as to deny altogether the ethical relevance of natural ends or of an ultimate end, and they coin the distinction already mentioned between *objectivity*, realizable in ethics through reflection on one's own judgments of value, and *nature*, in itself a mere fact of no ethical relevance. On this view, the mistake of the conventional theory is not to have absolutized the particular natural ends or goods, losing sight both of their hierarchical ordering to the ultimate good and of the consequent intrinsic link between the intentionality of particular goods and that of the ultimate good (but more on this in chapter three). Rather, the error of conventional theory is to have referred at all to natural ends, that is, to the world of facts, in order to derive from it ethical criteria of behavior.

In reality, for anyone who, like the neoclassicists, intended to undertake a careful rereading of the Thomistic doctrine of natural law, the most obvious criticism of the conventional theory's typical syllogism should have been that a human act is intrinsically immoral not when it simply prevents the attainment of a natural end, but rather when it prevents *man* from attaining his *true* (natural) end, that is, his ultimate end. For St. Thomas, such an impediment arises when man, distracted by the pleasurable good (*bonum delectabile*), forgets the moral good (*bonum honestum*), i.e. the natural order with its three elements of proper end, natural measure, and hierarchy (again, I will return to this in chapter three).

Furthermore, to say that a human act is intrinsically immoral when it prevents the attainment of its natural end is a clear contradiction in terms. The natural end of a *human act*, i.e. whatever is *willed* by the agent at the moment of carrying it out, is always whatever end he has set for himself, and not the natural end of the means used to accomplish this, whether they are instruments or parts of the body. As a matter of fact, the only thing that can prevent a human act from attaining its natural end is an external factor that takes away from man the capacity to move and to think. If, on the other hand, the agent changes his mind, *he does not prevent his act from attaining its natural end*—he simply carries out a different act.

This ought to have been the response of a *neoclassical* theory to a conventional theory mistakenly thought to be the *classical* one. Finnis and Grisez, however, having rejected any connection between the good known by practical reason and the *facts* of nature, and thus having eliminated the only point of view from which an objective, mutual ordering and hierarchy between the different human goods can be achieved, take the impractical route of basic, "pre-moral" values.[57] Before explaining what exactly the neoclassical alternative to the conventional theory consists of, a brief summary of the foundational premises of neoclassical theory is in order.

The neoclassicists maintain that all our choices are determined by a few value judgments, which depend on primordial intuitions and are not in any way derived from the facts of nature. Consequently, the only way to enhance our knowledge of them is to reflect on the intuitions themselves. These judgments (for example: life is good, friendship is good, knowledge is good, etc.) are the sole sources of the rationality of our actions, in the sense that every time a choice is freely carried out, the good intended can be traced back to one of the basic values grasped in these judgments. The basic values are therefore pre-moral, in the sense that their pursuit as basic values is entailed by both good and evil actions. Unlike the particular values involved in individual choices, the basic values are mutually irreducible and, for this reason, incommensurable. As such, they cannot be ordered to a further end, and are thus themselves the *ultimate ends* of human action. From these premises, the neoclassicists deduce—in a somewhat mysterious fashion, given their *factual* premise concerning the rationality of all human actions—that it is irrational to act directly against one or more of the basic values, and this becomes the fundamental principle of their ethics.[58]

Essentially, the neoclassical theory accepts the fragmentation of the human good, and the absence of any reference to the ultimate end, that characterize the conventional theory; it then attempts to criticize that theory by means of a self-defeating logical strategy. More particularly, it says that the different human goods are not *absolutely obligatory* ends—that is,

57 I explain the fundamental inconsistency of this position in my article, "I valori fondamentali nella teoria neoclassica della legge naturale."

58 See Finnis-Grisez-Boyle Jr., "Practical Principles, Moral Truth, and Ultimate Ends"; and *Nuclear Deterrence, Morality and Realism*, pp. 275–94.

ends that must always be pursued when one is acting in the contexts in which they are implicated—but that they do somehow constitute *limits* upon the range of possible choices, in the sense that one ought never intentionally and directly act against them.

On this view, an intrinsically evil act is not one that prevents the attainment of its natural end, but one that *of itself does nothing but* damage one of the basic human values.[59] Now before I go on, I must defend myself against the potential criticism that the first moral principle formulated by the neoclassical school is in reality something else, namely: "In voluntarily acting for human goods and avoiding what is opposed to them, *one ought to choose and otherwise will those and only those possibilities whose willing is compatible with integral human fulfillment*."[60] In fact, however, it emerges clearly from the writings of the neoclassicists that the only actions *incompatible with integral human fulfillment* are those that do nothing but damage one of the basic human goods, and the latter is therefore the criterion one must fall back on in ethical arguments about intrinsically evil acts.

It is also worth noting that, apart from the adjective "basic," the claim that an intrinsically evil act is one *that does nothing but damage one of the human goods* is compatible with the hierarchy-based Thomistic ethic. Indeed, one could legitimately say that for St. Thomas a morally evil act is precisely one that damages a human good without such damage being justified by an objective ordering to the ultimate end.

The neoclassicists, however, reject the notions of hierarchy and of an ultimate end, and given the fact that every properly human (that is, free and rational) act is necessarily carried out in view of a certain good (which can always be traced back to one of the basic values), clearly the only way there could be an action that does nothing but damage one of the basic human goods, is if it were not a human action—in other words, if such an action were neither free nor rational. This is the basic logical problem with the neoclassical theory of natural law. Finnis, Grisez and their followers, having posited an intrinsic link between free, rational action and the intentional pursuit of the basic values, have sought in every possible way to find an intentional alternative to these values that might ground the possibility of moral and immoral *human* actions.

59 See J. Finnis, *Natural Law and Natural Rights*, p. 118–25.

60 See Finnis-Grisez-Boyle, *Nuclear Deterrence, Morality, and Realism*, p. 283. See also my introduction, section 4, "The Neoclassical Theory of Natural Law."

To this end, they at first put forward the idea that immoral actions are those in which the agent allows himself to be guided only by feelings. However, given that feelings cannot constitute an intentional alternative to value, a free and therefore ration action will always be directed toward at least one of the values. Therefore, whatever the influence of feelings, it is not logically possible to define this action as immoral. If, on the other hand, feelings indicate pleasure as an intentional alternative to value, then in the neoclassical construction there is no reason not to list pleasure itself as one of the basic values, and the problem reappears in the same way as before.

Given the failure of this first attempt, the neoclassicists attempt to resolve the dilemma by distinguishing between those effects directly sought by the agent and "side effects." They argue that since every morally relevant action is always carried out in view of one or more of the basic values *to the detriment of* the others, immorality will occur when, instead of accepting the necessary harm to other values as mere "side effects," it is sought directly. It is clear, however, that this argument cannot avoid being reduced to a mere play on words: by hypothesis, what the agent pursues directly in every free action, even the worst that one could imagine, is always a basic value, and so necessary negative effects on the other values cannot be willed directly but only as side-effects (and not as means, because the means cannot be willed as a negative effect on something else but only as a positive effect on the end being pursued).

6. The Antinominalism of Neoclassical Theory

The transcendental attitude of the neoclassical school, that is, the rigid way in which it conceives the separation between practical and theoretical reason, lies at the root of its theorization of the "pre-morality" of values, and of its rejection of any hierarchy or ultimate end in morality. With these premises, however, the neoclassical school is unable to produce any penetrating criticism of the conventional theory's model of ethical justification, and is incapable of explaining the moral dimension of human acts.

Now, however, we must return to our main theme. Recall that the conventional model based the binding character of natural ends (i.e., of nature) on the remote reference to an indeterminate absolute principle, and ultimately to the will of God. It is precisely at this aspect of the conventional theory, usually traced back historically to Suárez's doctrine, that the neoclassicists aimed their main criticism. It is now time to touch on the neoclassical theory's approach to the problem of ethical autonomy and heteronomy, and in so doing to reevaluate the problem of the will of God in ethics (and perhaps, in this context, to do Francisco Suárez a little more justice). In this regard, I would like to begin by defending myself against the possible criticism that I am excessively emphasizing the contrast between the neoclassical theory and Suárez. I make use of this contrast mainly to correct some of the overly reductive references to the Suárezian and post-Suárezian[61] tradition, and to frame better the theoretical intentions of the neoclassical critics.

In brief, it does not seem to me that one can properly attribute to Suárez a factualistic conception of human nature, or say that his reference to the will of God is nothing but a vain attempt to avoid the naturalistic fallacy. Suárez probably never imagined the naturalistic-fallacy criticism, because reason is, for him, capable of knowing man's rational nature as *good*, that is, in a practical mode. He simply shrinks from the idea that man can bind himself, give himself the law: in other words, from the idea that the obligation of which conscience becomes aware is ultimately based on human reason itself. Responding to Gregory of Rimini, he rejects the notion of an ethics that is godless or totally autonomous, along the lines of the modern Kantian model. Rather, in knowing nature man grasps the wisdom and will of God, and it is in God that the meaning of moral goodness ultimately lies. The will of God cannot be interpreted here as a mere fact; it assumes a strictly moral value: that is to say, for man it is a good and it is practical knowledge. Since it refers to the order that God's own wisdom has conceived of as intrinsically good, it is not arbitrary. Finally, one cannot speak of a lack of connection between particular goods of human nature and the ultimate end, because man knows the will of God *precisely in the act of knowing the intrinsic goodness of nature*.

Up to now, we have spoken of the autonomy-heteronomy dichotomy in two senses. On the one hand, it signifies the opposition between an ethics that is ultimately based exclusively on human reason (autonomy), and an ethics whose sense of obligation or of the moral good ultimately rests on obedience to the order willed by God (heteronomy). On the other hand, it signifies two distinct interpretations of practical reason: one in which norms are imposed on it from without, as something extraneous

61 See, for example, J. Finnis, *Natural Law and Natural Rights*, pp 49, 342–43, 350. David Williams criticizes the neoclassical theory along the same lines in "The Immutability of Natural Law according to Suárez," *The Thomist*, 1 (1998), pp. 97–115.

(heteronomy); and the other in which the perception of normativity depends on a prior perception of the good that is the reason for the norm (autonomy). It is only by assuming this second sense of heteronomy that we can speak of it as the source of the naturalistic fallacy, or that we can have factualistic conceptions of human nature or rationalistic consequences in moral reasoning. It is clear, however, that if we refer to the will of God as a good for man, we do not deal with the second sense of heteronomy, but with (practical) reflection upon the (ultimate) meaning of the good perceived by human reason.

The neoclassicists believe that reference to the will of God, in the context of philosophical reflection on ethics, is a sure sign of heteronomy in the second sense, and of a reason that is blind to the good. Their project is therefore situated within the typically modern project of constructing an ethics without God,[62] and is inclined to attribute to human reason complete moral autonomy. The following statement of intent by Finnis is representative of this approach: "Thomas Aquinas [...] considers that the first principles of natural law are self-evident, but that (i) the existence of God is *not* self-evident to the human mind, (ii) a knowledge that friendship with God is our last end is *not* available by 'natural' reasoning but only by revelation, (iii) attainment of that end is not possible by natural means but only by supernatural grace; and (iv) the will of God insofar as it concerns creatures (such as mankind) cannot be discovered by reasoning [...] Part II of this book offers a rather elaborate sketch of a theory of natural law without needing to advert to the question of God's existence or nature or will."[63]

The first point is uncontroversial; all of St. Thomas's metaphysics depends on it, and it is explicitly and systematically asserted in his work.[64] However, the neoclassicists tend to overemphasize the notion of self-evidence. Therefore, it is well to recall at this point that, for Aquinas, *lack of self-evidence* does not mean *lack of knowledge* or *lesser importance*, and that for him *verum et bonum convertuntur*. Even the third point, for reasons that we cannot develop here, does not present difficulties. The second

62 For the idea that our current pluralistic context necessitates a "theory of natural law" without God, and for another attempt in this vein, see more recently J. Stout, "Truth, Natural Law, and Ethical Theory," in R.P. George (ed.), *Natural Law Theory: Contemporary Essays*, pp. 71–102.

63 J. Finnis, *Natural Law and Natural Rights*, pp. 48–49.

64 See for example, Aquinas, *ST*, I, q. 2, a. 1.

and fourth, however, as statements about St. Thomas, are extremely problematic, and are indicative of a broad metaphysical foundation driving the neoclassicists' radical conviction that the will of God, outside of the sphere of grace and supernatural revelation, is ethically irrelevant.[65]

Roughly, the neoclassicists agree that it is possible for human reason to posit the existence of an uncaused cause of the universe. We do not, however, understand this cause as a personal God who creates and loves, but as a "situation" without which nothing could exist, and which we do not therefore need to call "God" but only "D." The existence of a personal God can only be *hypothesized* on the basis of an "analogy" with the free choices of human beings. The reasoning proceeds more or less as follows: we hypothesize that the relationship between situation "D" and the universe is like that between a human act and the artifact which it produces; in this case, situation "D" could be thought of as an intelligent and free being. This argument serves the neoclassicists' apologetical goal of explaining the rational possibility of Revelation, in which God reveals Himself to man as the One who created the natural order and loves it, and wants to elevate it to a supernatural plane in which He himself becomes the end of human efforts.

Even given only these brief remarks, it is very difficult to connect this view with the Thomistic one. Think, for example, of the removal of any real basis from the analogy of being, reducing it to a mere scientific hypothesis; or think of the separation of arguments about God's existence from arguments about his essence; or again, think of the difficulty of reconciling in a person in a state of grace the pursuit of two qualitatively different ends, one (or several) natural, and the other supernatural.

For the moment, it suffices to emphasize that the Thomistic notion of eternal law—which includes natural law as a "participation in the eternal law by a rational creature"—is reduced, at the level of natural knowledge, to a mere hypothesis, and can only assume moral significance in supernatural theology, in relation to revelation and the action of grace. All that is left to natural reason is a bitter longing for the possibility of a "deeper explanation," and a hope that the meaning of moral life does not end in the "subjectivity of the '*merely* relative to us.'" It is only thus that the neoclassical authors, having based ethics on human reason alone, leave the

65 See in particular G. Grisez, *Beyond the New Theism: A Philosophy of Religion* (Notre Dame: University of Notre Dame Press, 1975); J. Finnis, *Natural Law and Natural Rights*, ch. XIII.

door open for a reflection on God that is not moral, but exclusively metaphysical.[66]

Having revisited with Suárez the basic terms of the dispute between the nominalists and the anti-nominalists, we should not be surprised that the objective of avoiding legalistic ethical attitudes by highlighting the intrinsically practical and rational character of moral norms inherently involves the risk of leading from an initial suspicion regarding any reference to the will of God to the explicit project of a *natural law without God*, or of an *ethics without God*. There is, however, a further important consequence of the propensity toward the *etiamsi daremus* that recalls in a dramatic way the *lex indicans/lex praecipiens* debate, and which must be underlined: deprived of reference to the authority of God, the very expression, "natural law," becomes excessively showy, superfluous, and metaphorical, or useful only to signify the link between philosophy and theology. If natural law is nothing more than an explanation of the dynamism of human reason oriented toward action, to continue to call it "law" may be just a source of ambiguity and misunderstanding. Natural law without God easily becomes a *lex naturalis without lex*.

In the neoclassical theory of *natural law*, this terminology is adopted solely "to use the classical phrase"; but since it is the result of a simple "word-play" of the Stoics, it is said to be an "unhappy term." Indeed, Finnis, when he takes up the theme of human law, deliberately avoids using it, in order to avoid a confusion of meanings: "'Natural law'—the set of principles of practical reasonableness in ordering human life and human community—is only analogically law, in relation to my present focal use of the term: that is why the term has been avoided in this chapter on Law, save in relation to past thinkers who used the term. These past thinkers, however, could, without loss of meaning, have spoken instead of 'natural right,' 'intrinsic morality,' 'natural reason, or right reason, in action,' etc."[67]

Generally speaking, the trend toward a natural law (or ethics) *without God and without law* can be found in other recent interpretations of St. Thomas's ethics that appear to be driven by two principal goals: first, as already mentioned, to repudiate an old and now recognized legalism; second, in a world in which God is merely a private question, to outline an ethics valid for believers and atheists alike. On the whole, two basic ten-

66 See again J. Finnis, *Natural Law and Natural Rights*, ch. XIII.
67 Ibid., pp. 31, 280–81, 294, 374.

dencies among the various authors can be easily distinguished: some, like the neoclassicists, concentrate on tracing the specific norms of the natural law back to the primordial apprehension of human goods by the practical intellect, while others attempt to deemphasize the normative aspect of natural law by reappropriating Thomistic morality essentially as a virtue ethics. All such interpreters more or less concur in defining natural law by concentrating exclusively on the autonomy of practical knowledge, and by depreciating the meaning of the term "law." It may be helpful, therefore, to survey (without pretending to be exhaustive) some contemporary interpreters outside the neoclassical school. This will be done not in order to offer a general evaluation of their thought, but in order to display a few examples of how the expression "natural law" and reference to the "will of God" tend to become worrisome to contemporary thinkers.

For example, in his excellent textbook on moral philosophy, it is only after giving an ample description of Thomistic ethics as a virtue ethics that Martin Rhonheimer mentions natural law, and he specifies that "'natural law' means nothing but the principles of practical reason on the basis of which the intentional aspiration to moral virtue is guided by cognition." Indeed, he makes a point of stressing that, for this reason, "*lex naturalis*, 'natural law' or 'law of nature' is an exceedingly insidious term."[68] He then asks, "But what becomes of God in an ethics of virtue? Has He become superfluous?" and he replies: "Virtue ethics does not need to insure moral obligations through recourse to God." The will of God can become "a further source of motivation" only after an argument that does not pertain to ethics but to the *metaphysics* of creation, in which natural law can be considered part of divine providence, and in which it can make "sense to designate the order of practical principles as *natural* law"; "but in order that the moral obligation may become a practical 'motive' in Thomas there is no need for a religious support." Is it therefore "possible, in principle" to have "an ethics without God?" "The structure of reasonableness which leads to knowledge of practical principles and their realization in concrete action, and the consciousness of moral obligation based on the rational understanding of the good, and thus the possibility of moral virtue: none of this can depend upon the recognition of the existence of God."[69]

68 M. Rhonheimer, *La Prospettiva della Morale: Fondamenti dell'etica filosofica*, pp. 227–.230.

69 Ibid., pp. 260–69.

A less pronounced but substantially analogous position is that of A. R. Luño. For this author, the natural law "consists of the natural light of intelligence and the moral judgments or rational dictates that we formulate in this light" (epistemological dimension) on the basis of the "inclinations of non-rational components of human nature toward their ends" (anthropological dimension); he too therefore tends to minimize the relevance of the concept of law, and natural law receives no more than a cursory treatment in his ethical treatise. Luño rejects the *etiamsi daremus* hypothesis on an objective level, but he accepts it on a subjective level because the *theonomic* dimension of the natural law pertains to the sphere of ultimate explanation in ethics, which belongs to a creationist metaphysics and "is not intelligible from an atheistic perspective." Strictly ethical discourse about the human good and obligation, being grounded on moral experience, can prescind from discourse about God. "This is the thesis sustained by, among others, Thomas Aquinas, and it is also the one that seems to us most adequate."[70]

Indeed, De Finance himself had already found the definition of law, insofar as it was applied to natural and eternal law, "difficult" and "contrived," especially in reference to the notes of promulgation and ordering to the common good that are typical of positive law[71]—precisely the two features that necessarily make reference to the (superior) authority from which law emanates. Javier Hervada, on the other hand, one of the most renowned contemporary natural law theorists, who devotes ample space to an original rereading of Thomistic natural law, does not even speak of God, and traces moral obligation back to a simple dictate or rule of practical reason regarding the ends of the natural inclinations.[72]

Giuseppe Abbà is, in many ways, a paradigmatic case of the approach we are describing. The considerable space that he devotes to the history and concept of natural law[73] is motivated solely by the need for a strong reaction against "legalistic morality"—a morality based upon the complete heteronomy of the "third person point of view," and upon the concepts of God as Legislator and of obligation, and which, unrivalled, has

70 A.R. Luño, *Etica*, pp. 71–75, 205–19.

71 J. De Finance, *An Ethical Inquiry*, pp. 298–309.

72 J. Hervada, *Introduzione critica al diritto naturale*, p. 144 ff.

73 See especially G. Abbà, *Lex et Virtus: Studi sull'evoluzione della dottrina morale di san Tommaso d'Aquino* (Rome: Las, 1983). The theses of this book are taken up without variation in *Quale impostazione per la filosofia morale?*, p. 53 ff.

dominated the Christian tradition. In the constructive part of Abbà's ethics, neither natural law nor God assumes any special relevance.[74] In moral philosophy, the expression "natural law" signifies only an initial theological legitimation of a metaphysical character: "man, *qua* rational creature, is an absolutely unique effect of God," and "consequently, the practical knowledge that we possess as authors of our good works—that is, our *phronesis* or *prudentia* and the practical science we construct upon it—is a participation in the *ratio* by which God governs creatures and in particular man, namely, the eternal law. In this way, practical wisdom or prudence, and 'moral science,' become precisely our way of knowing the eternal law."[75]

Once this most noble origin of our prudence has been posited at the outset, morality, both theoretical and practical, can proceed with a sure step, as an "ethics of virtue," without any further need to refer to God or to the natural law, save the obvious detail of introducing God (on the natural plane, which is *different* from the supernatural) as *one of* the goods, albeit the most important one, that make up "man's true happiness."[76] In virtue ethics the law, whether natural or human, understood as *universal*, as opposed to the *particular action* guided by prudence, must have at most the subordinate end of contributing to and facilitating "the formation of virtue."[77] If, on the other hand, the expression "natural law" were to be given an immediately practical, i.e. an ethical significance, we would be moving in an exclusively (supernatural) theological sphere, in which the same natural moral duty can be seen "in a religious style, as an expression of the belonging to and obligation toward God."[78]

Abbà's approach affects his exegesis of Aquinas, which hinges on the idea of a profound discrepancy between the works prior to the *Summa theologiae* (in particular the *Scriptum super Sententiis*, the *De veritate* and the *Summa contra gentiles*) and the *Summa theologiae* itself. The early works, according to Abbà, are deeply influenced by a theology of law in the Augustinian vein, which has nothing to do with "true and proper morality," for which one must adopt the first-person point of view. The

74 Indeed, in his work *Felicità, Vita buona e virtù: saggio di filosofia morale* (Rome: Las, 1989), they do not even appear among the arguments he discusses.

75 G. Abbà, *Quale impostazione per la filosofia morale?*, pp. 60–61.

76 G. Abbà, *Felicità, vita buona e virtù*, pp. 61–62.

77 G. Abbà, *Quale impostazione per la filosofia morale?*, pp. 67, 71.

78 G. Abbà, *Felicità, vita buona e virtù*, pp. 187–88.

Summa theologiae, on the other hand, especially in the second part, is the outcome of a total and decisive rethinking following the concept of virtue found in Aristotle[79] (I will return to Abbà's ideas in chapter three).

From this angle, the landscape does not appear to change with the new demands of "narrative natural law"[80] (very congenial to Abbà). For this school of thought "law" ends up signifying not (*simpliciter*) a relationship with authority, but the general and abstract norm; the aim is to save the norm from the attacks of some neo-Aristotelians who, affirming the primacy of virtue as the moral criterion, lament the inflexibility, nonhistoricity and inhumanity of the norm itself.[81] The specific concern of narrative natural law theorists is to emphasize the role that the virtue of prudence plays in the knowledge and formulation of norms, and consequently, the intrinsic interdependence between norms and particular historical and social knowledge and conditions.

Obviously, none of Thomas's interpreters denies that God is the *ultimate* source of moral duty, but the general tendency is to banish Him from ethics and from the doctrine of natural law. Although they all have elements of originality, novelty, and interest, the outcome is still that in so doing, they miss something—and something important—in Thomistic ethics.

79 G. Abbà, *Quale impostazione per la filosofia morale?*, pp. 57–68.

80 See for example A. MacIntyre, *Whose Justice? Which Rationality?* (Notre Dame: University of Notre Dame Press, 1988); P.M. Hall, *Narrative and the Natural Law: An Interpretation of Thomistic Ethics* (Notre Dame and London: University of Notre Dame Press, 1994); R. A. Gahl Jr., "From the Virtue of a Fragile Good to a Narrative Account of Natural Law," *International Philosophical Quarterly*, 4 (1997).

81 On this subject it is worth mentioning the recent works of Martha Nussbaum, *The Fragility of Goodness: Luck and Ethics in Greek Tragedy and Philosophy*; and *Love's Knowledge* (Oxford: Oxford University Press, 1990).

Chapter 2
The Presupposition of *Lex Naturalis*: Man as *Capax Dei*

1. Introduction

The idea of a natural law of human action, if viable, implies a harmony and interaction between the key concepts of nature and will of God. Even the sure knowledge of an objective natural order would not be sufficient to explain the ultimate meaning of moral action and the perception of duty, or obligation, on the part of the human conscience. In the last chapter, we saw that behind the current trend among some interpreters of St. Thomas toward a natural law without God is concealed another trend toward an excessive separation between metaphysics and ethics, so that philosophical discourse about God, even if acceptable, does not have a direct bearing on moral philosophy. I suggested that both of these tendencies imply a reductive vision of both the metaphysics and the ethics of the Angelic Doctor. I have also suggested that reference to the will of God does not necessarily imply an arbitrary or voluntaristic foundation for the moral order, because its relevance for practical reason depends on a prior perception of God Himself as man's authentic and ultimate good.

In this chapter I will proceed directly to a study of St. Thomas himself. In section 2, first of all, "The Ethical Relevance of the Will of God," I will clarify the importance that Aquinas attributes at the natural level—prior, that is, to the strictly theological level—to obedience to God's will, which he identifies as the very essence of moral action: according to him, man is morally good only when he wants something because he knows that God wants it. Then in section 2.1, "How We Know God's Will," I will indicate the manner in which, according to St. Thomas, man can come to know the will of God; we will see that this knowledge is given precisely by the natural order of things, through our understanding of its intrinsic teleology. This section will be a first way of reconciling nature and the will of God. It will be followed, in section 2.2, "Will and Law," by some clarifications of the important and defining role that the will assumes in the Thomistic concept of law.

The argument of section 2.1, "How We Know God's Will," follows a downward path in which the connection between the will of God and the natural order is taken for granted but not yet explained. The explanation, by contrast, presupposes the upward path by which man attains knowledge of God philosophically, and, at the same time, comes to characterize philosophically all other existing things as *created*, i.e., willed by God. All of section 3, "The Natural Knowledge of God," is devoted to this upward path. Obviously, we are here facing one of the most difficult and disputed aspects of Thomistic thought, so I have decided to address it, albeit briefly, without discounting any of the problems that it raises and that require a response. In this way, we will ultimately reach the conclusion that, as far as Aquinas is concerned, there is in the very essence of every human act of intellectual knowledge a cognitive tension pointing toward the being of God. Such a conclusion is surprising, but, if we think the question through carefully, it is the only one capable of theoretically justifying the role Aquinas assigns to God in moral action.

The first argument I will consider in this upward stage will be the non-self-evidence of God's existence. Many commentators, including the neo-classicists, have linked the claim that we can have an ethics without God to the Thomistic assertion that the existence of God is not self-evident to the human mind. They have taken this assertion to imply that not all men know God, and consequently that not everyone can have Him as an actual foundation for moral action. In fact, however, the assertion of non-self-evidence must be interpreted to mean that the idea of God is not the starting-point for the knowledge we have of Him (3.1, "The Non-Self-Evidence of God's Existence").

For Aquinas, the idea, concept, or content of the mind, although the proper object of intellectual knowledge, can never be the starting-point for the knowledge that man has of the being and existence of things. The idea is, for the intellect, only the *object of second intention*, while the *object of first intention* is always material reality, which presents itself to human knowledge as immediately evident. This theory of knowledge places Aquinas irremediably in opposition to any idealistic theory, and lies at the root of the well-known definition of his theoretical approach as *philosophical realism*. Thomistic realism implies that knowledge of God will be different in each person, will be inaccessible to the imagination, and will not necessarily be reflexive. I will examine all these concepts in section 3.2, "The Object of Human Knowledge," where I will also reevaluate the well-known but often misunderstood concept of truth as *adaequatio rei et intellectus*.

Another important consequence of Thomistic realism is that neither man's judgment nor his reasoning can ever have any truth-value unless they start from the immediately evident data (*of first intention*) of material reality. When the object of human reflection is not found immediately in material reality, the only way it can be more than a pure fantasy or hypothesis is by referring *mediately* to that same reality; that is, it must be a concept coined in the attempt to understand an immediately evident aspect of corporeal things (see 3.3, "Judgment and Reasoning").

Our natural knowledge of God, then, if it is not to be purely fantastic or hypothetical, must somehow be an explanation of sensible reality itself, and this raises the problem of the *presence of God in things*, which I address in section 3.4, "God in Reality." There we will see that for St. Thomas, God is present in all things as the first uncaused cause of their being, in such a way that if He did not exist, they would fall into nothingness. The procedure for reaching God is therefore a *quia* demonstration: one that seeks to move *backward* from effect to cause. In speaking of the presence of God in things, I will introduce for the first time the concept of a cause's *actuality*, which will become increasingly important in subsequent sections.

The *quia* demonstrative procedure has two importance consequences: first, one cannot know what the cause is like in itself; second, there must be an essential resemblance between the effect and the cause. From these consequences come the *via negativa* and *positiva* respectively, the two cognitive approaches to the being of God that characterize Thomistic philosophy. The interaction of these two ways will enable us to understand why, according to Aquinas, it is not possible to separate the question of the existence of God from that of His essence, and why and to what extent the knowledge of created things implies at the same time a knowledge of the essence of God. This doctrine corresponds perfectly with Aquinas's philosophy of language, according to which some names that we attribute to God express in a proper sense the very essence of God. All of these concepts are the subject of section 3.5, "Via Negativa and Via Positiva."

In section 3.6, "The Idea of God: Premise and Object of the Proofs," taking a cue from an objection to Aquinas's procedure, I will explain in greater depth the nature of the demonstration *quia*. In so doing, I will explain in what, exactly, consists the knowledge (idea) of God that man can attain, through such a demonstration, by the use of his reason alone. I will then formally lay out the rational sequence of the demonstration *quia* for each of St. Thomas's five well-known "ways" to God.

By this point (3.7, "The Insufficiency of Being"), it will be clear that the real theoretical problem with the five ways lies in their major premises, each of which connects a particular mode of being of sensible reality with the necessity of an actual and transcendent first cause of that mode of being. I will then move on to a detailed study of each way (3.7.1.–3.7.6.). In so doing, I will link the first three ways, together, with a negative knowledge of God, and the last two with a positive knowledge implying that God is intelligent and free. Then, I will show how Aquinas's doctrine of the participation of being is the common foundation of all five ways, though differently with respect to each of the two groups just distinguished. The upward path will come to an end with section 3.8, "The Metaphysical Experience of Being," where I will explain how human intellectual knowledge is always in cognitive tension with God.

Knowledge of God and of the natural order as willed by God obviously constitute essential starting points, but they do not yet explain the central ethical relevance that St. Thomas attributes to the will of God. To this end, there must be a further *practical* dimension to the will of God: in other words, God must be *important* for man, indeed, the most important thing of all, more important even than man himself. Is there a principle in Thomistic philosophy that ensures this importance? Section 4, "The Inclination To God," is devoted to this conclusive question. In contrast to the previous section, which focuses on the intellectual knowledge of God, this last section should be understood as an explanation of the openness and inclination of the human will to God. Whereas in section 3 we see that for Aquinas intellectual experience is characterized at its highest point in terms of a *tension with the Absolute*, in section 4 we see that moral (appetitive) experience is characterized in terms of a *tension toward the Absolute*.

My primary concern at this stage will be to clarify how we ought to understand the *practicality* of knowledge of the good (as opposed to theoretical reason), particularly with regard to the knowledge of God (4.1, "God as a (Moral) Problem for Man"). I will then briefly highlight the principal features of human moral experience in which the philosophical tradition of natural law has seen reflected the transcendent dimension of morality and the ethical centrality of the problem of God (4.2, "The Meaning of Moral Experience"). I will also try to find traces of these last two aspects in some recent neo-Thomistic philosophical reflection on the object of ethics and the meaning of the moral question (4.3).

Finally, I will turn specifically to the explanation that St. Thomas offers, in the *Summa theologiae*, of the nature of the human will, in which he concludes that man is naturally inclined to love God before himself and with a greater love (4.4, "By Natural Love, Man Loves God Before Himself and with a Greater Love").

2. The Ethical Relevance of the Will of God

In question 23, article 7 of *De veritate*, St. Thomas explicitly asks: "are we obliged to conform our will to the divine will?"[1] Notably, the first negative thesis he reports concerns precisely man's alleged incapacity to know the divine will. "It seems," the article begins, "that we are not . . . for no one is held to the impossible. But it is impossible for us to conform our will to the divine will, since the divine will is unknown to us. Therefore we are not held to the conformity mentioned." St. Thomas's response to the question is clear and sharp: "Everyone is obliged to conform his will to God's." And his specific response to the first objection is as follows: "The will of God cannot be fully known to us. Hence, neither can we fully conform our will to His. But we can conform it in proportion to the knowledge which we have, and we are held to this."

Right from the *incipit* of the article, we understand that Aquinas's target is not (at least principally) God's will as communicated to creatures by means of supernatural Revelation. This can be gathered not so much from

1 St. Thomas Aquinas, Truth, vol. 3, Questions XXI–XXIX, translated from the Leonine text (*Quaestiones disputatae de veritate*) by Robert W. Schmidt, S.J. (Chicago: Henry Regnery Company, 1954) [Translator's note: The edition used for the original book is Aquinas, *Le questioni disputate: La verità*, ed. P.R. Coggi O.P. (Bologna: ESD, 1992–93), in three volumes. I have occasionally altered the English translation slightly to better reflect both the original Latin and the Italian translation.]

the tenor of the reply, which in itself is general, as from the tenor of the objection. Not only would it be odd to object that God's revealed will is unknown, but above all, it seems obvious that Aquinas is referring to the *esse Dei est ignotum* that constitutes the core of all of his theodicy, or philosophy of God.

This first impression is fully confirmed by the argument of the article as a whole, because Aquinas's solution turns on the similarity and natural proportion between the being of God and the being of creatures (more of this in section 3.5), such that "His intellect is the measure of all knowledge; His goodness, of all goodness; and, to speak more to the point, His good will, of every good will. *Every good will is therefore good by reason of its being conformed to the divine good will*" (my italics). At this point, then, it might seem that reference to the will of God as the source of morality signifies an ultimate foundation of a metaphysical character. The rest of the argument clearly indicates, however, that there is something more going on.

Thomas first distinguishes two ways in which conformity can be considered, one regarding the human will as act and the other regarding the will as potency. In fact, the will of God is not only "an act of will" but also the "cause of all things that exist." The conformity of the human will as potency, i.e., as the effect of its cause, "is natural, belonging to the image" and "accordingly does not fall under any commandment." The will as act, on the other hand, is conformity of the will to another will, "and so an act of our will conforms to the divine will by reason of the fact that we will what God wants us to will."

But this is not yet sufficient, Thomas continues, because the object of the will can be considered in two ways: either "materially," as "the thing itself that is willed," or "formally," as "the reason for willing, which is the end." In this second sense, the human will conforms itself to the divine will not simply when it wants what God wants, but when it wills something "for the same reason for which God wills it," that is, when it "wills something from charity." Aquinas is even more explicit in the subsequent article (a. 8): "Are we obliged to conform our will to the divine will as regards its object so as to be bound to will what we know God wills?"

In this article, we are told clearly that "righteous wayfarers . . . conform to the divine will" *even against their personal preferences*, "because it pleases them that the order of the divine will be fulfilled in all things."[2]

2 Ibid., q. 23, a. 8 c., but see also q. 22, a. 2 c.: "All things naturally tend to God

This same approach is reflected in the Thomistic teaching on moral culpability. Having explained that evil in the strict sense (*simpliciter*) does not consist in the mere privation of a good, like blindness, but rather in the fault, which renders man and his will evil, Aquinas attributes the evil of the fault to a direct offense against God and not to an indirect offense such as would be involved in simply opposing created goodness. "The evil of fault is properly opposed to uncreated good: for it is opposed to the fulfillment of the divine will, and to divine love, whereby the divine good is loved for itself, and not only as shared by the creature."[3]

From these few remarks alone, it is evident that the will of God is not seen by Aquinas as a remote metaphysical foundation, but precisely as *the* (only) *practical motive*, which, actually present in the intention of the agent, makes his will and thus himself good *sic et simpliciter*. What this presupposes—here less evidently but clearly nonetheless—is that loving God, even against one's own personal preferences, is in some sense connatural to the human will. These few elements are already sufficient for us to state with confidence that in Thomas's ethics, even were it possible for an atheist to do exactly what God wants (in a "material" way), he and his actions would not thereby be morally good, and he himself would not know the moral good, that is, conformity to the divine will. Is Thomas a voluntarist, then, and is his morality impractical and far removed from the human good? In order to address these questions we must firstly come to a deeper understanding of how he conceives of human knowledge and of knowledge of God in particular. Hence I will begin with the most obvious question, given the sequence of the argument: Where is the will of God, in which the meaning of moral goodness appears to reside, and of what does it consist?

implicitly, but not explicitly," because "a secondary cause can influence its effect only in so far as it receives the power of the first cause"; but the first agent wills the secondary end "only by reason of the principal end existing in it"; now "only a rational nature can trace secondary ends back to God by a sort of analytic procedure so as to seek God Himself explicitly. In demonstrative sciences a conclusion is correctly drawn only by a reduction to first principles. *In the same way the appetite of a rational creature is correctly directed only by an explicit appetitive tendency to God, either actual or habitual*" (my italics).

3 Aquinas, *ST*, I, q. 48, a. 6. c.: "Malum vero culpae opponitur proprie ipsi bono increato: contrariatur enim impletioni divinae voluntatis, et divino amori quo bonum divinum in seipso amatur; et non solum secundum quod participatur a creatura."

2.1. How We Know God's Will

The first clue is to be found in the eighth article, precisely in the remainder of the sentence cited above: "[unlike sinners] righteous wayfarers . . . whose will adheres to the divine goodness but who yet do not so perfectly contemplate it that they clearly perceive every relation to it of the things to be willed, conform to the divine will as regards those objects for which they perceive the reason."[4] Something more precise can be found in the first book of the *Summa contra gentiles*, where Thomas dwells at some length on the way in which the will of God is related to the reasons for things.[5] There the basic principle guiding the entire argument is that the *end* is the reason for which the will wants something. Consequently, we know the will by understanding its end, which is the first principle in the practical sphere and for this reason is always a *good* for the acting subject.

The structure of the *Summa contra gentiles* follows a downward path from God to creatures. In chapter 74 of book one, Thomas explains that "the ultimate end," "the principal object of the divine will is the divine essence," among other reasons because the will wants the good that is intellectually known, and what the divine intellect knows principally is its own essence.[6] The object known, then, is what moves the subject's will to action, so that "if, then, the principal object of the divine will be other than the divine essence," there would have to be "something higher than the divine will moving it," and this would contradict the simplicity of God, which implies that there cannot be any real distinction in God between will and essence.[7]

God, St. Thomas continues, *necessarily wills* "His own being and His own goodness,"[8] because "every being endowed with will necessarily wills his own ultimate end," which is the reason for which all other things

4 Aquinas, *De veritate*, q. 23, a. 8 c.; see also a. 6 ad 6.

5 For the Latin text of the *Summa contra gentiles* I have used the Leonine edition, published in Thomas Aquinas, *Liber de Veritate Catholicae Fidei contra errors Infidelium seu Summa contra Gentiles* (Rome: Marietti, 1961). Hereafter *Summa contra gentiles* will be abbreviated *CG*. [Translator's note: I have followed the English translation of *CG* by A.C. Pegis (Book I), James F. Anderson (Books II-III), and C.J. O'Neill (Book IV) (Notre Dame and London: University of Notre Dame Press, 1956), except where the English translation conflicts with the Italian text.]

6 See also *CG*, I, chap. 44.

7 Ibid., I, chap. 73.

8 Ibid., I, chap. 80.

are willed as means; and "it is impossible for God not to will something in act, for He would be willing only in potency, which is impossible, since His willing is His being." However, he *does not necessarily will* all other things.[9] And this is because of an extremely important principle in the general explanation of rational obligation, namely, that "a will does not of necessity tend to the things that conduce to it, unless they are such that the end cannot be attained without them."[10] And since "the divine Goodness can be without other beings . . . God is under no necessity of willing other things from the fact of His willing His own goodness."

Aquinas at this point defines the relationship between the divine will and created things as a relationship of "hypothetical necessity."[11] God does not, in an absolute sense, necessarily will anything beyond Himself, but once He wills something, since His will is immutable and eternal, it is hypothetically necessary for Him to will it—and not only to will its existence, but to will everything required by that thing, because "whoever wills something, necessarily wills whatever is necessarily required for it, unless there be a defect in him either because of ignorance or because he is led astray through passion from the right choice of that which leads to the intended end. This cannot be said of God. If God, then, in willing Himself wills something other than Himself, it is necessary that He will for this object whatever is necessarily required by it. Thus, it is necessary that God will the rational soul to exist supposing that He wills man to exist."

Using these premises, St. Thomas recapitulates in chapter 86 the way in which one "can determine the reason of God's will." To begin with, the goodness of God is the end, "the reason why He wills the other things which are different from Himself," because, as has already been said, "the end is the reason for willing the things that are for the sake of the end," and God wills His own goodness as an end, and other things as means. The existence of created things, then, is the necessary starting point for deter-

9 Ibid., I, chap. 81.

10 See also Aquinas, *ST*, I, q. 19, a. 3 c.: "Now in willing an end we do not necessarily will things that conduce to it, unless they are such that the end cannot be attained without them; as, we will to take food to preserve life. . . . Hence, since the goodness of God is perfect, and can exist without other things inasmuch as no perfection can accrue to Him from them, it follows that His willing things apart from Himself is not absolutely necessary."

11 Aquinas, *CG*, I, chap. 83.

mining the reasons of God's will: once God has willed the order of the whole universe in relation to Himself, He also wills the reciprocal ordering of the parts of it, and the individual goods on which that order depends.[12] The order of the universe is thus the end, the good, "the reason why God wills each particular good in the universe"; and the existence of individual goods is "the reason why God wills the things that are required for each thing [each of those goods]."

But this is not yet sufficient, and St. Thomas adds an extremely important qualification: "But that which imposes necessity on another is the reason why that other exists." In order to understand this brief phrase, let us consider by way of comparison a human artifact. The existence of a car *necessarily* implies that it be capable of moving; whereas that it have doors, that it have this shape rather than that, that it have an odometer, all correspond to other, secondary objectives. When man invents and constructs a car, then, the end at which he necessarily aims is that it move: this is the reason for the existence of the car. In the same way, man can perceive in existing things various motives of the divine will: motives of convenience, motives of utility, and motives of (hypothetical) necessity, which are precisely *the natural ends of things*.

It is, therefore, in Aquinas's discussion of the will of God that we find the origin of the doctrine of natural ends. As we will see more fully in chapter three, we can find in Aquinas even the most striking examples of this doctrine, such as "walking on one's hands, or using one's feet for something usually done with the hands"[13]—but always in a context that fully reveals the connection between these examples and both the will of God, which is the ultimate source of morality, and the good of man. It will emerge clearly, for example, that the "disordered" use of one's hands, one's feet or any other human organ is not necessarily immoral, as long as it does not impede the realization of the only natural end or good without which man cannot exist as man; and this observation is anything but banal or superficial, as it might appear on the standard account of the so-called "conventional" theory.

"Thus, therefore, can we proceed," concludes chapter 86, "in determining the reason of the divine will. God wills man to have a reason in order that man exist as man; He wills man to be so that the universe may

12 See also ibid., I, chap. 78.

13 Ibid., III, chap. 122. In particular, see chap. 3, sect. 4.6, below: "Fornication and Marriage."

be complete; and He wills that the good of the universe be because it befits His goodness. However, this threefold reason does not proceed according to the same relationship. For the divine goodness neither depends on the perfection of the universe nor is anything added to it from this perfection. For, although the perfection of the universe necessarily depends on certain particular goods that are its essential parts, yet on some of them it does not depend of necessity, but nevertheless a certain goodness or adornment accrues to the universe from them, as from those things that exist only for the support or adornment of the other parts of the universe. A particular good depends necessarily on the things that are absolutely required for it, even though this too has certain things that are for its embellishment. Hence, at times the reason of the divine will contains only a befittingness; at other times, usefulness; at still other times, a hypothetical necessity; but it contains a necessity that is absolute only when God wills Himself."

2.2. Will and Law

The fact that the will of God is revealed to man in the reasons for things cuts off, right from the start, any charge of voluntarism against Thomistic ethics, because it refers the will to the order of wisdom. Furthermore, given the necessary simplicity of God, Thomas explains that in Him both intellect and will are nothing other than His very being and essence.[14] The accent upon the will remains important, however, because the will expresses the intention and the action of the subject with respect to the known good: the will brings into being, *binds*, and constrains; to the will is connected, first and foremost, the most evident characteristic of *law*, namely, *obligation*.[15] Hence, among the many places in his work in which Aquinas refers the will back to the intellect, it is appropriate to dwell for a moment on the passage immediately preceding that with which we opened our discussion: question 23, article 6 of *De veritate*, entitled "Does Justice as Found Among Created Things Depend Simply upon the Divine Will?"

Aquinas's intention in this article is clear, so there is no need to stress it any further. His solution is based on the general doctrine of rational action, according to which "will does not have the character of a first rule;

14 Aquinas, *CG*, I, chs. 22, 45, 73.

15 [Translator's note: without asserting a real etymological connection, the author's original vocabulary highlights the conceptual connections at work in this passage: The will binds (*lega*), and to it is connected the most evident character of law (*legge*), obligation (*l'obbligo*).]

it is rather a rule which has a rule," since it necessarily wills what the intellect knows beforehand. This holds both for us and for God "although in us the will is really distinct from the intellect. . . . For this reason the will and its correctness are not the same thing. In God, however, the will is really identical with the intellect, and for this reason the correctness of His will is really the same as His will itself. Consequently the first thing upon which the essential character of all justice depends is the wisdom of the divine intellect."

The general thrust of the article, including the tenor of the individual objections, already testifies to the central ethical role of the will of God: that is why it is important, if we are to avoid falling into a voluntaristic interpretation, to trace the will of God back to His wisdom. But for now, I wish to highlight the argument of the second objection, in which the will is explicitly connected to the meaning of law and of obligation. "Something is just," the objection says, "by reason of its agreement with law. But a law seems to be nothing but the expression of the will of a sovereign because 'what has pleased the prince has the force of law,' as the Legislator says. Since the sovereign of all things is the divine will, it therefore seems that the whole character of justice depends upon it alone." Now what is surprising about Thomas's reply to this objection is obviously not the fact that he relates the will to the primacy of reason, but that in so doing, he stresses the intrinsic link between the obligation of law and the will: "The will of the prince, by the fact of its being a will, has the coercive force of law (*vim legis in cogendo*), yet it does not have the character of justice except from being led by reason." In other words, reason by itself does not make law, nor does it create obligation.

The essential importance of the will in St. Thomas's concept of law has often been underestimated due to a superficial approach facilitated by the extraordinarily systematic nature of his final work. In the *Summa theologiae*, indeed, it is easy to identify a *treatise* on *lex*, which, as is well known, treats as its first subject of inquiry "whether law is something pertaining to reason" (*utrum lex sit aliquid rationis*).[16] For this reason many interpreters, moved especially by haste to offer a synthetic interpretation of the subject-matter, have immediately focused on rationality as the defining character of law, forgetting that the *proprium* of law is really the command.

16 Aquinas, *ST*, I-II, q. 90, a. 1.

To understand this, we need only widen our angle of vision from the treatise on law to the structure of the entire second part of the *Summa theologiae*, in which this treatise is contained. Law then emerges first of all as an action proceeding from a free agent; as such, it shares with every free act knowledge and love of the end, which is "the first principle in the sphere of action," and reason, which as the faculty that permits the ordering of acts to their known end is the "first principle" of the free action itself. From this point of view, it is not the rational character of law that distinguishes it from other free acts; rather, this rational character locates it within a genus without indicating its specificity. Furthermore, it is clear that the specific nature of law cannot be given by the notion of an ordering to the common good, because anyone can aim at the common good without thereby producing a law.

Within the systematic structure of the *Summa theologiae* (but also in the *Contra gentiles*), the fact that explains the specific nature of law among all free acts is rather its status as an "external principle" of action, which implies an authority capable of imposing itself with its will upon other subjects. Even prior to the problem of the law's rational character, the treatise on *lex* in the *Summa theologiae* opens with these words: "We have now to consider the external principles of acts." Basically, besides a series of internal principles provided by the various faculties (or powers) and virtues (or habits), human action for Aquinas is guided externally by means of authority. It is for this reason that he explains the meaning of *lex* (the question of his etymological error is irrelevant here) by tracing it back to the root of *ligare*, "because it binds one to act." The systematic role of the external principle, besides returning the concept of law to its common sense meaning, also points to its fundamentally heteronymous character, and explains the fact that Aquinas's primary concern when he begins to speak about law is to trace it back to reason rather than to the arbitrary will of the commanding authority—exactly the same concern that we have just seen in *De veritate*. It is illuminating, from this viewpoint, that Aquinas defines "command" as an act of reason, specifying at the same time that "it is due to the power of the will that reason moves by way of command. Hence, to command is an act of reason presupposing an act of the will." Here too, the specific character locating command among the various the acts of reason is provided by the will.[17]

17 Ibid., I-II, q. 17, a. 1. I explain this point better in two articles—"Natural Law as

These observations will prove very helpful when it comes to interpreting Aquinas's direct treatment of law, in chapter three. However, what has already been said about the will of God, and about its relation to His wisdom and to the concept of law, is sufficient to see that reference to the will of God or to the heteronomy of law is certainly not what sets apart the interpretation of either Suárez or the conventional theory from Aquinas's authentic thought.

After these digressions on the relationship between law and will, we must now consider our knowledge of the will of God. We have seen that for Aquinas, man perceives the will of God in the existence and order of things in accordance with reasons of convenience, utility, and necessity; and that to the extent that he knows this will, he is bound to conform himself to it by contemplating it, loving it, and insofar as it depends on his own free action, realizing it. But the downward path that we have taken in the *Summa contra gentiles* is based on a connection that must still be explained, namely, that between the existence of things and the divine will; and it leaves open the question of how it can come about that man refers all things to the will of God, and to God Himself as the ultimate end. To address this question, we must take an upward path, and see how St. Thomas conceives of man's natural knowledge of God.

3. The Natural Knowledge of God

Given that I am about to address briefly an extremely subtle and complex aspect of Aquinas's thought, I should immediately clarify what exactly my objective is. I maintain that, for Aquinas, man's moral sense is not only inseparable from his sense of God, but coextensive with it. In other words, I want to argue that the sense of God is, for the Angelic Doctor, like the *formal reason* of the moral sense, and that moral obligation can therefore be accurately characterized as *obedience to the order willed by God.* Just as it is impossible to find any person who has absolutely no moral sense—unless, due to some particular disease, or for reasons associated with the social or historical nature of man (think, for example, of men raised by animals or instances of primitive man), he has not developed his properly human powers—so also is it impossible to find any person who is absolutely deprived of a sense of God, and who does not know Him, at

Inclination to God" and "Law as 'Act of Reason' and 'Command'"—which are still unpublished.

least inchoately. Here, I intend to show how this is both possible and reasonable in St. Thomas's philosophy.[18]

The theme of knowledge of God is often misunderstood because St. Thomas's theoretical aims are thought of more or less in the following way: Among the many objects that man can know by means of his natural reason is God, and an adequate philosophical explanation can be provided for this. Moreover, once we know God's existence we will be in a position to say something about his essence.

This way of framing the issue is misleading. Instead, the question ought to be presented like this: according to Aquinas, whatever man knows, and insofar as he knows it, he also knows God and His mode of being, because the being of things (a) resembles essentially the being of God, and (b) leads the human intellect back to God in way that, even if mediated, is necessary. The natural knowledge that man has of God is thus directly proportionate to the knowledge he has of the being of the reality that surrounds him, and the philosophical explanation of the existence and essence of God is simultaneously a part of the explanation of human knowledge in general.[19]

3.1. The Non-Self-Evidence of God's Existence

Following the approaches of Grisez and Finnis, and the logical structure of Aquinas's own work, I will focus primarily on the problem of the self-evidence of God's being (*utrum Deum esse sit per se notum*).[20] Here I use

18 On the subject of this section, see in general C. Fabro, *Dio: Introduzione al problema teologico* (Rome: Studium, 1953), *Dall'essere all'esistente* (Brescia: Morcelliana, 1965), *L'uomo e il rischio di Dio* (Rome: Studium, 1967); R. Garrigou-Lagrange, O.P., *God: His Existence and His Nature* (St. Louis, MO.: B. Herder Book & Co., 1934); Etienne Gilson, *Elements of Christian Philosophy* (New York: Doubleday & Co., 1960); *Christian Philosophy: An Introduction*, trans. Armand Maurer (Toronto: Pontifical Institute of Mediaeval Studies, 1993); Jacques Maritain, *Distinguish to Unite: The Degrees of Knowledge*, trans. Gerald B. Phelan (Notre Dame: University of Notre Dame Press, 1995); *Sept leçons sur l'être et les premiers principes de la raison speculative* (Paris: Tequi, 1934); *Court traité de l'existence et de l'existant* (Paris: Hartmann, 1947); A. L. Gonzalez, *Filosofia di Dio* (Florence: Le Monnier, 1988); M. Grison, *Corso di filosofia tomista, Volume 6: Teologia naturale o teodicea* (Brescia: Paideia, 1967); J. Choza, *Manual de antropología filosófica* (Madrid: Ediciones Rialp, S. A., 1988).

19 See for example Aquinas, *De veritate*, q. 22, a. 2 ad 1: "all cognitive beings . . . know God implicitly in any object of knowledge."

20 Aquinas, *ST*, I, q. 2. It is well known that Aquinas addresses the question "*an Deus*

the term *being* deliberately, to avoid from the outset any appearance of separating the discussion of God's existence from that about his essence. Some think that when Aquinas denies that God's being is self-evident to the human mind, he is also affirming the possibility that there are men who do not know Him—in other words, that there are people who lack the idea of God; and that it is for this reason that he believes it necessary to proceed with a proper rational proof. This belief may be facilitated by the fact that the argument for the non-self-evidence of God's existence is inextricably linked to the critique of what Kant later called the ontological argument. This argument is generally understood as the proof whereby the existence of God is inferred, *a priori*, from an idea or concept present in the human mind.[21] It is not difficult to slide from a critique of the ontological argument to the devaluation of the very idea of God.

St. Thomas's intentions are best understood, however, if we recall that before Kant, the argument was known as an *a simultaneo* proof, because it did not consist in seeking out an inference, but in attempting to demonstrate that the idea of God necessarily implies His existence, given that the concept of "God" includes that of "the existence of God." In the proposition "God exists," then, the existence is self-evident because it is included in the concept of God, and the proof is *a simultaneo* because to think of God is simultaneously (*statim*) to think of His existence. "But as soon as the signification of the word 'God' is understood, it is at once seen that God exists. For by this word is signified that thing than which nothing greater can be conceived. But that which exists actually and mentally is greater than that which exists only mentally. Therefore, since as soon as the word 'God' is understood it exists mentally, it also follows that it exists actually."[22] The proof concludes that given this idea that we have of God, it is not necessary to demonstrate His existence.

Self-evident, in this discussion, simply means "already known." A proposition is self-evident to the human mind when the notion of the predicate is "already known" in knowing the subject of the proposition (*aliqua propositio est per se nota, quod praedicatum includitur in ratione*

sit" as the first topic of his treatise on the divine essence, and that in doing so he explains in sequence: (a) the non-self-evidence of God's existence; (b) the demonstrability of His existence; and (c) the proofs of His existence that can be adduced.

21 For a brief history of the ontological argument, see A.L. Gonzalez, *Filosofia di Dio*, pp. 53–84.

22 Aquinas, *ST*, I, q. 2, a. 1, obj. 2.

subiecti),[23] but also when one already possesses, beforehand, the notion of the subject.[24] If we apply analogically the concept of self-evidence as "a notion already known," we can say that the self-evidence for man of the existence of God (the predicate of "God exists") depends on the self-evidence for man of the being of God (the subject of the proposition).

Now, Thomas accepts (and explains) this concept of self-evidence, but he also accepts that the idea of God is present in everyone, i.e., that it is impossible for any human to lack the idea of God. And what is particularly significant for our purposes is the fact that in those places where he claims that this knowledge is necessary and universal, part of his certainty is derived from the fact that God is the ultimate (practical) end of human action. In other words, since "God is man's happiness," and since "man naturally desires happiness . . . , what is naturally desired by man, must be naturally known by him."[25] To deny the existence of a natural knowledge of God would be to deny that man is naturally a religious being, which would be to deny that the first signs of civility and humanity (such as the burial of the dead) are accompanied by religious forms; and such a denial is foreign to Thomistic thought.[26]

What Thomas denies, however, is that the idea of God can be the starting-point for coming to know His reality and for attaining certainty about His existence and His mode of being. This is because the concept, the "intelligible species," is not "what is actually understood"; otherwise science would not have as its object "the real things outside the soul," and the truth would be "that which appears to each one."[27] Aquinas holds that in fact, our natural knowledge of God is "general and confused," and is not

23 Ibid., c.

24 See also Aquinas's *De veritate*, q. 10, a. 12 c.: "For something to be immediately evident in itself (*per se notum secundum se*), it is only required that the predicate belong to the notion of the subject (*nihil aliud requiritur nisi ut praedicatum sit de ratione subiecti*): indeed, then the subject cannot be thought of without the predicate appearing as inherent in it. But for something to be immediately evident to us (*per se notum nobis*), we have to know the notion of the subject in which the predicate is included."

25 Aquinas, *ST*, I, q. 2, a. 1; *CG*, I, chs. 10–11.

26 On the natural religiosity of man see M. Guerra, *Storia delle religioni* (Brescia: La Scuola, 1989); and for an original and pleasant discussion, in which religiosity is connected to an appreciation of freedom, see also L. Polo, *Chi è l'uomo*, trans. P. Bonagura (Milan: Vita e Pensiero, 1992), chap. X.

27 Aquinas, *ST*, I, q. 85, a. 2 c.

the same for everyone. He writes, "many ancients said that this world itself was God," "some believed God to be a body," and "some believe He is not just"—but "God is known not only in the works which proceed from His justice," so from the fact that one does not know Him as just, "it does not follow that one does not know Him at all." In order to have certainty, Aquinas maintains, it is therefore necessary to reach God "through reasoning," to make use of "ratiocination."[28]

For the Angelic Doctor, an idea or concept (the universal nature of a thing, which exists in act in the intellect only) is not reliable, because it changes from subject to subject, and, in the same subject, from one moment to the next: it is not a stable reality and it cannot provide a basis for knowing the existence of anything. The concept constantly indicates the relationship between the knowing subject and the known reality, in proportion to and according to the degree of knowledge that the subject actually possesses[29]—that is, the concept is always intentional.[30] To attain certainty it is necessary to bring the concept back to the reality existing before us, and, through our reasoning, to constantly refine our knowledge of the object.[31] But in the reality before us, God does not exist, at least not upon a preliminary examination. In the words of Etienne Gilson: "Now, however we look at it, no given fact answers to our notion of God."[32] And according to Cornelio Fabro, "it is a generally accepted fact that God is not the object of immediate experience, and therefore neither is He the object of direct or indirect intellectual cognition,[33] as are sensible things and their essences."[34]

Note that, corroborating both this interpretation and the appeal of the ontological argument, Aquinas explicitly recognizes with Aristotle that *no* concept—except that God—implies of itself the self-evidence of the existence of the known thing, because only the concept of God necessarily requires His existence. The proposition, "the dog is," is not self-evident

28 For the last few quotations see Aquinas, *ST*, I, q. 2, a. 1 ad 1–2; *CG*, I, chs. 10–11; *De veritate*, q. 10, a. 12.

29 Aquinas, *ST*, I, q. 85, a. 3.

30 On the intentional nature of human knowledge, see for example G. Basti, *Filosofia dell'uomo* (Bologna: ESD, 1995), p. 197 ff.

31 Aquinas, *ST*, I, q. 85, a. 5.

32 E. Gilson, *God and Philosophy* (New Haven: Yale University Press, 1941), p. 109.

33 That is, intuitive knowledge as opposed to knowledge that is the product of reasoning.

34 C. Fabro, *L'uomo e il rischio di Dio*, p. 135.

because the concept of dog does not require the dog's existence; in other words, it is possible to think that the dog does not exist without taking anything away from the concept of "dog." In man, the certainty of the existence of known things does not involve a logical, but an *existential* evidence, so to speak, through the givenness of the reality before us. The only logically evident existence possible is that of God: "But since the essence of God is not evident to us, the fact of God's existence . . . is not immediately evident to us, [and we] need a demonstration" through those things whose existence is, for us, an immediately evident given.[35]

In other words, to use the more technical terminology that St. Thomas develops for this discussion, "a thing can be self-evident (*per se notum*) in either of two ways: on the one hand, self-evident in itself (*secundum se*), though not to us; on the other, self-evident in itself, and to us (*quoad nos*)."[36] On the basis of this distinction, one could say regarding the predicate of existence that the only judgment that is self-evident *secundum se* is that concerning the existence of God, but because God is not to be found in the reality that falls immediately before us, His existence cannot be evident *quoad nos*. And in spite of this, Aquinas admits that all men know God, that is, that they have an idea of Him, and since that idea is the only one that implies the existence of its object, the temptation to take it not as a point of arrival, but as a starting-point from which to deduce the *quoad nos* self-evidence of the existence of God, is always strong for one who devotes himself to serious reflection on the type of knowledge he finds within himself.

35 See Aquinas, *De veritate*, Q. 10, a. 12 c.: "Now, existence (*esse*) is not included in the concept of any creature (*in nullius creaturae ratione includitur*), for the act of existence (*esse*) of every creature is something other than its essence (*quiditate*). Hence, it cannot be said of any creature that its existence (*esse*) is immediately evident (*per se notum*) even in itself. But, in God, His existence (*esse*) is included in the concept of His essence (*in suae quiditatis ratione*), for in God *essence* and *existence* (*quod est et esse*) are the same, as Boethius says. And *that He is* and *what He is* (*an est et quid est*) are the same, as Avicenna says. . . . But since the essence of God. . . ." See also Aristotle, *Posterior Analytics*, II.7, 92b24 ff., trans. Jonathan Barnes (Oxford: Clarendon Press, 1994). All English translations of Aristotle, except the *Nicomachean Ethics*, are taken from *The Complete Works of Aristotle*, revised Oxford translation, ed. Jonathan Barnes (Princeton, NJ: Princeton University Press, 1984). See also, more recently, V. Possenti, *Terza navigazione: Nichilismo e metafisica* (Rome: Armando, 1998), p. 64.

36 Aquinas, *ST*, I, q. 2, a. 1 c.

3.2. The Object of Human Knowledge

In reality, behind Thomas's criticism of the self-evidence of God's being is concealed the entire doctrine with which, overcoming the Platonic ideas in favor of Aristotelian realism, he claims that the human intellect's knowledge derives from the corporeal things present in reality. By means of the light of the active intellect, we abstract the quiddities of such things, and only by reasoning about such data can we achieve, through analogy, some knowledge of God.[37] To state my conclusion about knowledge of God more precisely, therefore, I must discuss Aquinas's account of human knowledge in greater detail.

The object of intellectual knowledge is the intelligible universal, but the reality existing before man is made up of particular sensible things in continual change. "Wishing to save the certitude of our [universal] knowledge of truth through the intellect," says Thomas, Plato admitted, besides "things corporeal, . . . another genus of beings, separate from matter and movement, which beings he called *species* or *ideas*"[38]; these are the unmoving, subsistent and matterless forms of corporeal things, intelligible in act, the immediate object of the human intellect.[39] This opinion, Thomas continues, is unacceptable for two reasons: firstly, because the proper object of the natural sciences, inseparable from "knowledge of movement and matter," would be excluded from our knowledge, as well as "all demonstration through moving and material causes"; secondly, "because it seems ridiculous (*derisibile videtur*), when we seek for knowledge of things which are to us manifest, to introduce other beings, which cannot be the substance of those others, since they differ from them essentially: so that granted that we have a knowledge of those separate substances, we cannot for that reason claim to form a judgment concerning these sensible things."[40]

From Plato and Aristotle on, the history of theoretical philosophy has been characterized by the difficulty of reconciling the particular knowledge of corporeal reality with the universal knowledge of the mind. Moreover, the refusal to admit the presence of the intelligible universal in

37 See, in particular, ibid., I, q. 84, a. 7 ad 3; q. 88, aa. 2–3; and also I, q. 4, a. 3; q. 8, a. 1; q. 12, a. 12; q. 13, a. 2; q. 79, aa. 2–3.

38 Ibid., I, q. 84, a. 1 c.

39 Ibid., I q. 79, a. 3 c.

40 Ibid., I q. 84, a. 1 c.

particular sensible reality is characteristic of the starting-points of both Humean empiricism and Kantian transcendentalism.

Aquinas's Aristotelian solution, on the other hand, is well known. Aristotle "does not allow that forms of natural things exist apart from matter" and holds instead that they are given in reality. They are not, however, *actually* intelligible because they exist only in particular things. Because of this, the human intellect must be not only potentially receptive of the universal form, but it must also have an active capacity to abstract the intelligible species from sensible particulars, making them actual so that it can know them.[41] Intellectual knowledge is thus a true knowledge of reality, which proceeds from sensible objects by abstraction of the intelligible forms under the light of the active intellect.[42]

This doctrine is recapitulated by Aquinas in the first part of the *Summa theologiae*, question 85, article 2, where he explains that, though the object of our intellect is "the intelligible species abstracted from the phantasm," this species is not "what is actually understood" but "that by which the intellect understands." The proper object of our intellect is rather the material thing itself, the *res*, insofar as this is intrinsically intelligible (the "quiddity of a material thing"[43]).

To know means somehow to have within oneself the object known; it is the *intentional possession of a form*, according to the well-known Aristotelian notion. It is thus clear that the intellect cannot have as an object the "reality existing outside the soul," but only the universal intelligible species. The idea or concept, however, is an image or likeness of the intelligible object, just as the visible form is an image or likeness produced in the organ of sight by the visible object. "But since the intellect reflects upon itself, by such reflection it understands both its own act of intelligence, and the species by which it understands. Thus the intelligible

41 Ibid., I q. 79, aa. 2–3.

42 Ibid., I q. 84, a. 6; q. 85, a. 1.

43 Ibid., I, q. 84, a. 7 c; q. 86, a. 2 c. In the Italian edition of this book—and also in my article, "The Concept of Truth and the Object of Human Knowledge," in F. T. Arecchi (ed.), *The Scientific and Philosophical Challenge of Complexity* (Milan: ASRui, 2000)—I slightly misunderstood the notion of the proper object of intellectual knowledge in Aquinas. I revisited this notion in greater depth in my article, "What Nature? Whose Nature? Reflecting on Some Recent Arguments in Natural Law Ethics," in M. Waddell (ed.), *St. Thomas and Nature* (South Bend, IN: St. Augustine's Press, 2002) and have modified this paragraph accordingly. I thank Stephen Brock for his helpful suggestions in this regard.

species is that which is understood secondarily; but that which is primarily understood is the thing (*res*), of which the species is the likeness."[44]

This solution is proposed by Aquinas in direct contradiction to the opinion of those who thought that the idea was the true object of intellection, or, to put it in more general terms, "that our intellectual faculties know only the impression made on them." "This, however, is manifestly false," says St. Thomas, precisely for the two reasons to which I earlier alluded: "First, because the things we understand are the objects of science; therefore if what we understand is merely the intelligible species in the soul, it would follow that every science would not be concerned with things outside the soul, but only with the intelligible species within the soul; thus, according to the teaching of the Platonists all science is about ideas, which they held to be actually understood. Secondly, it is untrue, because it would lead to the opinion of the ancients who maintained that *whatever seems, is true*, and that consequently contradictories are true simultaneously."[45]

Only in light of these explanations can one fully appreciate the logic of the criticism leveled by the Angelic Doctor at the argument for the self-evidence of God's existence. His critique is framed in terms of the *logical impossibility* of proceeding from the mental existence of the premises to the real existence of the conclusion: "Yet, granted that everyone understands that by this word *God* is signified something than which nothing greater can be thought, nevertheless, it does not therefore follow that he understands that what the word signifies exists actually, but only that it exists mentally. Nor can it be argued that it actually exists, unless it be admitted that there actually exists something than which nothing greater can be thought; and this precisely is not admitted by those who hold that God does not exist."[46]

This epistemological approach has important consequences. For now I will highlight three in particular, which explain how, according to Aquinas, natural knowledge of God is different in each person, is inaccessible to the imagination, and is not necessarily reflexive. The first consequence can be summed up by saying that the measure of human knowledge is always sensible reality, never the perception of the knower (or, in intellectual knowledge, the intelligible species). In other words, one could

44 Ibid., I, q. 85, a. 2 c.

45 Ibid.

46 Ibid., I q. 2, a. 1 ad 2.

easily be led to believe that the only difference between Platonism, on the one hand, and Thomas's Aristotelianism, on the other, rests in the *origin* of the ideas present in the human mind: immediate evidence in Plato, and abstraction from sensible particulars in St. Thomas. This would be deeply mistaken. The true difference is that the ideas, as a means that the intellect employs in order to know reality, are neither immutable nor eternal, but are variable and always perfectible, just as the knowledge each person can have of the reality that surrounds him is variable and perfectible.

Thomas explains clearly that when man perceives things, "confused knowledge" is always "prior to distinct knowledge."[47] This is not only true for intellectual cognition, in which a "confused and general" knowledge of the more universal notion precedes the knowledge of the less universal, as generic knowledge of the notion of animal precedes the more specific knowledge of man; it is also true for sensory cognition: (a) in the spatial order, as when "a thing is seen approaching from afar off" and "it is seen to be a body before it is seen to be an animal; and to be an animal before it is seen to be a man, and to be a man before it is seen to be Socrates or Plato" and (b) in the temporal order, as "a child," who "can distinguish man from not man before he distinguishes this man from that."[48]

The human intellect, in order to know, requires judgment and reason. In St. Thomas's words, it "necessarily compares one thing with another by composition or division," in a constant intentional relationship with reality, because it "does not acquire perfect knowledge by the first act of apprehension; but it first apprehends something about its object, such as its quiddity, and this is its first and proper object; and then it understands the properties, accidents, and the various relations of the essence. Thus it necessarily compares one thing with another by composition and division; and from one composition and division it proceeds to another, which is the process of reasoning."[49] It is entirely possible, then, that "some understand a thing more profoundly than do others."[50] And this, at bottom, is the reason that in St. Thomas's philosophy, every act of the human intellect, both in the speculative and in the practical order (think, for example, of practical norms), can express a true knowledge of the object, but never a definitive knowledge.

47 Ibid., I q. 85, a. 8 c.
48 Ibid., I q. 85; a. 3 c.
49 Ibid., I q. 85, a. 5 c.
50 Ibid., I q. 85, a. 7.

These considerations allow us to re-evaluate the widely discredited notion of truth as "*adaequatio rei et intellectus*." The truth, St. Thomas says, does not refer primarily to reality but to the intellect. We do not say, for example, that the dog is true, but that our judgment, "the dog is beside us" (or "is a German shepherd" or "exists") is true or false, and the measure of our judgment can only be the actual reality of the dog: our intellect is true if the dog is really beside us; otherwise it is false. Truth *simpliciter* is the "logical truth" belonging to judgment, which always expresses the relation of conformity between the knowing intellect and the known thing. But, given the intentionality of our knowledge, our judgment will not be true only when it says *everything* about the known object, but when it expresses something about it, however minimal, that really corresponds to it.

A child's knowledge of the elephant may be limited to the fact that it is bigger than a dog, and the scientist's knowledge will be much more specialized than that of the layman: none, however, will be false if it expresses a (real, *true*) aspect of the elephant. It is only *secundum quid* that we subsequently predicate truth of the things themselves (*verum*), thus signifying their *real being* as object and measure of the intellect's knowledge.[51]

Clearly, this is the only way in which we can speak of the truth, because even if one were to deny such a notion, one would have to argue that it (as a judgment concerning the notion of truth) *does not conform to* what is really meant by "truth." Note, moreover, that such a notion does not imply that reality is somehow static or immutable but simply that it is always the measure according to which man judges his own judgments. For example, the opinion of a historian about the regime change brought about by the French Revolution is more or less credible to the extent that it more or less grasps what really happened, i.e., to the extent that it *conforms to* the facts, to people's real motivations, etc. The opinion of a political theorist about the best form of government must be supported by (that is, it must *conform to*) the facts. Anyone who wanted to maintain that nature changes would have to measure his judgment by changes actually observed, and would thus affirm an *intelligible aspect* of reality, for instance, the law of natural evolution. Even judgments about chance, or chaos, fall well within our notion of truth, since they express in an intelli-

51 Aquinas, *De veritate*, q. 1. For a concise exposition of the concept of truth in St. Thomas, see T. Alvira-L. Clavell-T. Melendo, *Metafisica* (Florence: Le Monnier, 1987), pp. 132–37.

gible or universal way our incapacity to explain something or everything: even with such judgments, albeit in a negative way, the intellect conforms to the reality that it knows.

In the Thomistic conception of the *adaequatio rei et intellectus*, it goes without saying that *one man's truth is not another's*, but it also goes without saying that there is only one objective truth. Truth, in fact, is always first and foremost the intentional relationship of *my* intellect with the reality that *I* know, and it therefore depends on *my* particular point of view. Each person's knowledge is, in a sense, a world of its own. But only reference to the same reality, to the same unit of measurement, so to speak, permits dialogue and comparison with other points of view on particular issues, and consequent agreement or disagreement.

Here, I believe there could be an interesting point of convergence with modern, post-analytic, constructivist theories of truth, intended as a critique of objectivistic descriptivism, which is seen as simplistic and naive. Substituting for the metaphor of the "mind as a mirror" that of the "mind as a reflector," constructivism seeks to underline the fact that all descriptions of reality are guided by the particular viewpoint (i.e. the evaluation or choice) of the subject that observes it, and that they cannot, therefore, be purely objective. Now if we add to this, following St. Thomas, that objectivity is reality as known (that is, as object of the intellect) and that everyone's knowledge is always intentional (that is, personal, perfectible, and gradual), then the connection with constructivism seems clear and promising.[52]

The concept of truth as *adaequatio rei et intellectus* is also valid when it is not the intellect that conforms to reality but, conversely, reality as the object of the agent's action that conforms to the intellect (practical truth: *adaequatio rei ad intellectum*). Indeed, the truth of actions is their conformity to the idea that the subject has in mind to realize. The measure of practical truth is thus the end, both in *praxis*, in which the end is immanent in the subject, and in *poiesis*, in which the end is external.

Turning now to our main topic, it follows from what has been said so far that in Thomistic philosophy, assuming that everyone has an idea of God and that such an idea corresponds to a real, existing, Being, it is

52 On the constructivist theory of truth and the metaphor of the mind as reflector, see for example V. Villa, *Conoscenza giuridica e concetto di diritto positivo* (Turin: Giappichelli, 1993); and N. Rescher, *The Coherence Theory of Truth* (Oxford: Oxford University Press, 1973).

entirely logically consistent to affirm that everyone will have his *own* idea of God, and that it will be original and different from that of others. But, at the same time, we must say that everyone's idea will be more or less true or false, according to the degree of its conformity or lack thereof to the knowable reality of God Himself, the objective measure of everyone's knowledge.

The second consequence of the Thomistic approach worth underlining is that the intellect cannot conceive the intelligible species without the actual mediation of images. In other words, the quiddity of a material thing, the direct object of the intellect, does not exist in itself but only as a form of the really existing particular presented to the mind by the senses through an image (phantasm); and this fact makes the mind incapable of conceiving its object, whether of first or of second intention, apart from the mediating image.

Aquinas explains this in two ways. First, he draws attention to the fact that the intellect, albeit an inorganic and immaterial faculty with an intelligible universal as its object, is impeded in its activity by those injuries to the organic faculties that make impossible the use of the imagination and memory, i.e. the faculties that have as their object images of corporeal reality. Second, Aquinas invites us to engage in a very interesting exercise: to try to think of any concept without forming an image in one's mind, however vague, confused, or deformed, of corporeal reality. "Anyone," in this way, "can experience this of himself, that when he tries to understand something, he forms certain phantasms to serve him by way of examples, in which as it were he examines what he is desirous of understanding. For this reason it is that when we wish to help someone to understand something, we lay examples before him, from which he forms phantasms for the purpose of understanding."[53] Try to think of concepts like chaos, reflective equilibrium, the dynamic sublime, or quantum mechanics: nobody can understand them until he forms images—albeit confused and changeable—of them, which are distinct from the reasons for concepts, but necessary for the intellect to think of them.

Hence, spiritual things are thinkable but not representable: the term "spirit" signifies breath, air, a puff of wind. This is important for our present subject because it means that the idea of God cannot be conceived without images, even though there is no image that can represent it. The idea of God is, for the human mind, like a concept perpetually fleeting and in tension, which employs available images to approach what cannot be

53 Aquinas, *ST*, I, q. 84, a. 7 c.; q. 86, a. 1 c.

imagined or represented in any way. This explains in part the intrinsic difficulty of the idea of God for man. In this regard Gilson, drawing our attention to a daring expression of Sertillanges, defines the Thomistic view as an "agnosticism of representation."[54]

Finally, the third consequence is that man does not necessarily have a complete and developed reflexive knowledge of those things he knows by means of conceptualization, judgment, or reasoning. In fact, we have seen that the intellect has reality itself as an *object of first intention* and that it is only due to its capacity to reflect upon itself that it can have its own thought as an *object of second intention*. Now it is natural for the intellect to reflect upon itself, but this does not mean that it always does so for everything it knows; what is more, it is a given of shared experience that we have never in fact reflected upon *most* of the things we know. Finnis offers an evocative example of this when he writes: "We often say 'Too late!'; but how often do we formulate the presupposition on which our conclusion rests, the guiding presupposition that time cannot be reversed?"[55]

When we speak of "natural knowledge" of God, we are referring primarily to knowledge of first intention. Consequently, not everyone need fully realize *reflectively* what he knows and what exactly God means for him. On the contrary, there will be few who ever engage this problem; and fewer still who manage to find a satisfactory solution to it. The knowledge of God of *first intention* does not automatically overflow into that of *second intention*, although it does necessarily manifest itself in language, and, in general, in communicative cultural symbols. In fact, all human knowledge tends to express itself outwardly (toward the other) in communicative forms that are culturally determined; hence, every culture has names, gestures, artistic expressions, etc., that refer to God and contain some sense and knowledge of the divine.

If we mean by *common sense knowledge* the portion of nonreflective (first-intentional) human knowledge—made up of more or less immediate concepts, judgments, and trains of reasoning—without which man cannot act or think as man (and which a normal, developed person must therefore possess), then we can say that on my interpretation, natural knowledge of God is for Aquinas common sense knowledge.[56]

54 E. Gilson, *Christian Philosophy: An Introduction*, pp. 33–44.

55 J. Finnis, *Natural Law and Natural Rights*, p. 64.

56 On this subject, see in particular A. Livi, *Filosofia del senso comune* (Milan: Ares, 1990).

3.3. Judgment and Reasoning

To sum up briefly what we have been discussing until now, we can say that for Aquinas ideas are not reliable, and cannot be the starting-point for human knowledge. The *object* of our knowledge is rather material reality, whose being is immediately evident to us. The intellect employs ideas, understood as intentional concepts, as means of knowing reality, abstracting them from corporeal things and making them the objects of judgment and reasoning. Finally, since God does not exist among corporeal things, His being is not self-evident to us and His existence can only be reached through a process of reasoning.

In order to further clarify the terms of the discussion, however, we need to dwell a bit longer on the function that judgment and reasoning have in human knowledge, because the most surprising aspect of Thomistic realism is that the being of any thing—its existence—can never be *deduced*. That is, being or existence cannot be *derived* from the mind either through judgment (which is the union of several concepts) or through reasoning (which is the union of several judgments). "Being," in fact, "is not included in the concept of any creature," and the judgment of existence ("the dog is") does not confer existence on the thing. The knowledge of existence in man depends simply on the evidence of sensible reality, and there is *no other existence* that man can know. It is for this reason that St. Thomas maintains that one cannot come to grasp philosophically the existence of angels, and he admits them as a philosophical issue—in order to understand what their nature might be—only on the *hypothesis* (here the term is entirely appropriate), or on the testimony of faith, that pure, intelligent spirits exist. If God exists, therefore, and if man can know Him by natural reason alone, then He must somehow reside in the being of sensible reality, and be part of the evidence of human knowledge.

This, however, seems contradictory. I have just reiterated that for St. Thomas we can only reach God through a process of reasoning, precisely because His being does not fall immediately before our senses, and our idea of Him does not therefore contain within it the evidence of His existence. Now I am saying that reasoning cannot lead us to the existence of *anything*, and therefore neither can it lead us to the existence of God. What exactly does this mean?

The *immediate evidence* of the being of corporeal things is not something isolated in time but is rather continuous, constant, and *intentional*. The senses, in constant relation with reality, produce and continuously improve the images from which the intellect abstracts its concepts, and the intellect returns constantly to those images and to its own concepts by means of judgment and reasoning. In Thomistic philosophy, then, human knowledge grows through experience, which, to quote Luño's beautiful definition, is the "contact of man with being (with the world, with himself, with other people) that takes place thanks to the cooperation between the senses and the intellect."[57]

Judgment and reasoning have the primary function of increasing and improving our immediate knowledge of the reality that falls before us. But this is not enough. They also constantly produce and refine additional concepts, or ideas, which can be of two types: fantastic and purely hypothetical, on the one hand, and real but mediated, on the other. In the first case, assembling and disassembling the images and concepts it already possesses, the intellect can create the idea of a flying horse or of a fairy; it can hypothesize the existence of another dimension, of extraterrestrials, or of pure spirits. In so doing, it must use images and concepts from immediately evident corporeal reality (wings, horses, dimensions, living beings, etc.), but it cannot logically pronounce judgments of real existence concerning the new ideas—at least not until it discovers, around it, clues justifying the passage from fantasy (e.g. a flying man) or pure hypothesis to scientific hypothesis, or indeed to reality itself. In the case of real but mediated ideas, on the other hand, the new ideas necessarily imply judgments of existence because they are coined precisely in the effort to deepen one's understanding of the existing reality. The ideas of atom, energy, electromagnetic waves, the law of gravity, chaos, etc., are neither fantastic nor purely hypothetical. They may be the result of a mistaken explanation, but their reality is nonetheless that of a real event that they are attempting to rationally penetrate: the structure of matter, falling bodies, the transmission of wireless messages, light, the complexity of things, etc. The concept of truth, finally, can be applied analogically to every type of new idea; thus the truth of fantastic and purely hypothetical ideas is their mental existence, but the truth of real, mediated ideas consists of that aspect of immediately evident corporeal reality that they are meant to express.

In this way, our dilemma concerning the existence of God is resolved: if the being of God does not somehow fall before our senses, we can never know His existence through reasoning, not even mediately. Or, to put the point even more radically, if the being of God is not from the very outset

57 A.R. Luño, *Etica*, p. 30.

a part of the immediate (and constant) evidence of the existence of those things from which our knowledge begins, it will *never* be known by us. Thus understood, reasoning about God is for St. Thomas nothing other than making explicit and further deepening our knowledge of particular aspects of sensible reality. And this raises the basic question concerning Aquinas's arguments for reaching God through reason: where is God in the sensible reality that falls before us?

3.4. God in Reality

To answer this central question we need only say that God is present in sensible reality just as a cause is present in an effect that cannot subsist without it, in such a way that the presence of the effect necessarily implies the presence of the cause. More specifically, God is present in reality as the first, uncaused cause of the very being of things.

St. Thomas addresses this issue directly in the question in the *Summa theologiae* devoted to the presence of God in things (*De existentia Dei in rebus*), in which the first query is "whether God is in all things" (*Utrum Deus sit in omnibus rebus*).[58] The response goes as follows: "God is in all things; not, indeed, as part of their essence, nor as an accident; but as an agent is present to that upon which it works. For an agent must be joined to that wherein it acts immediately (*in quod immediate agit*), and touch it by its power; hence it is proved in *Physic.* vii that the thing moved and the mover must be joined together. Now since God is very being by His own essence, created being must be His proper effect; as to ignite is the proper effect of fire. Now God causes this effect in things not only when they first begin to be, but as long as they are preserved in being; as light is caused in the air by the sun as long as the air remains illuminated. Therefore as long as a thing has being, God must be present to it, according to its mode of being."

God is thus in things in an intimate manner because being inheres in all things in the most intimate and profound way, as "formal in respect of everything found in a thing." Most importantly for our purposes, however, God is found in all things in an *actual* way. Just as a table is actually present to everything resting on it, which would otherwise fall to the ground, so—to assist our intellect with an image—we can consider that God is in all existing things like a table on which they rest, so that if the table were not there, they would fall into nothingness. The causality of God is like

58 Aquinas, *ST*, I, q. 8, a. 1.

that of an efficient cause whose presence must be simultaneous—is required *per se* (the hand that moves the staff, the staff that moves the stone), not *per accidens* (the grandfather who begets the father, the father who begets the son)[59]—if the effect is to be produced. To use a more recent terminology, God's causality should be thought of after the manner of those causes "essentially subordinate in the present," not of those "accidentally subordinate in the past."[60]

Now if the presence of God in reality is the presence of the actual ultimate cause of being, the immediate evidence we have of His presence is that the being of reality intrinsically presents itself as an effect. In other words, in Thomistic philosophy the being of sensible things, whose existence constitutes our primary certainty (*"res sunt"*),[61] necessarily discloses itself to our knowledge from the very beginning as requiring a cause, i.e. as insufficient in itself to account for its own existence. The starting-point of St. Thomas's theodicy is not simply reality, but the *being of reality as effect*, or *created being*: "there is no experience, properly speaking, of the Infinite, but only of the being (*essere*) that shows the insufficiency of the being (*ente*) and moves the finite spirit to transcend it."[62]

59 Ibid., I q. 46, a. 2 ad 7.

60 See A.L. González, *Filosofia di Dio*, p. 93, who on this point refers to J. García López, *Nuestra sabiduría racional de Dios* (Madrid: Instituto "San José de Colosony" de Pedagogía, 1950).

61 See E. Gilson, *Elements of Christian Philosophy*, p. 102: "Among the data of sense experience, the most strikingly evident information to be found about things is that they are. To say that they are and that they have actual being, or actual existence, is to say the same thing." See also A. Livi, *Il punto di partenza della filosofia secondo Gilson* (Rome: Pontificia Università Lateranense, 1960).

62 C. Fabro, *Dall'essere all'esistente*, p. 69. Cornelio Fabro is undoubtedly the scholar who has most effectively highlighted the centrality of the principle of causality in the proofs of the existence of God; his remains the best available philosophical defense of this principle. See in particular *L'uomo e il rischio di Dio*, in which the author's best essay on the argument is reproduced in the appendix, "La difesa critica del principio di causa," originally published in *Rivista di filosofia neoscolastica* (1936), pp. 102–41. Garrigou-Lagrange focuses correctly on "created being" as the starting-point of the five ways, but he does not see that this starting-point must be taken from the material, perceptible, reality. See Garrigou-Lagrange, *God: His Existence and His Nature*, pp. 245–46: "These five arguments . . . may truly be called metaphysical, for they are based on the highest metaphysical principles . . . , in this sense that *any created being whatever* can be taken as the starting-point in the argument, ranging from stone to angel and ending in those five attributes which can be predicated only of that being that subsists above all—*Ipsum esse*

It is clear, then, why the idea of God and the judgment of His existence should be understood as *mediated but real*: our intellect reaches God precisely as the proper cause of an effect whose existence, as such, is immediately evident to us. Thus, when St. Thomas asks about the *demonstrability of the existence of God*, he explains that, in this case, the procedure to be followed is not that which moves from knowledge of the cause to knowledge of the effect (demonstration *propter quid*), but that which seeks to move *backward* from the effect to its cause (demonstration *quia*). In fact, "when an effect is better known to us than its cause, from the effect we proceed to the knowledge of the cause. And from every effect the existence of its proper cause can be demonstrated, so long as its effects are better known to us; because since every effect depends upon its cause, if the effect exists, the cause must pre-exist. Hence the existence of God, insofar as it is not self-evident to us, can be demonstrated from those of His effects which are known to us."[63]

3.5. *Via Negativa* and *Via Positiva*

We must now touch upon two important consequences of the causal relationship and the demonstrative procedure just described. The first consequence is that our knowledge of God is necessarily negative. Indeed, St. Thomas constantly reiterates in his work that even by reasoning "we cannot know what God is, but rather what He is not,"[64] and that the "way of negation" is therefore the only route we can take. To understand this, we need only recall that a necessary implication of demonstration *quia* is that the cause in itself cannot be known. Suppose we were to see a moving football. In the absence of any further evidence, we cannot infer that it was kicked by a player rather than by a dog, or whether its movement was perhaps caused by a hand grenade. Precisely because we have no *direct* knowledge of the cause, we can say nothing positive about its nature.

In the case of God, we have at our disposal an initial positive determination, insofar as we reach Him as the first (or ultimate) cause that

subsistens, subsistent Being itself, whence flow all the divine attributes. These five proofs are deduced from the laws of created being, viewed not inasmuch as they may happen to be of the sensible or of the spiritual order, but inasmuch as they are created. Every created being is mobile, caused, contingent, composite, imperfect, and relative. St. Thomas preferred to select his examples from the objects of sense perception, but he also applied these same proofs to purely spiritual things, to the soul and its intellectual and volitional movements."

63 Aquinas, *ST*, I, q. 2, a. 2 c.

64 See for example Aquinas, *ST*, I, q. 3, *Prologue*.

moves everything without being moved, or that causes everything without being caused. Such a causality implies the absence in God of any change or potentiality, and it is not hard to go on from this point to predicate of His Being attributes such as simplicity, perfection, infinity, immutability and unity. We do this not, however, as predicating something positively of His nature, but rather by negation, concluding that in Him there can be no composition, potentiality, limitation, change, or division such as we find in the things we know directly.[65] Thus, to the degree that we distinguish God from the being of things, always by specifying further "what He is not" (He is not a body, He is not an accident, etc.), we deepen our knowledge of His nature, "for we know each thing more perfectly the more fully we see its differences from other things." Since, however, not having direct knowledge of God we cannot attribute to Him positive differences, our knowledge of Him will never be "perfect, since it will not tell us what God is in Himself."[66]

Surprisingly, though, the second consequence safeguards in turn the *positive* character of our knowledge of God. Indeed, St. Thomas never tires of repeating another extremely important principle, namely, that between creatures and God there is necessarily an essential resemblance. The reason for this is that an effect as effect cannot be dissimilar from its cause as cause, even when there is, properly speaking, no proportion between them, as occurs between the finite and the infinite.[67]

Let us return to the earlier example. Observing a moving football, although we certainly cannot infer the nature of what brought about its movement, we can nevertheless infer that the cause is, in itself, capable of causing motion, and that its capacity is at least equal to the movement that we now encounter. We cannot say, on the other hand, that the cause is in some way *movement*, because by placing the cause in the same genus as the effect, this would already amount to an illicit inference. Given, then, that God is the cause of the total being of things, it follows that, knowing things, we can say that God is *really* everything that they are—"the effect pre-exists virtually in the efficient cause."[68]—but that he has this reality (we now return to the way of negation) in a perfect, infinite and eminent mode, which is in itself unknowable and incomprehensible to the human mind. "Since therefore God is the first efficient cause of things, the per-

65 Ibid., I, qq. 3–11.
66 Aquinas, *CG*, I, chap. 14.
67 Aquinas, *ST*, I, q. 2, a. 2 ad 3.
68 Ibid., I, q. 4, a. 2 c.

fections of all things [i.e. all of their actualities] must pre-exist in God in a more eminent way."[69]

The interaction of negation and affirmation permits us to determine which modes of being can be properly attributed to God, and in what manner. In a very limited sense, we can say that God is body, lion, plant, etc. (just as man, had he created the ball out of nothing instead of kicking it, would have to be, as cause, *at least* ball). Properly speaking, however, these modes of being cannot in any way express the divine essence, because they are intrinsically limited to reference to corporeal or specific existence.[70] But if there are modes of being not necessarily subject to these limitations, which can legitimately be predicated of being as such—"pure perfections" of being, as Cornelio Fabro calls them—then according to the ways of affirmation (God has that mode of being), of negation (He does not have it in the way in which we know it) and of eminence (He has it, as its ultimate cause, to a supreme and ineffable degree), it is entirely proper to attribute them to God.[71] Thus, from the fact that there is life, intelligence, will, goodness, etc. in things, Aquinas can affirm that God is properly and to a supreme degree life, wisdom, will, goodness and everything that necessarily depends on them.[72]

Let us consider a brief example. To be alive, explains the Angelic Doctor, formally signifies self-determination to action rather than action "as moved by another." Consequently, life does not imply a univocal mode of being, but can occur in different degrees insofar as "the more perfectly this power [of self-determination to action] is found in anything, the more perfect is the life of that thing." The analogous character of this mode of being allows us to attribute it, in an eminent way, even to God.[73]

When St. Thomas speaks explicitly of creatures' resemblance to God, he always starts with the principle of causality, explaining that since "each thing acts according as it is in act," that is, according to a certain formality (wood heats insofar as it is fire in act, that is according to the formality of heat), there must be a resemblance in form between creatures (effects)

69 Ibid. See also *CG*, I, chap. 28.

70 Any generic or specific existence directly involves a composition because the species has a difference outside to the nature of the genus. For this reason, St. Thomas concludes that God cannot be contained in any genus and is not definable "because every definition is given by the genus and the difference" (*ST*, I, q. 3, a. 5).

71 C. Fabro, *L'uomo e il rischio di Dio*, pp. 105–7, 159–63.

72 For these examples see Aquinas, *ST*, I, qq. 6, 14, 18, 19.

73 For St. Thomas's complete explanation, see in particular *ST*, I, q. 18, a. 3.

and God (cause).[74] Such a resemblance, however, cannot be according to a generic or specific form (or nature), but only "according to some sort of analogy; as existence (*esse*) is common to all."[75] For this reason, he can then say that God, as *causa essendi*, is present in all things *per essentiam*,[76] "according to [each thing's] mode of being"[77]; and that "in this life" we can know of God by our unaided (natural) reason *not only that He exists*, but also everything that "must necessarily belong to Him, as the first cause of all things, exceeding all things caused by Him."[78]

The basic reason that we cannot separate the question of God's existence from that of His essence is that in knowing the effects, we simultaneously know both the existence of the cause and, albeit imperfectly, its mode of being. St. Thomas's so-called ways to the existence of God intrinsically imply a knowledge of His mode of being: that He is the ultimate uncaused cause, that in Him there is no change or composition, that He is supremely good, beautiful, intelligent, free, etc. Thus, the image of the

74 Aquinas, *CG*, I, chap. 29: "It belongs to the nature of action that an agent produce its like, since each thing acts according as it is in act. The form of an effect, therefore, is certainly found in some measure in a transcending cause, but according to another mode and another way. For this reason the cause is called an *equivocal cause*"; and *ST*, I, q. 3, a. 3 c.: "since every agent reproduces itself so far as it is an agent, and everything acts according to the manner of its form, the effect must in some way resemble the form of the agent."

75 Aquinas, *ST*, I, q. 4, a. 3.

76 Ibid., I, q. 8, a. 3.

77 Ibid., I, q. 8, a. 1 c.

78 Ibid., I, q. 12, a. 12 c. Aquinas also has recourse to the principle of necessary resemblance between cause and effect in the context of a multi-faceted and evocative, *strictly theological* explanation of the "true first cause of the distinction of things" (see *CG*, II, chap. 45). It is interesting to read at least Aquinas's first argument on this point: "Since every agent intends to introduce its likeness into its effect, in the measure that its effect can receive it, the agent does this the more perfectly as it is the more perfect itself; obviously, the hotter a thing is, the hotter its effect, and the better the craftsman, the more perfectly does he put into matter the form of his art. Now, God is the most perfect agent. It was his prerogative, therefore, to induce His likeness into created things most perfectly, to a degree consonant with the nature of created being. But created things cannot attain to a perfect likeness to God according to only one species of creature. For, since the cause transcends the effect, that which is in the cause, simply and unitedly, exists in the effect in composite and multiple fashion—unless the effect attain to the species of the cause; which cannot be said in this case, because no creature can be equal to God. The presence of multiplicity and variety among created things was therefore necessary that a perfect likeness to God be found in them according to their manner of being."

table that we proposed a short time ago turns out to be insufficient, since God is not merely the table upon which all things rest, but the cause of their total being. Were it not for the danger that images can be not only insufficient but also misleading, we might even think of Him as a solid object, within which, *by diminution of being*,[79] all things exist.

St. Thomas's doctrine of creatures' resemblance to God corresponds perfectly, within his work, to his explanation of the divine names. "Words," he says, "are signs of concepts (*signa intellectuum*), and concepts are images of things. . . . It follows therefore that we can give a name to anything in as far as we can understand it." Hence, precisely because we *know God through creatures*, we can name Him with terms taken from creatures—terms that cannot, therefore, express "the divine essence in itself."[80]

For the same reason, however, some names attributed to God in an "absolute and affirmative" way—such as good, wise, living, etc.—not only signify His causality ("He is the cause of goodness") or what He is not ("He is living" in the sense that "He is not in the mode of inanimate things"), but express in a real though insufficient way His essence. Indeed, every creature represents and resembles God, even if imperfectly, "so far as it possesses some perfection . . . not as something of the same species or genus, but as the excelling principle of whose form the effects fall short, although they derive some kind of likeness thereto"; and "our intellect," according to each such perfection, "knows and names God." "So when we say, *God is good*, the meaning is not, *God is the cause of goodness*, or *God is not evil*, but the meaning is, *Whatever good we attribute to creatures, pre-exists in God*, and in a more excellent and higher way. Hence it does not follow that God is good, because He causes goodness, but rather, on the contrary, He causes goodness in things because He is good."[81]

79 See E. Gilson, *Christian Philosophy: An Introduction*, p. 103.

80 Aquinas, *ST*, I, q. 13, a. 1 c. On the "problem of divine names," see E. Gilson, *Elements of Christian Philosophy*, pp. 137–44.

81 Aquinas, *ST*, I, q. 13, a. 2. See also *CG*, I, chap. 30: "Since it is possible to find in God every perfection of creatures, but in another and more eminent way, whatever names unqualifiedly designate a perfection without defect are predicated of God and of other things: for example, goodness, wisdom, being, and the like. But when any name expresses such perfections along with a mode that is proper to a creature, it can be said of God only according to likeness and metaphor. . . . Such names are used to designate the species of a created thing . . . for to each species belong its own mode of perfection and being. The same is true of whatever names designate the properties of things, which are caused by the proper principles of their species. . . . But the names that express such perfections along with the mode

Such names, Aquinas continues, are attributed to God *in a proper sense* because, even though our intellect grasps the perfections they signify "in the way in which they are found in creatures," the *res significata* itself (goodness, life, etc.) is present first of all in God, "in a more eminent way."[82] "Hence as regards what the name signifies (*quantum ad rem significatam per nomen*), these names are applied primarily to God rather than to creatures, because these perfections [signified by the names] flow from God to creatures; but as regards the imposition of the names, they are primarily applied by us to creatures which we know first."[83]

One objection to this doctrine might be that attributing particular modes of being to God would seem, at first glance, to contradict his simplicity, and thus to imply some limitation. St. Thomas responds that the affirmative propositions that we formulate about God are valid because our intellect, though it knows God through various concepts, understands that a single reality corresponds to them, since it "does not attribute its mode of understanding to the things that it understands; for example, it does not attribute immateriality to a stone even though it knows the stone immaterially." Even if we attribute to God life, intelligence, goodness, etc., we know that the distinction between these attributes and His being is not a real distinction, since "if there is some diversity in the composition, it is referred to the intellect, whereas the unity is referred to the thing understood by the intellect."[84] "Therefore, although the names applied to God signify one thing, still because they signify that under many and different aspects, they are not synonymous."[85] Finally, just as created things' generic or specific modes of being cannot be attributed to God, the names that we predicate (nonmetaphorically) of God and of creatures cannot be predicated univocally, but only analogically[86]—that is, according to a partial similarity, in the *res significata* (affirmation), and a partial dissimilarity, in the *modus significandi* (negation).[87]

of supereminence with which they belong to God are said of God alone. Such names are the *highest* good, *the first* being, and the like."

82 Aquinas, *ST*, I, q. 13, a. 3.

83 Ibid., I, q. 13, a. 6 c.

84 Aquinas, *CG*, I, chap. 36; *ST*, I, q. 13, a. 12.

85 Aquinas, *ST*, I, q. 13, a. 4.

86 Ibid., I, q. 13, a. 5.

87 See, in particular, Aquinas, *CG*, I, chap. 30. On St. Thomas's philosophy of language, see Ralph McInerny's excellent book, *Aquinas and Analogy* (Washington, D.C.: The Catholic University of America Press, 1996), which I had the pleasure of translating into Italian (*Tommaso d'Aquino e l'analogia*, trans. F. Di Blasi [Rome: Armando, 1999]).

3.6. The Idea of God: Premise and Object of the Proofs

The intimate connection in Thomistic philosophy between things, concepts, and words, and the use of the *quia* proof to demonstrate the existence of God, allow us to reach a further conclusion especially relevant for our purposes: namely, that the idea of God possessed by everyone spontaneously not only necessarily precedes the demonstration, but is one of its premises and its proper object.

It is obvious that nobody can set about demonstrating the existence of something (the atom, extraterrestrials, etc.) without first having some notion of it: indeed, one cannot even raise the problem in the first place. A specific objection to which Aquinas responds, concerning the possibility of demonstrating the existence of God, allows us to lay out formally and to deepen our understanding of what is meant by this common sense observation. The objection is that "the essence is the middle term of demonstration." Think, for example, of the following sequence: (a) dogs cannot fly, have paws, etc.; (b) Bobby is a dog; therefore (c) Bobby cannot fly, has paws, etc. Now precisely because we cannot know in what the essence of God consists but only "in what it does not consist," it follows that "we cannot demonstrate that God exists."[88]

This objection in itself is flawless, but it is only valid in relation to demonstrations *propter quid*, which move from causes to effects. What is more, St. Thomas adds that with respect to this type of demonstration God is absolutely indemonstrable, beyond any rational discourse whatsoever, because demonstrations *propter quid* imply the predication of genus and difference (the middle term is a definition, and "a definition is from genus and difference"), and God cannot be contained within any genus.[89]

In demonstrations *quia*, on the other hand, Aquinas explains that in order to demonstrate the existence of a cause, the "effect must take the place of the definition [or nature] of the cause." At first glance, we might think of a syllogism such as the following: (a) the existence of flying saucers (effect) requires the existence of extraterrestrials (cause); (b) flying saucers exist; therefore (c) extraterrestrials exist. This example, however, is not yet sufficient to respond to the objection because it does not explain the use, in the major premise, of the notion of the cause (extraterrestrials): if we have no direct knowledge of the cause, neither can we have any notion of it. And so St. Thomas goes on to explain how exactly we can make use of the effect in place of the nature of the cause: "In order to

88 Aquinas, *ST*, I, q. 2, a. 2 ad 2.
89 Ibid., I, q. 3, a. 5 c.

prove the existence of anything, it is necessary to accept as a middle term the meaning of the word (*quid significet nomen*), and not its essence (*quid est*), for the question of its essence (*quid est*) follows on the question of its existence (*an est*). Now the names given to God are derived from His effects; consequently, in demonstrating the existence of God from His effects, we may take for the middle term the meaning of the word *God*."[90]

The explanation is now clear: the middle term is the notion that we have of the cause, by virtue of our direct knowledge of the effects. The correct sequence of the *quia* demonstration, in the case of the extraterrestrials, is therefore the following: (a) the existence of flying saucers requires the existence of intelligent, non-terrestrial beings capable of constructing them; (b) flying saucers exist; therefore (c) intelligent, non-terrestrial beings capable of constructing them exist. Assuming as given the existence of the relevant effect, we can now reformulate the syllogism using the term "extraterrestrial," as follows: (a) the existence of flying saucers requires the existence of intelligent, non-terrestrial beings capable of constructing them; (b) the term "extraterrestrial" signifies such beings; (c) that which the term "extraterrestrial" signifies exists.

In the case of St. Thomas's five ways, in turn, the sequence of the demonstration *quia* can be summed up as follows. *First way*: (a) The movement of things requires the existence of "a first unmoved mover"; (b) the term "God" signifies such a first mover; (c) what the term "God" signifies exists. *Second way*: (a) The order existing between efficient causes requires a first efficient cause; (b) the term "God" signifies a first efficient cause; (c) what the term "God" signifies exists. *Third way*: (a) The existence of contingent things requires the existence of a "being having of itself its own necessity"; (b) the term "God" signifies a being that is in itself necessary; (c) what the term "God" signifies exists. *Fourth way*: (a) the existence of being, goodness, truth, nobility and other such perfections in things, to a greater or lesser degree, requires the existence of a single cause that is good, true, etc., to the highest degree; (b) the term "God" signifies a highest good, a highest truth, etc.; (c) what the term "God" signifies exists. *Fifth way*: (a) the existence of finality in things requires an intelligent being ordering them to an end; (b) the term "God" signifies such an intelligent being; (c) what the term "God" signifies exists.

The term "God" thus indicates the mediated knowledge that we naturally (spontaneously) have of God as the ultimate cause of the being of things. In this sense, natural and spontaneous knowledge of God (the idea,

90 Ibid., I, q. 2, a. 2 ad 2.

the name) is not only a premise of the proof of His existence, but also its proper object. In fact, the proof concludes that God is precisely that cause which our intellect had identified and named, and so it does nothing other than reflectively make explicit the cognitive path upon which we had already spontaneously embarked.[91] For this reason, the five ways do not end by saying, *therefore God exists*, but rather in exactly the following ways: (1) "Ergo necesse est devenire ad aliquod primum movens, quod a nullo movetur: *et hoc omnes intelligunt Deum*"; (2) "Ergo est necesse ponere aliquam causam efficientem primam: *quam omnes Deum nominant*"; (3) "Ergo necesse est ponere aliquid quod sit per se necessarium, non habens causam necessitatis aliunde, sed quod est causa necessitatis aliis: *quod omnes dicunt Deum*"; (4) "Ergo est aliquid quod omnibus entibus est causa esse, et bonitatis, et cuiuslibet perfectionis: *et hoc dicimus Deum*"; (5) "Ergo est aliquid intelligens, a quo omnes res naturales ordinantur ad finem: *et hoc dicimus Deum*."[92]

3.7. The Insufficiency of Being

It is now clear that the whole problem of St. Thomas's ways resides ultimately in the major premises that we have listed. These premises contain the observation of several modes of being of sensible reality and affirm their *essential insufficiency*: their very existence requires an ultimate, actual cause of their being, which "everyone calls God." This insufficiency, moreover, must be an immediate and primordial datum for human knowledge.[93] Movement does not have within itself the reason for its existence (I); the same holds for the efficient causes that we experience (II) and for the contingency of corporeal things (III); finally, the very being of things that fall beneath our senses immediately calls for the existence of a cause (IV and V).

The actuality of the cause that we are discussing also explains why St. Thomas's starting-point does not (even virtually) require the consideration of all existing things. If movement does not have the reason for its being

91 Gilson, addressing this topic, speaks of "a sort of spontaneous inference, wholly untechnical but entirely conscious of its own meaning, in virtue of which every man finds himself raised to the notion of a transcendent Being by the mere sight of nature in its awesome majesty" (E. Gilson, *Elements of Christian Philosophy*, p. 51).

92 Aquinas, *ST*, I, q. 2, a. 3 c. (my italics).

93 See C. Fabro, *L'uomo e il rischio di Dio*, pp. 217, 223.

within itself, it is sufficient that "in the world some things are in motion" for us to affirm the existence of a cause of the being of movement. Similarly, it is sufficient that we encounter among things in our experience "an order of efficient causes," or that we find "some [causes] that can be and non be," or "some . . . that act for an end." Even in the fourth way, a virtual consideration of the being of all things is not required; it is sufficient that there be gradation among the things that we know for us to affirm the existence of a Being of the highest degree that transcends them and is their cause.

One might object, at this point, that at least some of the modes of being from which the ways begin, and the causality that they imply, are not as immediate in our knowledge as St. Thomas requires. Therefore, we need to consider again what was said regarding the function of judgment and reasoning. Our immediate knowledge of the being of reality is *intentional*, i.e., it grows over time and can be greater or less depending on the degree of rational penetration we have attained in any given moment. St. Thomas's ways will therefore be more evident to the human intellect the less interpretation is required of the modes of being upon which they are based, and the greater our experience of the causality linked to each of them. What is important is that our starting-point remain within that reality whose existence is *immediately* (i.e., without mediation) present to our knowledge: namely, the reality of sensible things.

The movement of bodies is certainly a more evident datum than their natural finality, and the causality of motion is more evident than that required by participation in being in varying degrees: the way of motion is therefore, of all of the ways, "the most evident." However, the more or less immediate evidence of first intention need not correspond to that of second intention. For example, the concept of contingency might turn out to be difficult to grasp compared, for example, with that of motion, but this does not mean that at the level of experience, the contingency, the majesty or the order of things is less evident to common sense than their motion. If it is true that philosophy first reached God as the "Unmoved Mover," it is also true that even the most primitive of religious sacrifices implicitly contains knowledge, however imperfect, of a personal God: that is, of a God who can become angry, be appeased, *want* something, or change His mind. As the human intellect cognitively penetrates various modes of being of the things before it, it constantly refines its understanding of their intrinsic existential insufficiency, and in this way is moved more and more to turn to an ultimate cause, which it nevertheless does not know directly.

This is the cardinal principle connecting the starting-point of the ways to our knowledge of things, a principle of which we should not lose sight.

Finally, let us read in its entirety the concise exposition of the ways offered by Aquinas in the *Summa theologiae*, an exposition that, as Fabro puts it, "it is not permissible to spoil with an arid summary."[94]

First way: "The existence of God can be proved in five ways. The first and more manifest way is the argument from motion. It is certain, and evident to our senses, that in the world some things are in motion. Now whatever is in motion is put in motion by another, for nothing can be in motion except it is in potentiality to that towards which it is in motion; whereas a thing moves inasmuch as it is in act. For motion is nothing else than the reduction of something from potentiality to actuality. But nothing can be reduced from potentiality to actuality, except by something in a state of actuality. Thus that which is actually hot, as fire, makes wood, which is potentially hot, to be actually hot, and thereby moves and changes it. Now it is not possible that the same thing should be at once in actuality and potentiality in the same respect, but only in different respects. For what is actually hot cannot simultaneously be potentially hot; but it is simultaneously potentially cold. It is therefore impossible that in the same respect and in the same way a thing should be both mover and moved, *i.e.*, that it should move itself. Therefore, whatever is in motion must be put in motion by another. If that by which it is put in motion be itself put in motion, then this also must needs be put in motion by another, and that by another again. But this cannot go on to infinity, because then there would be no first mover, and, consequently, no other mover; seeing that subsequent movers move only inasmuch as they are put in motion by the first mover; as the staff moves only because it is put in motion by the hand. Therefore, it is necessary to arrive at a first mover, put in motion by no other; and this everyone understands to be God."

Second way: "The second way is from the nature of the efficient cause. In the world of sense we find there is an order of efficient causes. There is no case known (neither is it, indeed, possible) in which a thing is found to be the efficient cause of itself; for so it would be prior to itself, which is impossible. Now in efficient causes it is not possible to go on to infinity, because in all efficient causes following in order, the first is the cause of the intermediate cause, and the intermediate is the cause of the

94 Ibid., p. 143.

ultimate cause, whether the intermediate cause be several, or one only. Now to take away the cause is to take away the effect. Therefore, if there be no first cause among efficient causes, there will be no ultimate, nor any intermediate cause. But if in efficient causes it is possible to go on to infinity, there will be no first efficient cause, neither will there be an ultimate effect, nor any intermediate efficient causes; all of which is plainly false. Therefore it is necessary to admit a first efficient cause, to which everyone gives the name of God."

Third way: "The third way is taken from possibility and necessity, and runs thus. We find in nature things that are possible to be and not to be, since they are found to be generated, and to corrupt, and consequently, they are possible to be and not to be. But it is impossible for these always to exist, for that which is possible not to be at some time is not. Therefore, if everything is possible not to be, then at one time there could have been nothing in existence. Now if this were true, even now there would be nothing in existence, because that which does not exist only begins to exist by something already existing. Therefore, if at one time nothing was in existence, it would have been impossible for anything to have begun to exist; and thus even now nothing would be in existence—which is absurd. Therefore, not all beings are merely possible, but there must exist something the existence of which is necessary. But every necessary thing either has its necessity caused by another, or not. Now it is impossible to go on to infinity in necessary things which have their necessity caused by another, as has been already proved in regard to efficient causes. Therefore we cannot but postulate the existence of some being having of itself its own necessity, and not receiving it from another, but rather causing in others their necessity. This all men speak of as God."

Fourth way: "The fourth way is taken from the gradation to be found in things. Among beings there are some more and some less good, true, noble, and the like. But 'more' and 'less' are predicated of different things, according as they resemble in their different ways something which is the maximum, as a thing is said to be hotter according as it more nearly resembles that which is hottest; so that there is something which is truest, something best, something noblest, and, consequently, something which is uttermost being; for those things that are greatest in truth are greatest in being, as it is written in *Metaph.* ii. Now the maximum in any genus is the cause of all in that genus; as fire, which is the maximum of heat, is the cause of all hot things. Therefore there must also be something which is to all beings the cause of their being, goodness, and every other perfection; and this we call God."

Fifth way: "The fifth way is taken from the governance of the world. We see that things which lack intelligence, such as natural bodies, act for an end, and this is evident from their acting always, or nearly always, in the same way, so as to obtain the best result. Hence it is plain that not fortuitously, but designedly, do they achieve their end. Now whatever lacks intelligence cannot move towards an end, unless it be directed by some being endowed with knowledge and intelligence; as the arrow is shot to its mark by the archer. Therefore some intelligent being exists by whom all natural things are directed to their end; and this being we call God."

3.7.1. The Way of Motion

Aquinas dwells especially on the evidence of the causality required by the first way, according to which "whatever is in motion is put in motion by another," and which, in its most perfect metaphysical formulation, is expressed through the concepts of act and potency: "nothing can be reduced from potentiality to actuality, except by something in a state of actuality." Why does the existence of motion necessarily require an actual cause of its being? Motion simply indicates the fact that something moves. And the fact that something moves means that the thing in act is only potential with respect to the end or completion of the movement it is carrying out, that is, the moving thing *is not* yet what it is becoming: hence motion, as Aristotle explains, is "the fulfillment [the act] of what is potentially, as such."[95] Now, precisely because what is in motion *is not yet* what it is becoming, it cannot be the cause of its own motion, since otherwise, it would have to be already what it has not yet come to be. Wood cannot start burning (i.e., become fire in act) by itself, just as a dead body cannot begin to live by itself: a living body is a body in which the principle of that particular motion we call life acts actually, as cause. The essential insufficiency of movement is thus reducible to the principle of non-contradiction, according to which "it is not possible that the same thing should be at once in actuality and potentiality in the same respect, . . . *i.e.*, that it should move itself." A thing's movement is a reality that can neither occur nor be conceived without immediate reference to some other thing that has produced it: herein lies the evidence of its being caused, and this is why

95 Aristotle, *Physics*, III, 1, 201 at 10.

the experience of any movement whatsoever leads the intelligence spontaneously to search for a cause that might explain it.

"Therefore, whatever is in motion is put in motion by another," but the actuality of the cause also requires the simultaneous operation of an ultimate cause *that moves without being moved*, since otherwise, *nothing would move*. This is the famous step establishing the impossibility of an infinite regress of *actual* causes, which should be clear in light of what has already been said on this topic. The point is generally represented by the images of the train car and of the chandelier. To explain the movement of a train car another car will not suffice, nor even an *infinity of cars*: a locomotive is required. Likewise, to explain the suspension of a chandelier in the air, a metal ring supporting it will not suffice, and neither will an infinity of rings in a chain: we require *at least one ring* attached to the ceiling.[96]

There is no need at this point to undertake a detailed analysis of each of the elements of the various ways, of the objections that have been raised against them, and of the corresponding replies; for this I refer the reader to the works already cited. On the other hand, it is interesting to note the analogies and differences between the first three ways and the last two with regard to the mode of being from which they start and the causality by which they lead to God.

The most evident difference that emerges in the text of St Thomas is that in the fourth and fifth ways there is no reference to the impossibility of an infinite regress. It is often held that this is, in reality, a logical step essential to all the ways, and that Aquinas's attitude can be explained by his "love of brevity" or by the fact that the step is "implicitly present in the starting-point." Other differences, however, which we should not overlook, seem to suggest another explanation. Following the distinction we have sketched between negative and positive knowledge of God, we can easily appreciate the following striking difference between the two groups of ways: the first, unlike the second, do not come to predicate anything *positive* of God's being except His uncaused causality. This difference is reflected by, and depends upon, the modes of being from which the ways depart: those of the first three ways (motion and contingency) are intrinsically imperfect, and cannot therefore be predicated properly of God; those

96 On the way of movement see also, in particular, Aquinas, *Compendium Theologiae*, I, chap. 3, in *Opuscola Theologica*, ed. R.A. Verardo, O.P. (Rome: Marietti, 1954), and *CG*, I, chap. 13, where Aquinas examines in detail the explanations provided by Aristotle in books VII and VIII of the *Physics*.

of the latter two, on the other hand, express pure perfections of being and lead to God as the eminent cause of such perfections.

3.7.2. The Way of Efficient Causality

From the point of view of this last claim, the second way might be misleading, because it seems to start from the same notion as is later applied to God: that of an *efficient cause*. However, the mode of being that is the starting-point of the second way cannot be efficient causality, for a simple reason: for something to be an efficient cause does not by itself imply that it has been caused; this characteristic cannot, therefore, give rise to a chain leading back to a first, uncaused efficient cause. Everything that moves is necessarily moved by something else: therefore motion cannot be predicated of God, Who is the Unmoved Mover. But everything that causes is not necessarily caused by another; therefore God can properly be said to be a cause.

The starting-point of the second way is thus the efficient cause inasmuch as it, in turn, is *moved*: that is, it is the *order* of efficient causality that is presented to us in our sensible experience. The value of the second way as a proof lies in its being another way of looking at the first, and this is why St. Thomas does not feel the need here to repeat his detailed explanation of the essential insufficiency of the starting-point. If it is not viewed in conjunction with the first way, the exposition of the second appears incomplete precisely because it lacks an explanation of why the efficient causality we observe must, of necessity, have been caused by something else.[97]

3.7.3. The Way of Contingency

The third way, on the other hand, does not initially create any difficulty with respect to the distinction between positive and negative knowledge, because *contingent being*, however one interprets this notion, is not predicated of God. Rather, problems arise in considering the impossibility of an infinite regress, and they arise precisely because necessary being does not as such need to be caused by another necessary being. As we have seen for the notion of an efficient cause, this is why the notion of necessary being is also applicable to God. Nonetheless, unlike the case of efficient causality, we have no *experience* of caused, necessary beings. Therefore,

97 On the substantial coincidence of the first two ways, and the grounds for the distinction between them in St. Thomas, see also E. Gilson, *Elements of Christian Philosophy*, pp. 83–84.

even assuming that the first part of the way leads to the existence of a necessary Being, how can one apply the argument against an infinite regress to arrive at a necessary being that does not receive from others its own necessity?

In fact, the point that prevents an equivocal interpretation of the notion of contingency, clarifies the starting-point of the third way, and determines its probative value, is precisely the application of infinite-regress argument, which requires that the starting-point, the (experiential) mode of being, be some sort of *motion*, and thus manifest of itself the necessity of an external cause. The directly experienced temporal movement of corruptible beings, their generation and corruption—in other words, their passage from non-being to being—requires as an *actual* cause a necessary being that, precisely as an actual cause, must be *ultimate.* Misunderstandings of the third way, by contrast, arise from a strong temptation to read it as a journey backward through time (where the series of causes can indeed be infinite), forgetting the actuality of *causal dependence* that it necessarily requires.

The third way becomes intelligible, then, in the following terms: what moves in time between being and non-being (and therefore *can not be*) does not have within itself the reason for this actual movement; otherwise it would neither begin (pass from non-being to being) nor end (pass from being to non-being) but would give and take being from itself, which is a contradiction. Such a thing must not only have been produced in time by something else (by generation or creation) but also requires an actual *non-contingent* cause that maintains in being the movement of generation and corruption—if this cause were not present *now, as before, nothing would move in time*: "nothing would exist." The first step of the way simply says that behind sensible things' movement of generation and corruption there cannot be pure contingency, but rather a necessary being (in the pure and simple sense of *not being subject to generation and corruption*), as the actual cause. But the actual cause of a movement, as we have already seen, entails an ultimate cause that causes without itself being caused: in the case of the third way, a necessary being "having of itself its own necessity, and not receiving it from another." Consequently, the starting-point for the infinite-regress argument in the third way is not the being of caused necessary beings but the movement of corruptible beings.[98]

98 Even Fabro, in *L'uomo e il rischio di Dio* (p. 271), does not appear to have noticed this, and refers this logical step of the third way to the notion of participated being.

If we understand contingency in this way, we can see how the phrase that appears in the first step of the way, "*quod possible est non esse, quandoque non est*" (that which is possible not to be at some time is not), is consistent with the philosophical possibility of a *contingent* cosmos that is caused (i.e., created) *ab aeterno*.[99] Indeed, the phrase refers to corruptible beings, affirming precisely the need for necessary beings as a condition of their existence: "Therefore, if everything is possible not to be, then at one time there could have been nothing in existence. Now if this were true, even now there would be nothing in existence, because that which does not exist only begins to exist by something already existing. Therefore, if at one time nothing was in existence, it would have been impossible for anything to have begun to exist; and thus even now nothing would be in existence—which is absurd. Therefore, not all beings are merely possible, but there must exist something the existence of which is necessary." If the cosmos, then, were *merely contingent* (in the sense that this term is given in the third way), it could not exist.

The further need, in the order of actual causes, for a necessary being that does not derive its own necessity from something else, does not speak to the question of whether such a being willed the world from eternity or only from a given moment; it simply says that the actual existence of the world requires the action of an ultimate transcendent cause to maintain it in being.[100] In reality, when people speak of the philosophical possibility of a *contingent* cosmos that is caused *ab aeterno*, they give a different meaning to the concept of contingency, understanding it in relation to the composition of essence and act of being. This notion of contingency turns out to coincide with that of participation, which we will consider in the following section.[101]

99 It is well known that in the tradition of Christian thought, to which Aquinas fully adhered, the fact that the world was created at a particular moment (that it "has a beginning") and was not *always* there, is not demonstrable by philosophical argument but is known only as a truth of faith: philosophy can only grasp the necessity of God as the transcendent cause. See Aquinas, *ST*, I, q. 46, a. 2.

100 I have given careful study to the connection between the concept of contingency in the third way and the passage "*quod possibile est non esse, quandoque non est*," following a fruitful exchange of ideas with Vittorio Possenti, whom I thank.

101 It is probably because he focused too much on the general sense of contingency that Garrigou-Lagrange did not see that the starting-point of the third way is given precisely by "the contingency of material things." See Garrigou-Lagrange, *God: His Existence and His Nature*, p. 248.

3.7.4. The Doctrine of Participation

The third way can also be traced back to the essential insufficiency of motion as the passage of a being (*ens*) from non-being to being.[102] But what is the relation between motion, the *via negativa*, and the infinite regress? It is that motion immediately calls for the existence of a cause, but does reveal anything about the thing moved other than its extrinsic relation to the thing that moves it; in fact, "the relation to its cause is not part of the definition of a thing caused."[103] The essential insufficiency of motion is immediate but extrinsic to being: the path to God must therefore be *mediated* by denying the possibility of an infinite regress in the series of actual causes of motion.

It is clear, however, that if, in the entities that present themselves to our experience, there were an *intrinsic, essential insufficiency*, in other words, if their very being were actually causally dependent, the passage to God would be immediate (because the *actual* cause of being, as such, must be the creative cause),[104] and would not be attained through negation but through the affirmation of the proper cause of the being that is given in existence.

This is what Aquinas expresses through the doctrine of the participation of being, most explicitly in the *Summa theologiae*, I, q. 44, a. 1, where he explains why anything that exists must have been created by God.[105] His

102 This unification of the ways around the concept of movement can be appreciated by considering how one may contemplate God *ex aeternitate*, as described in the prologue to the commentary on St. John's Gospel, which was written after the *Summa theologiae*: "Alii vero venerunt in cognitionem Dei ex eius aeternitate. Viderunt enim quod quicquid est in rebus, est mutabile; et quanto aliquid est nobilius in gradibus rerum, tanto minus habet de mutabilitate: puta, inferiora corpora sunt secundum substantiam et secundum locum mutabilia; corpora vero caelestia, quae nobiliora sunt, secundum substantiam immutabilia sunt; secundum autem locum tantum moventur. Secundum hoc ergo evidenter colligi potest, quod primum principium omnium rerum, et supremum et nobilius, sit immobile et aeternum" (Aquinas, *Expositio in Evangelium sancti Ioannis*, in *Catena Aurea in Quattuor Evangelia*, ed. A. Guarienti, O.P. [Rome: Marietti, 1953], *Prologus*).

103 Aquinas, *ST*, I, q. 44, a. 1 ad 1.

104 Ibid., I, q. 45, aa. 1 and 5.

105 See also, in particular, Aquinas, *Quaestio disputata de potentia*, q. 3, a. 5; and q. 5, a. 5, ad 1. The English edition used here is *On the Power of God*, translated by the English Dominican Fathers (Westminster, Maryland: The Newman Press, 1952). [In the Italian edition, the author drew attention to a recent translation of qq. I–VII, *La potenza di Dio*, ed. A. Campodonico (Florence: Nordini, 1991)].

argument runs as follows: "It must be said that every being in any way existing is from God. For whatever is found in anything by participation, must be caused in it by that to which it belongs essentially, as iron becomes ignited by fire. Now it has been shown above (Q. 3, A. 4) when treating of the divine simplicity that God is the essentially self-subsisting Being; and also it was shown (Q. 11, AA. 3, 4) that subsisting being must be one; as, if whiteness were self-subsisting, it would be one, since whiteness is multiplied by its recipients. Therefore all beings apart from God are not their own being, but participate in being. Consequently, it is necessary that all things which are differentiated according to their diverse participations of being, so as to exist more or less perfectly, are caused by one First Being, Who possesses being most perfectly. Hence Plato said (*Parmen.* xxvi) that unity must come before multitude; and Aristotle said (*Metaph.* ii., text. 4) that whatever is greatest in being and greatest in truth, is the cause of every being and of every truth; just as whatever is the greatest in heat is the cause of all heat."

The formula of causal dependence is clear and the passage is immediate: from participated being to being by essence. "Whatever is found in anything by participation, must be caused in it by that to which it belongs essentially." Aquinas's reference to white-hot iron clarifies the actuality that we should understand as characterizing this causal relation: being hot, unlike, for example, being in one particular shape rather than another, requires a cause of heat outside the iron itself actually acting on it. To have something "by participation" means to possess it *not* "*by essence*," and this presupposes an actual causal dependence on something possessing the same characteristic by essence. St. Thomas also uses the example of an illuminated body: such a body, insofar as it is illuminated, does not possess light by essence but participates in it by virtue of something that possesses it of itself—for example, fire.[106] The concept of participation thus understood includes the causal dependence of motion and expresses, in the most radical way, the evidence for the principle of causality:[107] "The evi-

106 Aquinas, *Quaestiones quodlibetales*, II, q. 2, a. 3, ed. R.M. Spiazzi, O.P. (Rome: Marietti, 1949).

107 See C. Fabro, *L'uomo e il rischio di Dio*, p. 221: "The possibility of the critical defense of the principle [of causality] using the notion of participated being occurred to me while seeking in St. Thomas the ultimate metaphysical reason for which a thing can be said to be dependent." See also C. Fabro, *La nozione metafisica di partecipazione (secondo S. Tommaso d'Aquino)*, 3rd rev. ed. (Turin: Società Editrice Internazionale, 1963).

dence and self-existence (*perseità*) of the principle are assured because participated being appears to our mind in an immediate relation of dependence on being by essence, both in the order of knowledge and in that of reality: this means that '*if*' being by participation is a given, '*if it exists*,' with this existence and givenness, the relation of dependence must also exist."[108]

Now, what St. Thomas means to say in the first article of question 44 is that the being of the things that surround us, their total, universal, intensive being, presents itself as participated being because such things "are not their own being": "*nulla enim creatura est suum esse, sed est habens esse*."[109] This characteristic depends on the radical composition, present in all finite entities, of essence and act of being; all in fact *are* (act, action of being)—but not only *are* they, simply; they are *something* (essence), and this something does not in itself require being but limits and circumscribes it as a *determinate* being. "Being," as we have already seen, "is not included in the concept of any creature, for the act of existence of every creature is distinct from its essence."[110] The fact, then, that right now something *is* but is not by essence implies an immediate actual causal dependence upon the *only* being that, as being by essence (being "self-subsisting") is capable of conferring being and maintaining in being all things that "are not their own being." Clearly, *there cannot here be a mediated passage*, as there is in the case of motion, since there is nothing preceding the first being of things (*esse absolute*) to which a secondary (or intermediate) cause could extend its action. Hence also the passage from absolute non-being to being—creation—is not a movement or motion.[111]

For Gilson, Aquinas's discussion in this article amounts to *another* proof of the existence of God.[112] For Fabro, the doctrine of participation is not only not "metaphysically derived," i.e. "secondary," but represents "the ultimate theoretical requirement" that precedes and grounds, but does not exclude, "inferior levels of metaphysical consideration according to the different real conditions that different entities occupy in the hierarchy of the real. For this reason, St. Thomas has been able to offer, in his mature

108 C. Fabro, *L'uomo e il rischio di Dio*, p. 223.
109 Aquinas, *Quaestiones quodlibetales*, II, q. 2, a. 3.
110 Aquinas, *De veritate*, q. 10, a. 12 c.
111 Aquinas, *ST*, I, q. 45, aa. 1–5.
112 E. Gilson, *Elements of Christian Philosophy*, p. 56; *Christian Philosophy: An Introduction*, p. 95

thought, not one but five *ways* to ascend to God."[113] For our purposes, it is sufficient to underline that if we take as our starting-point for reaching God the total being of the things that present themselves immediately to our knowledge, then there is no need to raise and reject the possibility of an infinite regress in the series of causes.

Let us return momentarily to the third way. The appeal of absolute contingentism, according to which this way has often been interpreted, is largely due to the strong intellectual temptation to confuse the immediate causal dependence of the intensive being of participated entities with the mediate dependence of mere *existence*, that is, of the mere extrinsic fact of their actual movement in being. Contingentism amounts to a misunderstanding of the third way and a partial but distorted intuition of participation.

The only *existence* we know directly is that of corruptible material entities, and from their *movement*, we can work our way back to a *necessary* cause, and, by the infinite-regress argument, to a necessary uncaused cause. We do not know the existence of necessary, caused (*contingent*) entities directly; but because the notion (essence) of such beings does not imply their existence, even if we did know them directly we could only use them as a starting-point for the infinite-regress argument. With regard to the contingency of existence, therefore, the only possible starting-point is material things and the only path we can take lies through the infinite-regress argument. (From this point of view, it is hardly surprising that contingentism has proliferated in idealistic environments, where the tendency has been to start with the *notion* of contingency, forgetting the real meaning of the existence of things). Ultimately, it is only if we keep in mind not merely the existence, but the total being of material entities and its participated character, that we can immediately reach the causality of God.

3.7.5. The Fourth Way

Let us now move on to the fourth way. Given what we have already said, it is obvious that if (as Fabro explains in detail) one traces the fourth way directly back to the notion of participation, one avoids "all the uncertainties and complications that we came across in [its] formulation," and its probative value immediately becomes evident: the "*magis et minus* dialectic . . . does not appear to be essential to [its] structure."[114] And yet, we

113 C. Fabro, *L'uomo e il rischio di Dio*, pp. 141–42, 240.
114 Ibid, pp. 258–59.

might add, there is a reason for this dialectic. The fact is that besides movement, Aquinas has in mind at least two other modes of being that effectively express the causal dependence of entities that present themselves to our knowledge: multiplicity and gradation. Gilson illustrates these two forms of dependence with particular clarity, commenting on *De potentia*: "when one thing is found in common in several beings, a single cause must be responsible for its presence in them. Indeed, the presence in common of the same thing in several different beings can be explained neither by their differences nor by a number of different causes." As regards gradation, moreover, whereas multiplicity "simply affirmed the one as the cause of the many," the argument from gradation "affirms the absolute, or the supreme degree in every genus, as the cause of everything that differs more or less within the same genus."[115]

The fact that several entities have something in common pushes us back to a cause of that something external to them, and if they possess it to different degrees, i.e., according to a "more" and a "less," we need a cause that possesses it to a supreme degree. If the common feature, then, does not belong to the essence of the entities in question, the external cause must be actual, and we are again dealing with the concept of participation. Let us take an example: if we see several illuminated bodies, we say that they have light and that there must be a single cause of this light external to each of them; otherwise they could not all possess it in the same way. If, in addition, they possess it to different degrees (i.e., some are brighter than others), we must say that there is a single cause that possesses light to a supreme degree compared with the gradation that we observe, and which could not otherwise exist. Again, if there are illuminated bodies but the light is not part of their essence, there must be a single cause, in act, that possesses light by essence; otherwise nothing would be illuminated. Inasmuch as light (like heat) is reducible to a *movement* of material things, this argument can lead to God as uncaused cause, through the rejection of an infinite regress. The peculiarity of this procedure is that the starting-point immediately makes evident the *unicity* of the required cause.

What St. Thomas does in the fourth way is to start from the being of things as intensive act that is *common* to them according to *different degrees*. All things *are*, as we have seen. But they *are* according to differ-

115 E. Gilson, *Christian Philosophy: An Introduction*, pp. 19–20. The text being discussed is Aquinas, *Quaestio disputata de potentia*, q. 3, a. 5.

ent modes. With respect to their total being, moreover, the only possible difference is one of degree, i.e. of more and less. The intensive being of things, extrinsic to their essence, immediately pushes us back (in a way exceptionally evident to the intellect), through the commonality and difference of degree with which it presents itself, to the only Being that *is* to an eminent degree and is self-subsisting, as to its proper cause. Thus the special evidence of the fourth way, compared with the preceding three, and the full value of that aspect of its formulation that has given rise to so many debates[116]—the passage from the dialectic of degrees to the causality of the supreme degree—come clearly into view.

One last point remains to be clarified: the connection between the terms of gradation taken in the fourth way as starting-points ("goodness, truth, nobility and other such perfections") and the total being of things. In this regard, it must be pointed out that the "perfections" that the Angelic Doctor takes into consideration express in themselves precisely the being of things, as related to intellect and will. The truth of things is the intrinsic rationality of their being, which makes them intelligible. The goodness of things is the intrinsic virtue of their being, which renders them *useful* (in a broad sense) for something, and thus attractive and desirable: it is the rationality of being observed in its *finality*, that is, the being of things as *ordered*, whether in themselves or in relation to something else. The same holds for the other perfections in the orders of truth and goodness, such as nobility, beauty, etc.

To contemplate the truth of things, then, means to observe their *total* being as rational, and thus to see it (according to participation) in an immediate relation of dependence on the intelligent cause that produced it from nothing: things *are* rational but they *are not the rationality*. In addition, the gradation of truth in things increases the immediacy of the passage to the unique intelligent cause of being. Similarly, to contemplate the goodness of things means to observe the more or less complex and articulate dynamism with which they move toward an end, and thus to turn one's attention to the intelligence that created in them such a rational ordering—and so on. Beginning with the individual perfections, Aquinas links the very being of things to an intelligence that conceives of them, and a will that posits them. In this way he increases still more the immediacy of our passage to God as Creator. In any case, for our purposes it is sufficient to stress that the *real* reference to goodness, truth, etc., is equivalent to a reference to intensive being, and points to a *res significata* that,

116 See C. Fabro, *L'uomo e il rischio di Dio*, p. 242 ff.

according to the way of negation and of eminence, can express *in a proper sense*, in human language, the *essence of God.*

3.7.6. The Way of Finality

These clarifications allow us to penetrate the content of the fifth way as well. The point of departure here is, in fact, the goodness of things—the rational order present in their being—and I have already sufficiently emphasized that the doctrine of participation, applied to being as such, permits us to proceed immediately to the only Being by essence as cause of all other being, while gradation makes this passage easier without constituting an essential step. The passage from the order of things to creative intelligence is exceptionally evident to common sense, and this allows Aquinas—who has already dealt on several occasions and from different angles with the existence of God and the procedure for proving it—to give a simple and succinct formulation of this way.

Despite the many endless debates about the finality of nature, the relevant data are macroscopically incontestable; moreover, Aquinas makes clear that their use does not require a quasi-mathematical proof, but only the simple, *minimal* observation that "some things . . . without intelligence . . . act always, or nearly always, in the same way": even a limited and imperfect repetition of the same behavior is opposed by definition to pure chance. The fourth and fifth ways, which among the pure perfections of being take as their starting point the rationality of things, necessarily entail that in Thomistic philosophy man's natural knowledge of God is knowledge of a personal God, intelligent and free.

A final clarification may be helpful in this regard: the conclusion concerning the personal being of God does not depend on man's existence. Indeed, confronted with the reductive idea that philosophical reasoning can only reach the existence of an impersonal God (as First Cause or Unmoved Mover), one might at first think that the way to show the personal nature of God is to be found in the existence of man himself: if a *free, created effect* exists, and if "the effect pre-exists virtually in the efficient cause,"[117] then the existence of man necessarily implies that the Creator too is free, according to the way of negation and eminence. Now this reasoning is correct, but also reductive, and it makes the occurrence of natural religion at any level quite problematic.

The experiential point of departure for demonstrating the existence of a personal God is the intrinsic rationality that *all* things have, and cannot

117 Aquinas, *ST*, I, q. 4, a. 2 c.

give themselves, understood in relation to the intelligent and free cause that produces this rationality from nothing. Such rationality is all the more evident, as a starting-point for reaching God, the more it is manifested in the corporeal things that man finds before him. Human freedom, on the other hand, not only does not pertain to corporeal reality, but is an object of experiential knowledge that is extremely difficult to grasp in its intrinsic (natural) rationality, in such a way as to lead back to God as its cause. If the idea of a personal God depended on human freedom as its experiential starting-point, few would reach it with the spontaneity of common sense.

The rationality of material things makes inference to a personal God objectively possible, in Thomas's account, even if man did not exist. At the same time it is true that with respect to his cognitive faculty man is capable of opening himself up to the personality of God only *by extension*, through the prior experiential knowledge of his own free being. In this way, as Antonio Livi aptly stresses, the notion of *I* necessarily precedes that of *God* in human noetic knowledge.[118] Thus, if we wish to understand natural religion and the idea of God, it is important to come to a deeper understanding of our own personal being, and the way in which man knows himself and his freedom.

3.8. The Metaphysical Experience of Being

Our discussion began with the claim that "according to Aquinas, whatever man knows, and insofar as he knows it, he also knows God and His mode of being, because the being of things (a) resembles essentially the being of God, and (b) leads the human intellect back to God in way that, even if mediated, is necessary." These points have been adequately explained by highlighting the principle that created thing must resemble God, and by showing how they lead back to Him as their cause. I have also brought out the plausibility of an intentional notion of God present in every man, and the necessity, for the Angelic Doctor, that such a notion precede rational, demonstrative discourse. We must still, however, say something about the *necessity* of the human intellect turning to God, by showing how *every act* of human intellectual knowledge involves a tension with, and an openness to, the Absolute.

At the beginning of the *De veritate* we find the famous Thomistic formula according to which the *ens* is "*quod primo intellectus concipit quasi notissimum et in quod conceptiones omnes resolvit . . . unde oportet quod*

118 A. Livi, *Filosofia del senso comune*, p. 51.

omnes aliae conceptiones intellectus accipiantur ex additione ad ens": that which the intellect first conceives as, in a way, the most evident, and to which it reduces all its concepts . . . all the other conceptions of the intellect are had by additions to being.[119] But since there is nothing that is *not* encompassed by the notion of *ens*—there is nothing that is not something—this notion cannot be understood univocally, as if other concepts were related to it as specific differences to a common genus. Consequently, St. Thomas immediately adds: "*sed enti non possunt addi aliqua quasi extranea per modum quo differentia additur generi vel accidens subiecto, quia quaelibet natura est essentialiter ens, unde probat etiam Philosophus in III Metaphysicae [8] quod ens non potest esse genus; sed secundum hoc aliqua dicuntur addere super ens in quantum exprimunt modum ipsius entis qui nomine entis non exprimintur*": But nothing can be added to being as though it were something not included in being—in the way that a difference is added to a genus or an accident to a subject—for every reality is essentially a being. The Philosopher has shown this in III Metaphysicae [8] by proving that being cannot be a genus. Yet, in this sense, some predicates may be said to added to being inasmuch as they express a mode of being not expressed by the term *being.*[120]

Everything the intellect conceives, then, is based on the notion of being (*ens*), which signifies *that which is* (*id quod est*), i.e., that which has being. Being (*ens*) is therefore the first and most universal[121] notion, "*quod primo intellectus concipit,*" and indicates a determinate, essential, mode of being: being *something*. *Ens*, however, is not a flat, generic concept, which needs subsequently to be *specified* in relation to the different modes of being: it expresses intentionally the entire being of the thing that is known, in such a way that other notions serve only to make explicit the various aspects of which the thing is composed. *Ens* is thus an analogical notion, since it simultaneously expresses the mutual resemblance of all things in being, and the difference of each one in its proper and determinate mode of being.[122]

The notion of being in its universality—"*ens universale,*" "*ens in universale*"[123]—signifies what is usually called the common formal object

119 Aquinas, *De veritate*, q. 1, a. 1 c.
120 Ibid.
121 Aquinas, *ST*, I, q. 85, a. 3.
122 On various aspects of the notion of *ens* see Alvira-Clavell-Melendo, *Metafisica*, pp. 14–28.
123 See, for example, Aquinas, *ST*, I, q. 78, a. 1 c; I, q. 79, a. 2 c.

of the intellect (as distinct from the proper formal object, that is, the "quiddity" of sensible things),[124] and allows Aquinas to distinguish the intellectual powers as such, since "the powers of the soul are distinguished generically by their objects" and there are some that embrace "*universaliter omne ens*."[125]

To express this with an image, the notion of *ens* is like the chink through which the human intellect looks at reality; however—and this is the point that matters most for our purposes—such a notion is composite and in itself implies a tension. On the one hand, it always refers to a determinate essence, to a mode of being that is not shared by other things, and on the other, it expresses the being that is common to all. In St. Thomas's terminology, the notion of *ens* is composed of the notions of essence and act of being, both of which, to the extent that they precede "*quod primo intellectus concipit*," are not conceptual or definable.

Cornelio Fabro, as is well known, distinguishes three basic moments in the process of determination of the real: phenomenological, ontic, and metaphysical.[126] The first is the moment of perceptual *experience* (where experience "should be understood in the sense of direct and proper apprehension, as opposed to deduction or inference"): at this stage, reality is based "on appearance." He speaks, in this regard, of "first degree immediacy," characterized by an "active determination," since the object imposes itself immediately upon the knower in its particularity, "in a given moment and in function of the isolated presence that separates it, not only from the field of objects of other spheres of consciousness, but also from objects in its own field not actually present, given that only one object at a time can be present to experience so understood." The immediacy of the active determination leads consciousness not toward openness and commonality but toward "particularity," "limitation," and, precisely, "determination."[127]

Active determination also pertains to the second moment, not more perceptual but more intellectual, in which the real is based on being but "the immediacy . . . is given by the knowledge of abstract essences," that

124 For a succinct exposition of these distinctions see S. Vanni Rovighi, *Uomo e natura: Appunti per una antropologia filosofica* (Milan: Vita e Pensiero, 1980), pp. 178–96; R. Lucas Lucas, *L'uomo spirito incarnato: Compendio di filosofia dell'uomo* (Milan: Paoline, 1993), pp. 118–23.

125 Aquinas, *ST*, I, q. 78, a. 1 c.

126 C. Fabro, *Dall'essere all'esistente*, pp. 60–69.

127 Ibid., pp. 62–63.

is, it is "constituted by the specifying limit of a difference." The sphere of the intelligible is that which has being (*ens*) as its principle. What is immediate in the knowledge of the *ens* is thus the essential difference: the *something* by which each *ens* differs from the others.[128] It follows from this that the *synthesis* of the first two moments, of "the sensible data of perception and the intelligible contents of abstraction," "intensifies the aspect of active determination" because "it encloses being [*esse*] in *a* being [*ens*], and therefore provides only an experience of this being [*ens*] which is precisely a *composition* and therefore something posterior and derived."[129]

The composition of an *ens*, however, contains a flight from the determinacy of definition attained by the ontic moment, and a constant reference to the common being that, precisely as common, breaks the isolation of essences with the transcendent fact that they *are*. This step, both permitted and required by the intrinsic composition of the *ens*, leads the intellect back from abstract essences to real, *actual* being. This is the ontological moment, in which being reveals itself to consciousness as "the *act of presence* of the *ens* and the presence in the *ens* of the moments or elements that constitute it." Now what characterizes this *metaphysical experience* is not a particular and definite conceptual content but the unlimited and universal openness of being, which is "that *active-passive indeterminacy* of the primordial act that never ceases to subtend and sustain the active determination of the immediate and abstract experience and transcends it": it is "the *reality of a being's act of presence*, through which everything has, of being, that which it is, and is not nothing." To know reality, then, essentially means "*to illuminate* a being [*ens*] with being [*esse*], referring the being [*ens*] back to being [*esse*]. It is only in this 'return' or *regressive process*," concludes Fabro, "that we can have the metaphysical experience of being."[130]

At this point, we should emphasize why the intellect cannot help *living* the passage from the ontic moment to the metaphysical moment, and why the latter opens the human mind to God as the cause of being. To know something's mode of being means to determine, more and more, its

128 Ibid., p. 63: "immediate experience, or that which is presented as such, as has been said, on account of its abstract character of 'active determination' *does not in itself reach the truth of being*. Its object is precisely particularity, limitation, determination . . . : while being is reality and the universal act, unlimited, indeterminate and, in and of itself, infinite."

129 Ibid., pp. 63–64.

130 Ibid, p. 65.

difference from other things and thus to sketch with ever greater precision a relationship (of genus and difference) between a more particular notion and a more general one. To deepen our knowledge of dogs, for example, means to fill in our picture of what is specific to them with respect to other living beings. One cannot think of a dog except as a living being; in other words, one cannot think of the particular notion without an intentional reference to the more general one that precedes it. It is in this way that for Aquinas, the first data of intellectual cognition are necessarily the most universal.[131]

Being thus emerges as the most universal notion, even relative to the *ens* itself, but it is a notion that is not definable, since it precedes and grounds essence. Nor can being be understood in a generic sense, given that it encompasses the entire mode of (intensive) being of every *ens*. Hence, to know an *ens* is also to think of a common being that nevertheless does not exist as common except in the knowing intellect: in reality, there is only a *multiplicity* of beings (*entia*) that *are* according to different modes. The knowing intellect certainly concentrates more on the determinate particular than on the indeterminate universal, but it cannot avoid the call of the universal for long. The effect of the metaphysical experience of being, in short, is not only to refer essences back to the reality existing in act, but also to turn the intellect to the notion of intensive being as the act common to (participated by) all things, and thus to bring it immediately to the necessity of a *Being by essence*.

This concludes my analysis (in light of what I have said above about participation and the fourth way), because it shows precisely why the ontological moment puts man immediately in tension with God as Pure Act, and why Fabro says in the end that "it is not possible to conceive of the being [*esse*] of beings [*entia*] without 'opening oneself up' to a relation with the Absolute."[132]

4. The Inclination To God

The idea that morality essentially consists of obedience to the will of God, combined with the idea that the content of such a will is disclosed to man in the reasons for things (essentialist metaphysics), is precisely what the most recent critics, and especially the neoclassicists, have singled out as

131 Aquinas, *ST*, I, q. 85, a. 3 ("Whether the more Universal Is First in Our Intellectual Cognition").

132 C. Fabro, *Dall'essere all'esistente*, p. 67.

the cause of the voluntaristic and legalistic decay of modern, Thomistically inspired ethics. This is also what has provoked the reactions against the so-called "neoscholastic" or "conventional" accounts of ethics, and the criticisms of factualism and the naturalistic fallacy. In the last analysis, critics say, the will of God is nothing for man but a *mere fact*, extrinsic to his (moral) good, and one cannot logically derive an "ought" from the being of things.

It is for this reason that over the past fifty years many interpreters of Aquinas, occasionally emphasizing the concept of *non-self-evidence* or adducing the philosophical "unknowability" of a personal God, have tended to set God aside in their treatment of ethics, referring to Him only as the ultimate metaphysical foundation, and removing all value from the notion of the *will of God* in the determination of moral obligation. Such interpreters have instead taken up the concept of ethical autonomy, emphasizing the rational and intrinsic character of moral norms and their connection with the concrete goods of human existence. In line with Joseph De Finance, several of them have believed they needed to pursue an inductive method, which is not based on an initial determination of the ultimate end (i.e., does not start with God) in order subsequently to reach specific moral norms, but which has as its starting-point an understanding of moral experience. In this way, they have tried to preserve the *practical* character of ethical reflection, understood as a response to the real needs and aspirations of human beings.

In section 2, "The Ethical Relevance of God's Will," I stressed that for Aquinas man is morally good when "he wants something because God wants it," and that he is capable of recognizing the will of God in the reasons for things. However, we also saw in the first chapter that reference to the will of God can escape the charge of voluntaristic and legalistic heteronomy if it occurs in the context of a practical reflection on the meaning of the moral good that man lives and perceives. More specifically, Aquinas's demanding claim concerning the ethical role of God's will can be justified only if the *ultimate* meaning of the moral good to which man aspires can somehow be seen to reside in obedience to God's will, so that only an intentional reference to God can make (morally) good man's pursuit of any other good.

This position presupposes in Aquinas a concept of the natural knowledge of God so wide and pervasive that it can be applied to everyone—even to someone who denies God's existence or appears not to know Him. Indeed, we have seen in section 3, "The Natural Knowledge of God," that the Angelic Doctor's understanding of our natural knowledge of God encompasses right from the outset the very structure of human intellectual knowledge, so as to bring into view the being of the things we know (nature) as intrinsically dependent on a free and transcendent creative cause. In other words, the being of things presents itself primordially to man (in the tension of the ontological moment) as *willed* by God. Only with these premises can God assume such a practical importance in ethics that He is effectively the *foundation* of the morality of human acts.

The theoretical premises of the knowledge of God and of the natural order as willed by God do not yet explain, however, the *importance* of the will of God for man. In other words, they do not explain the practical dimension of our knowledge of God, which alone enables us to avoid a complete heteronomy of God's *commands*, a heteronomy that would reduce those commands, as perceived by the moral conscience, to nothing but a set of extrinsic impositions.

In anthropological terms, it could be said that St. Thomas's theonomic ethics presupposes a structure of the human being that is not only capable of relating to God as Supreme Truth and Supreme Good, but necessarily tends to do so. This structure is effectively expressed by the doctrine of natural inclinations, which we will address directly and at length in the next chapter. Here it is important to emphasize that at the root of Thomistic morality are the basic inclinations to God of the human intellect and will.[133]

The intellect's capacity to know the natures of other corporeal beings (to make itself *quodammodo omnia*)[134] and to open itself to God depends, in Thomistic philosophy, on its spiritual nature; indeed, as is well known, this capacity is the privileged philosophical way to argue for the spirituality of the human soul.[135] The operations of the intellect, however, depend on a natural inclination to know (to know the truth, obviously, because to know what is false is a contradiction in terms: "there are true and false beliefs, but knowledge is of the truth"[136]). This inclination, as we have seen, reaches its zenith in the ontological moment, which opens human knowledge to the eternal and transcendent, and puts man's intellectual life,

133 On the centrality of these inclinations see S. Pinckaers, *The Sources of Christian Ethics*, pp. 404–5.

134 See Aquinas, *ST*, I, q. 14, a. 1.

135 Ibid., I, q. 75, a. 2.

136 See J. Finnis, *Natural Law and Natural Rights*, p. 59.

in the measure of his intentional knowledge, in a necessary tension with the Absolute: the cognitive tension that each one reaches with the Absolute coincides perfectly with the intentional idea of God that he possesses at a given moment. All of section 3, "The Natural Knowledge of God," can also be read as an explanation of the human intellect's openness to and inclination toward God.

To the spirituality of the intellect, moreover, corresponds the spirituality of the rational appetitive power, which can turn to the various particular goods presented to it by the intellect without ever being satiated, and which is open to an appetite for the Absolute Good known by the intellect in the ontological moment. The operations of the will, like those of the intellect, depend on its basic natural inclination, which is to desire the good known by the (practical) intellect. This natural inclination reaches its zenith in knowledge of God as the Absolute Good. The inclination to, the desire for God elevates the end of human action to a transcendent dimension (above man himself), which is capable of conferring a character of absoluteness on the pursuit of that end, and can thus give rise to morality. If the cognitive experience of man can be characterized, at its highest level, as *tension with the Absolute*, the moral experience must be characterized as *tension toward the Absolute*.

The next chapter will deal with the way in which the moral goodness of human acts is concretely realized, in relation to the knowledge of nature, the ultimate end, and particular goods. The present section, however, should be read in connection with the previous, "The Natural Knowledge of God," as an explanation of the openness and inclination of man's will toward God.

4.1. God as a (Moral) Problem for Man

The practical question about God in a way precedes the theoretical one. If it is true that one cannot love or desire what one does not know, it is also true that nobody would speak about God, or engage in any discussion on this subject, if *what we usually call "God"* were not a problem for him. If there were not in man a tension, an aspiration, a desire, the question would be entirely meaningless.

In the existence of each person, however, the problem of God proves to be a crucial question from which, like it or not, there is no escape, and which emerges in the different moments and circumstances of life in more or less strong and demanding forms. Thus the discussion concerning God makes sense because *man is not indifferent to God*, just as he is not indifferent to members of the opposite sex, to friendship with others, to play, or to his own professional fulfillment.[137]

From an existential perspective, moreover, the question of God appears as the problem of problems, "the essential problem of the essential man," as Fabro has defined it.[138] Man's conscience links the thought of God to the question of the ultimate meaning of his own being, of his own actions, of the various spheres within which he moves and fulfils himself, and the question of good and evil in absolute terms. Not surprisingly, death (whether one's own or that of another), the event that in a single moment relativizes everything, is perhaps the moment in which man's relationship with God reaches its greatest tension. Faced with the experience of death, man prays or refuses to pray, but he does not remain indifferent to the Absolute. The denials of Nietzsche and Sartre are lived and preached as dramatic events.

The tradition of Catholic catechesis, of which St Thomas is one of the greatest exponents, clearly reflects this view. God's Revelation is not imposed on man from outside but responds to the needs of his nature. The first topic is therefore a philosophical one: man as *capax Dei*; and even before the natural knowledge of God (which, as we have seen, enjoys an epistemic priority), the introductory topic is the moral one: "the desire for God."[139] The emblem of this aspect of Catholic thought has always been, even in St. Thomas's time, the famous opening of St. Augustine's *Confessions* in which he outlines the so-called theology of the *restless heart*: "You are great, O Lord, and greatly to be praised: great is your power and to your wisdom there is no limit. And man, who is part of your creation, wishes to praise you, man who bears about within himself his mortality, who bears about within himself testimony to his sin and testimony that you resist the proud. Yet man, this part of your creation, wish-

137 See John Paul II, *Crossing the Threshold of Hope*, trans. Jenny McPhee & Martha McPhee (New York: Alfred A. Knopf, 1994), p. 31: ". . . *the response to the question 'An Deus sit?' is not only an issue that touches the intellect; it is, at the same time, an issue that has a strong impact on all of human existence*. It depends on a multitude of situations in which man searches for the significance and the meaning of his own existence. Questioning God's existence is intimately united *with the purpose of human existence*. Not only is it a question of intellect; it is also a question of the will, even a *question of the human heart*."

138 C. Fabro, *Dio: Introduzione al problema teologico*, p. 106. See also A.L. Gonzalez, *Filosofia di Dio*, p. 4.

139 See *Catechism of the Catholic Church* (Dublin: Veritas, 1995), chap. 1, "Man's Capacity for God," sub-section I, "The Desire for God."

es to praise you. You arouse him to take joy in praising you, for you have made us for yourself, and our heart is restless until it rests in you."[140]

It should be noted that the practicality of the good, that is, the attraction it exerts on man, is not the result of any mental deduction. Men and women do not find themselves attracted to each other as the conclusion of this or that rational argument; they do not *decide* to be attracted. Rather, having recognized the other (theoretically) as woman or man on the basis of the relevant attributes, they simply are attracted. It is in this way that St. Thomas asserts that the notion of good adds nothing to that of being but except a relation to appetite, just as the notion of truth adds nothing but the relation to a knowing intellect: *ens, bonum et verum convertuntur.*[141]

The Thomistic doctrine of the transcendentals is the mirror-image of the doctrine (also of Aristotelian origin) by which Aquinas distinguishes between theoretical and practical reason (or knowledge). The latter is constituted by an intellectual knowledge that has as its first principle an attraction to the thing known (the good), and that thus interacts actively with the will. The radical difference between intellect and will is that the former is a receptive faculty whereas the latter is what moves man toward things.

For Aristotle, the principle that acts as the efficient cause of moral action is "deliberate choice" (προαίρεσις), understood as the proper act of the intellect (or rational part of the soul) in its practical, or calculative function. The principles of deliberate choice, however, are λόγος, the calculation of means, and ὄρεξις, desire for the end. "Therefore," concludes Aristotle, "choice is either a desiring intellect (ὀρεκτικὸς νοῦς) or a reasoning desire (ὄρεξις διανοητική)." In spite of the many discussions about the exact interpretation of these elements of Aristotelian thought, it is evident that here the ὄρεξις, inasmuch as it determines the initial attraction toward a known end, is essentially rational appetite, and builds on the

140 Augustine, *Confessions*, trans. John K. Ryan (New York: Image Books, 1960), 1, 1, 1.

141 Aquinas, *De veritate*, q. 1, a. 1; *ST*, I, q. 5, a. 1.

142 The virtue of wisdom or prudence (φρόνησις) is the perfection of the inclination of the practical intellect toward its proper act: in other words, the perfection of the capacity to make deliberative choices.

143 Aristotle, *Nicomachean Ethics*, VI.2, 1139b4–5. See also ibid, III.4–5, and all of book VI. [Translator's note: All quotations of the *Nicomachean Ethics* are taken from the translation by H. Rackham (Cambridge, Massachusetts and London: Harvard University Press, 1934). The author originally used the Italian translation by M. Zanatta (Milan: Rizzoli, 1986)].

prior conceptual knowledge of reality attained by the speculative intellect (νοῦς). The ὄρεξις, in this sense, is the primordial conceptual knowledge of the end under the formality of the good, and coincides with what we call practical knowledge.

Human action is thus guided, both for Aristotle and for Thomas, by a sort of *appetitive knowledge*, which results from the interaction of the two rational faculties of intellect and will, and which we call practical reason. The first principle of practical reason for St. Thomas is not simply being as known, but the being as desired ("*faciendum et prosequendum*"), i.e., the good.

> Now as being (*ens*) is the first thing that falls under the apprehension simply, so *good* is the first thing that falls under the apprehension of the practical reason, which is directed to action: since every agent acts for an end under the aspect of good.[144]

The attraction of the good as such cannot in any way be deduced or demonstrated: that man is attracted by some things, and that he values them, conferring on them a greater or lesser importance, is simply a *fact of experience* that has a primordial character for practical reason. This fact points to both the validity and the limits of Hume's law, to which Finnis, Grisez and their followers correctly draw our attention.[145] But the attraction of the good depends on man's mode of being, that is, his needs and the way in which the things he knows are objectively capable of satisfying them. And here Veatch is certainly right to emphasize that moral questions always require a response that cannot be the mere tautology, "it is good because I am attracted to it," but one that makes sense only if grounded in human *nature*.

All of this also holds for St. Thomas's discussion about God. The ethical centrality that he attributes to God requires not only a direct confirmation in moral experience, but also a correspondence with the nature of the intellect and the will, both as openness and as inclination.

144 Aquinas, *ST*, I-II, q. 94, a. 2 c.

145 See for example J. Finnis, "Natural Law and the 'Is-Ought' Question: An Invitation to Professor Veatch," *Catholic Lawyer*, 26 (1981). See also A.R. Luño, *Etica*, pp. 37–40. Ricoeur makes a similar point, pointing out the primacy of the teleological aspect of ethics over the deontological aspect. See P. Ricoeur, *Oneself as Another*, trans. Kathleen Blamey (Chicago: University of Chicago Press, 1992), pp. 169–71.

4.2. The Meaning of Moral Experience

The cognitive tension reached by the intellect in the ontological moment described by Fabro flows entirely into practical reason, in terms of tendency and need. In this light it is not difficult to characterize the entire moral experience of man as *openness to* and *need for* God, or for "what men call *God*." But more specifically, the philosophical tradition of natural law has, over the course of its history, highlighted various aspects of moral experience that, although not in themselves proofs for God's existence, clearly reveal that "what men call God" is the most profound answer to man's needs. Without pretending to be systematic, I will now offer a brief outline of the most important of these.

The search for happiness. All men aspire to be happy, but this aspiration goes beyond the confines of space and time because no finite or limited, relative or contingent object is capable of entirely satisfying it. When man attempts to find the meaning of his life in a good of this type, he deceives himself and, in the long term, remains dissatisfied. The human desire for happiness automatically projects the moral life into a transcendent dimension. Even suicide bears testimony to this, since whoever carries out such an act does so either in the name of a cause so high as to *transcend* his own life, or in order to escape somehow from a world in which he believes he can no longer find the happiness he yearns for. The summons to God inherent in the desire for happiness is so strong that this desire has often in the history of thought been taken as sufficient proof for God's existence: the *eudaemonological argument.* How could that to which man aspires so strongly not exist? However, I agree with Gonzalez that an argument of this type would involve an illicit step from mental to real existence, and would be vulnerable to the Thomistic critique of the ontological argument.[146]

The desire for eternity. An inseparable aspect of the happiness to which man aspires is its *eternity*: eternal life. "Man rises from the earth and returns to it . . . : this is an immediately evident fact. Yet in man there is an irrepressible longing to live forever."[147] Eternity, from a certain perspective, indicates the very mode of thinking of the human mind. In fact, it is psychologically impossible for man to think of his own hypothetical

146 A.L. Gonzalez, *Filosofia di Dio*, pp. 133–34.

147 John Paul II, *Tertio millennio adveniente* (Boston: Pauline Books & Media, 1994), n. 9.

"ceasing to be": If he tries to do so, he can only observe himself from outside, with other eyes that continue to exist. Furthermore, when he reflects on his own future, he does so as if it were never to end; and when he declares his love for another, he instinctively says, "forever." The very prospect of death, far from constituting a limit to the desire for eternity, arouses it and projects it into the transcendent dimension where it clearly belongs.

The need for truth. Here truth must be understood in a directly moral sense: it is not mere curiosity, the inclination to know how things are, but the demand for a stable point of reference, a positive answer to the question of the meaning of life. Confronted not only with contradictions and sufferings, but also with the normal succession of events, the human being feels the need for existential answers that are not relative or hypothetical, but certain, and for a certainty not limited to simply *universal* truths, valid for everyone and for all times, but one that is *absolute*, transcending all the contingencies and relativities of this world.[148]

The need for justice. The need for an absolute truth is closely linked to an aspiration to absolute justice, in which all the wrongs and inequalities among human beings, humanly inexplicable and irremediable, would find redress. At bottom, even the egalitarian tendency of a Rawls, with its intolerance of arbitrariness in the distribution of wealth, talents and social positions (including family), implies the unsustainable adoption of a divine point of view, and the embracing of an ethics destined to remain frustrated by the obvious impossibility of its own declared objective. The need for absolute justice is also reflected in the common-sense intuition that our actions gain some sort of *merit*, or demerit, with respect to the eternal life and happiness to which we aspire.

The desire for importance. This aspect of moral experience subsumes all those listed above, and brings us to the heart of man's natural religiosity with its essentially relational character. Man is not self-sufficient; he needs to feel important, and to be important means to be important *for somebody*. He needs to know that he is *wanted*, or *loved*, notwithstanding and apart from any other consideration, simply because he exists, and is who he is: "for his own sake." Given our experience of the limitations and relativity of this world, and above all, given our experience of evil, this

148 For a dialectical critique of the possibility of denying the value of truth, see J. Finnis, "Scepticism, Self-Refutation, and the Good of Truth."

need can find its full answer and fulfillment only in the absolute and transcendent dimension of a divine love. Only in such a dimension can human existence be considered absolutely important, beyond the brief trajectory of an earthly life. Indeed, the man who opens himself to this dimension can truly stop worrying and, come what may, overcome the temptations of the absurd, of powerlessness, of discouragement and discomfort, certain that his life is always a good because God has willed it and even now wills it just as it is, and indeed is always looking after him. The desire for importance is the natural moral foundation of the doctrine of providence; this doctrine also has a metaphysical foundation, but we will deal with this in the next chapter.

The experience of duty. In the various objective and subjective circumstances in which it finds itself, the human conscience experiences the primordial presence of a duty that imposes itself universally and absolutely—"this is good," "that is evil"—even against one's own personal preferences. Such an experience is characterized by both universality and attention to circumstance, because it involves the judgment that anyone in a particular and determinate set of circumstances ought to act in a certain way. But above all, the experience of duty is characterized by the absolute and transcendent dimension of *sacrifice* ("not what I want, or what I like, but what I ought to do"), which raises moral truth above the agent's own will.[149] The consciousness of duty, which as we noted in the first chapter has always been considered the most important argument for the existence of a natural law, involves going out of and relativizing oneself, and can find its full meaning only in the higher ethical significance, for man, of the will of God ("The good," in an absolute sense, "is not what I want but what You Want").

Duty and good. At first glance, the desire for God as absolute and eternal good and the conflict inherent in the experience of duty appear to be in clear contradiction: what duty does, in fact, is precisely to negate desire. Nevertheless, the two can be reconciled, for behind duty is concealed the agent's truest and deepest will. Robert Spaemann clearly displays this phenomenon when he writes: "Every 'ought' has to be linked to

149 Jeff Goldsworthy takes a position along similar lines when he says that the force of moral duty (the obligatoriness of precepts) presupposes God because it is such that it transcends even the most noble personal interests; see J.D. Goldsworthy, "God or Mackie: The Dilemma of Secular Moral Philosophy," *American Journal of Jurisprudence*, 30 (1985).

a want of some kind, otherwise we would have no reason to act on it."[150] The real question, when faced with duty, has to do with what we really want in an absolute way—in other words, it is the question about the ultimate end or the Supreme Good. Behind the absoluteness of duty lies the absoluteness of willing. From a different angle, to highlight further the autonomous character of ethics, Spaemann claims that the conflict in conscience between what we want and what is good and right is, in reality, a conflict between what we want "now" and what we "basically, really want": "Conscience is an imperative we give to ourselves."[151]

In order to understand fully the significance of our experience of moral duty, we need to rethink the transition from the active determination of the ontic moment (immediate knowledge of abstract essences) to the indeterminate perception of God as *Being by essence*, the culmination of the ontological moment. The human will is naturally inclined to pursue the good known by the intellect, and always turns immediately to the particular goods clearly determined by the intellect in the ontic moment. However, the will also adverts, albeit vaguely (and mediately), to the constant presence of the Absolute Good presented to it by the intellect in the ontological moment, and in pursuit of this ultimate good it spontaneously assigns roles to (and relativizes) all particular goods as means, thus giving rise to the experience of duty with respect to these lesser goods.

4.3. The Formal Object of Ethics

It seems to me that the admittedly radical attribution of an intrinsic transcendent character to human moral experience, to the point of defining it as a *tension toward the Absolute*, dovetails nicely with some recent reflections on the object of ethics and the meaning of the moral question.

In his textbook on philosophical ethics, Luño defines this discipline using the classical distinction between material and formal objects.[152] The material object of ethics is "human acts," in particular those that are free, whether "elicited" (that is, proceeding immediately from rational deliberation and from the will, such as love, hatred, or desire) or "commanded" (that is, proceeding from the will but mediated by other powers, such as

150 R. Spaemann, *Basic Moral Concepts*, trans. T. J. Armstrong (London and New York: Routledge, 1989), p. 15.

151 Ibid., pp. 58–59. [Translator's note: Following the Italian translation, I have modified the English at this point to restore the distinctively Kantian term "imperative."]

152 A.R. Luño, *Etica*, pp. 6–11, 122–25.

speaking, working and striking). Ethics does not deal with mere "acts of man," i.e. acts that are not carried out freely "either because in the moment in which they are carried out the requisite knowledge and willingness are lacking, or because they are processes over which man has no direct control (physical development, circulation of the blood, etc)." The distinction between human acts and acts of man is also present in St. Thomas,[153] and it seems intuitively sound if one thinks of the conceptual difference between "acting" and "happening." Only "human acts," insofar as they "depend entirely" on the person as the "center of self-determination," "imply moral responsibility," and can be the object of praise or blame and a source of merit or demerit.

"The *formal object* of a field of knowledge is the aspect or property of the material object" to which that knowledge attends. The formal object of ethics, then, "is that according to which human acts," considered simply as such, "are qualified as good or bad"; in other words, it is *the morality of human acts.*

When we refer to the morality of human acts, there is no need either (a) to think of the "natural qualities that the person brings into play when acting," or (b) to confuse it with the "technical perfection" that the acts themselves may have with respect to determinate objectives or tasks. "Man's natural characteristics," indeed, "(intelligence, skill and physical energy, strength of personality, etc.) are morally ambiguous, since they can be used in either a positive or a negative way.[154] Intellectual acumen can be seen both in planning a robbery and in presenting the truth persuasively; the same can be said of composure, constancy, etc." On the other hand, when it comes to the technical aspect of acts, "it is sufficient to observe that common sense distinguishes without difficulty between the technical and the ethical uses of the qualifications 'good,' 'perfect,' etc.

153 Aquinas, *ST*, I-II, q. 1, a. 1.

154 In this context, as is well known, Aristotle distinguishes between "cleverness" and "prudence" with respect to the "intellectual part" of the soul, and between "natural virtue" and "virtue in the proper sense" with respect to the "moral part." "There is a certain faculty called cleverness, which is the capacity for doing the things aforesaid that conduce to the aim we propose, and so attaining that aim. If the aim is noble, this is a praiseworthy faculty: if base, it is mere knavery; this is how we come to speak of both prudent men and knaves as clever. Now this faculty is not identical with prudence, but prudence implies it"; "if a man of good natural disposition acquires intelligence (νοῦς), then he excels in conduct, and the disposition which previously only resembled virtue, will now be virtue in the true sense." See Aristotle, *Nicomachean Ethics*, VI.12–13, 1144a24–1144b15.

Someone who morally disapproves of robbery and terrorism has no difficulty speaking of a 'good' robbery or of a 'perfect' terrorist attack, since it is naturally understood that such evaluations, employed in a certain way, do not even touch upon the ethical status of the behavior in question."

"On the contrary," concludes Luño, "*when they are used in the ethical sense, good and evil have an absolute meaning.*[155] *Moral good and evil are good and evil that actions possess insofar as they are human,* and for this reason, they concern the human person as such, in his totality: they make man good or evil absolutely and without restriction, as a human person." It is the absoluteness of the moral good that makes possible an ethical judgment concerning the other limited and particular aspects of human acts, and that can give rise to remorse and repentance for something that nonetheless turned out well. For Luño, moral experience as the experience of absolute goodness or duty constitutes the common point of departure for both Kant's transcendental ethics—grounded on the *factum rationis* of the absolute necessity perceived by practical reason in the diverse situations of everyday life—and the classical, realist ethics of Aristotelian and Thomistic inspiration, grounded on the philosophy of being.[156]

As we have already seen for Spaeman, Luño too traces the experience of passing ethical judgment on one's own acts and those of others to a more basic will directed to the ultimate end: "the explanation of this common experience is that, at a deeper level than that of the goods that attract us here and now, there is 'something' that is desired in a necessary and irrenounceable way," and which "in reality is the cause and the constitutive measure of all our desires."[157]

Luño's reflections on the formal object of ethics coincide with those of Spaeman, who explains that philosophical ethics is defined as the discipline that inquires into the absolute good that presents itself to the human conscience with an imperative character.[158] Taken in a relative sense, the question of the good pertains to all the disciplines that deal with human action. For example: "The doctor says: 'It would be a good idea to spend another day in bed.' To be precise the word 'good' should be qualified in two ways. The doctor should say, 'It is a good idea for you,' and 'It is a good idea for you if your first priority is to get well.' . . . But with

155 On the absoluteness of the moral good in Aristotle, see for example ibid., VI.5.
156 A.R. Luño, *Etica*, pp. 30–32, 40–50.
157 Ibid., p. 11.
158 Spaemann, *Basic Moral Concepts*, pp. 1–12, 57–67.

regard to the question of whether or not it is 'good' to act in this way, the doctor, as a doctor, can make no pronouncement."

According to Spaemann, the philosophical quest for an absolute and universal answer to the question of the meaning of life and of good and evil originally comes from the observation of cultural diversity in ethical behavior. Confronted with the different and variegated customs of surrounding cultures, the Greek philosophers "began to look for a single standard by means of which different ethical codes and forms of life could be evaluated and compared, in the hope that it might be possible to decide, eventually, that some were better than others. They called this standard 'Physis' or Nature."[159] However, the certainty that there is an absolute and universal answer to the moral quest is discovered by man from the very beginning in the demands of his conscience, which may therefore be defined as "the focal point of an absolute perspective in a finite being, the means by which this perspective is anchored in that being's emotional structure." The moral conscience arises from a "movement of the spirit" that "leads man beyond himself," allowing him to "perceive his own interests as something relative" and to seek "what is good and right."[160]

Neither Spaemann nor Luño goes so far as to refer the moral question present in the human conscience directly to God; instead, they prefer to stop with the Aristotelian concept of the final end, understood as "a happy life" or "the fullness of meaning of the human condition" (Luño), or to stress the absolute value of the person as an "end in itself" (Spaemann). John Paul II, on the other hand, does refer the moral question to God in several passages that, in spite of their theological context, should be interpreted as strictly philosophical and as explanatory of the moral dimension of man as *capax Dei.*

At the beginning of the encyclical in which he sets out to expound the *sure* foundations of Catholic morality, the Pope writes that as a consequence of original sin, "man is constantly tempted to turn his gaze away from the living and true God in order to direct it toward idols," but that "no darkness of error or of sin can totally take away from man the light of God the Creator. In the depths of his heart there always remains a yearning for absolute truth and a thirst to attain full knowledge of it. This is eloquent-

159 Ibid. Using a similar argument, Leo Strauss considers cultural variety as the origin of the idea of natural right; see L. Strauss, *Natural Right and History* (Chicago and London: The University of Chicago Press, 1953), chap. I.
160 Ibid.

ly proved by man's tireless search for knowledge in all fields. It is proved even more by his search for *the meaning of life.* The development of science and technology, this splendid testimony of the human capacity for understanding and for perseverance, does not free humanity from the obligation to ask the ultimate religious questions. Rather, it spurs us on to face the most painful and decisive of struggles, those of the heart and of the moral conscience."[161]

As is well known, the entire first part of *Veritatis splendor* builds on the dialogue of Jesus with the rich young man described in the St. Matthew's Gospel (19:16), especially on the question, "Master, what good must I do in order to obtain eternal life?" Here, the Pope is unequivocal in relating the question of the young man in the Gospel to the "moral question" *naturally* present in the conscience of all men, and in connecting the young man's question to the natural desire for God and for eternal life.

Consider the following passages: "In the young man, whom Matthew's Gospel does not name, we can recognize every person who, consciously or not, *approaches Christ the Redeemer of man and questions him about morality*. For the young man, the question is not so much about rules to be followed, but *about the full meaning of life*. This is in fact the aspiration at the heart of every human decision and action, the quiet searching and interior prompting which sets freedom in motion. This question is ultimately an appeal to the absolute Good which attracts us and beckons us; it is the echo of a call from God who is the origin and goal of man's life."[162] "The question which the rich young man puts to Jesus of Nazareth is one which rises from the depths of his heart. It is *an essential and unavoidable question for the life of every man,* for it is about the moral good which must be done, and about eternal life. The young man senses that there is a connection between moral good and the fulfillment of his own destiny."[163]

There is a perfect correspondence between the approach that emerges from these passages and the doctrine set out in the second part of the encyclical on moral conscience—described as both "*man's dialogue with himself*" and "*man's dialogue with God*"—and the morality of human acts. "The first question in the young man's conversation with Jesus,"

161 John Paul II, *Veritatis splendor* (encyclical on the foundations of moral philosophy and moral theology), n. 1, in *The Encyclicals of John Paul II* (Huntington, Indiana: Our Sunday Visitor, Inc., 1996).

162 Ibid., n. 7.

163 Ibid., n. 8.

writes the Pope, "immediately brings out *the essential connection between the moral value of an act and man's final end,*" which is "God Himself, the supreme good."[164]

4.4. "By Natural Love, Man Loves God Before Himself and with a Greater Love"

The interpretation of moral experience described in the preceding sections and characterized by the absolute and overriding importance of God for man's conscience is so crucial to Aquinas that it forms the basis of his explanation of the nature of the human will. In fact, metaphysical knowledge of the spiritual powers or faculties, in the realist philosophy of St. Thomas, begins with knowledge of human action.

Beginning now from a slightly different angle, let us clarify the precise goal of this final section. Given the practicality of the good as the only possible basis of its nonextraneousness for moral conscience, and given that the practicality of the good depends on a primordial inclination of the will to pursue it, we can see that all of Aquinas's ethics, as described up to this point, is viable only if man is naturally inclined to love (i.e., to *will*) God "before himself and with a greater love." As we shall see shortly, St. Thomas affirms this most explicitly in the part of the *Summa theologiae* devoted to the angels (I, qq. 50–64), and in particular in question 60, "Of the Love or Dilection of the Angels (*De amore seu dilectione angelorum*)." By considering the understanding of natural love developed in this question, we can put the capstone in our discussion of *homo capax Dei.*

This location of this subject requires a brief explanation: St. Thomas's treatment of the angelic nature should also be read as a deepening and fine-tuning of his anthropology. Since angels are not, in fact, an object of human experience, reflection on them is based on an analogy with human beings, and any claim about their nature therefore presupposes a refinement in our understanding of the specificity of man's spiritual powers of intellect and will, as distinct from his corporeal nature. This said, we may now go straight to the relevant texts.

Question 60 begins by distinguishing between "natural love or dilection" and "love of choice" (*dilectio electiva*). Natural love is the necessary inclination toward the end that everything possesses in conformity with the movement of its own nature. Given this description, it should be pointed out that "it is common to every nature to have some inclination; and this

164 Ibid., especially nn. 57–61, 72.

is its natural appetite or love"; however, "this inclination is found to exist differently in different natures, but in each according to its mode of being." "In the intellectual nature there is to be found a natural inclination coming from the will; in the sensitive nature, according to the sensitive appetite; but in a nature devoid of knowledge, only according to the tendency of the nature to something."[165]

Without natural love no being could move or act. As for man, if his will did not naturally tend toward his ultimate end, or "beatitude," he too could not move, because "all other desires (*voluntates*) are caused by this natural desire (*naturali voluntate*); since whatever a man naturally wills he wills on account of an end." Natural love thus explains the love of choice, since the necessary appetite for the ultimate end makes all other goods attractive to the will as *means*: "therefore the love of that good, which a man naturally wills as an end, is his natural love; but the love which comes of this, which is of something loved for the end's sake, is the love of choice."[166]

St. Thomas's objective in this first article is to demonstrate that there is in angels, besides natural love, a love of choice, inasmuch as the existence of the latter does not depend on an imperfection of the human will. At first glance, indeed, one might think that the need to pass through the (desire of the) means in order to attain the end derives from the imperfection of the willing subject, whose corporeal nature impedes the mind from immediately enjoying the desired end—just as the need to pass through partial truths by means of reasoning derives from the human intellect's incapacity to attain knowledge of being directly, without passing through the material reality that falls beneath the senses.

Aquinas's discussion here is based on a famous and evocative parallel, of Aristotelian origin, between intellect (natural cognition) and reason (ratiocinative cognition), on the one hand, and will (*voluntas*) and free choice (*liberum arbitrium*) on the other. Compared to the simple and intuitive acts of intellect and will, reason and free choice are paths to be traveled as means to the attainment of intellectual truth or the desired end. "All deliberation," writes Aristotle, "is investigation,"[167] since to choose, or deliberate, means to try to attain one's end through the use of some means. Similarly, every step in reasoning (every use of reason) is nothing but the

165 Aquinas, *ST*, I, q. 60, a. 1.
166 Ibid., I, q. 60, a. 2.
167 Aristotle, *Nicomachean Ethics* III.3, 1112b21–23.

search for a particular intellectual truth. Reason is to the intellect, in this sense, as free choice is to will.[168]

In mentioning this parallel, I do not mean to underestimate in the least the complex and difficult dispute on the relation between the Aristotelian concepts of προαίρεσις and βουλησις and the Thomistic concepts of *electio* and *voluntas*. For our purposes, the only important thing is that both *dilectio naturalis* and *dilectio electiva* should be understood not so much in reference to the moment of the choice, i.e., freedom, as to the attraction of the good as such, i.e., inclination. In any choice that man makes, the attraction of the end appears as the primary datum, and the end is desired for its own sake; the means, on the other hand, is not attractive for its own sake but only for the sake of the end. Therefore, love of the means arises only subsequently to deliberation (or choice or election), which creates a means-end relation between a particular act and the desired end, transforming the former into a means that is desired precisely as such.

Let us now turn to the second article of question 60 (*Utrum in angelis sit dilectio electiva*). The fact that the human intellect does not immediately attain perfect knowledge of things, but must have recourse to reasoning, is due to an imperfection in human nature associated with corporeal existence, which cannot occur in angels. But "the act of the appetitive faculty," Aquinas tells us, "contrary [to that of the intellect], follows the inclination of man towards things (*est, e converso, secundum ordinem appetentis ad res*)." "Consequently it does not arise from imperfection in the person desiring (*appetentis*), for him to seek (*appetat*) something naturally as his end, and something else from choice as ordained to such end." In the angels, who possess a perfect intellectual nature, there is "natural cognition" only, and not "ratiocinative" cognition. Nonetheless, there is in angels both natural love and love of choice.[169]

With these broad premises in hand, St. Thomas can proceed with his discussion, explaining that angels, like men, love themselves both with natural love and with love of choice. This is not contradictory, he says, because there are two ways in which "a thing can be loved": either as "a subsisting good" or as "an accidental or inherent good." A subject, in other words, can simply tend by nature "to procure what is good for itself" (natural love), and this is also proper to non-rational creatures; but he can also desire "by means of a choice (*per electionem*) something which will ben-

168 See also S. Pinckaers, *The Sources of Christian Ethics*, pp. 384–86.
169 Aquinas, *ST*, I, q. 60, a. 2.

efit himself," and in this case he desires the good sought "for something else (*alteri*)," in this case himself, and in this way "he loves himself with the love of choice." The example that Aquinas gives clarifies his idea: when we desire *knowledge*, it is not loved for its own sake (*ut ipsi sit bonum*), but that it may be possessed (*ut habeatur*); this is the love "of concupiscence."[170]

The next step in the argument of question 60 is to show that an angel loves others with a natural love (in other words, is naturally inclined to the other) in a way *similar* to that in which he loves himself, since "everything loves another which is one with it in species, with a natural affection, insofar as it loves its own species." This love or inclination, precisely because it is natural, "cannot be diminished" even in the wicked.[171] Hence we finally arrive at the last and most important article of question 60 (the fifth), "Whether an Angel by Natural Love Loves God More Than He Loves Himself? (*Utrum angelus naturali dilectione diligat Deum plus quam seipsum*)."

The subtlety of the argument here leads Aquinas to make various qualifications before enunciating his thesis. First of all, he denies that the nature of God is "infinitely far from that of the angels," based on the principle of essential resemblance between God and creatures that we have already explained in section 3.5, "*Via Negativa* and *Via Positiva*." God is in fact the "whole cause of the existence and goodness" of things: He is not only "the good of one species," but "the universal good" (ad 1). Two other qualifications affect the philosophical character of the question: on the one hand, for the reason already mentioned, love of the "absolutely universal good" does not imply a movement extraneous to nature (ad 3), and on the other, reference to natural love does not concern "the supernatural love of charity" infused in the heart by God, by means of grace (ad 4). Another qualification concerns the natural necessity of the inclination inherent in the concept of natural love: in fact, "the love of God more than self" persists, albeit perversely, even in the sinner (ad 5).

What is much more interesting for our purposes, however, is the argument of the second objection, because like the principal argument of the article (the *respondeo*), it contrasts "the love of God more than self" with "the love of concupiscence." The difference between the second objection and the *respondeo*, as we will see, is that objection rejects the "love of God

170 Ibid., I, q. 60, a. 3.
171 Ibid., I, q. 60, a. 4.

more than self," on the basis of the love of concupiscence, whereas in the *respondeo* St. Thomas rejects the claim that "the love of God more than self" can in fact be traced back to the love of concupiscence. What reassures him about the truth of his thesis, on the other hand, is his awareness of revealed natural law, which, as is well known, explicitly contains "the precept to love God more than oneself" (*sed contra*).

The second objection runs as follows: "*That on account of which a thing is desired as such, is desired yet more so*. But every one loves another with natural love for his own sake: because one thing loves another as good for itself. Therefore the angel does not love God more than self with natural love." St. Thomas's reply is clear and sharp: "When it is said that God is loved by an angel *insofar* as He is good to the angel, if the expression *insofar* (*in quantum*) denotes an end, then it is false; for he does not naturally love God for his own good, but for God's sake (*propter ipsum Deum*). If it denotes the nature of love on the lover's part (*rationem amoris ex parte amantis*), then it is true; for it would not be in the nature of anyone to love God, except from this—that everything is dependent on that good which is God."

Let us now move on to the *respondeo*, which begins thus: "There have been some who maintained that an angel loves God more than himself with natural love, both as to the love of concupiscence, through his seeking the Divine good for himself rather than his own good; and, in a fashion, as to the love of friendship, insofar as he naturally desires a greater good to God than to himself; because he naturally wishes God to be God, while as for himself, he wills to have his own nature. But absolutely speaking (*simpliciter loquendo*), out of natural love he loves himself more than he does God, because he naturally loves himself before God, and with greater intensity."

This view, however, St. Thomas resolutely opposes, because our experiential knowledge of natural things (which includes the knowledge of human moral action as described in the preceding sections) demonstrates, in his view, that "everything which, as such, naturally belongs to another, is principally and more strongly inclined to that other to which it belongs, than towards itself." And he concludes his response unequivocally: "Consequently, since God is the universal good, and under this good both man and angel and all creatures are comprised, because every creature in regard to its entire being naturally belongs to God, it follows that by natural love angel and man alike love God before themselves and with a greater love (*naturali dilectione etiam angelus et homo plus et principalius diligat Deum quam seipsum*). Otherwise, if either of them loved self more than God, it would follow that natural love would be perverse, and that it would not be perfected but destroyed by charity."

This last claim reveals the degree to which Aquinas is aware of the full implications of his philosophical thesis about natural love. This thesis, in fact, suggests that natural love of God "before oneself and with a greater love" should be understood as a necessary presupposition of revealed doctrine. In other words, if man did not love God naturally in this way, human nature would have been created *evil*, and the supernatural intervention of God would not save it, but destroy it.

However, it is now important to highlight another implication of the argument. If, as I hope to have shown, the experience of the good and of moral duty is for St. Thomas a manifestation of the natural love that man has for God "before and more than" himself, then his ethics completely escapes the charge of hedonism directed by Kant against teleological ethics. Moral duty, in fact, does not arise from the "desire of one's own good," but precisely from the capacity to transcend it (or sacrifice it) for love of God. This love, furthermore, raises the natural love of self and of others to an ethical level, putting them on an equal footing (inasmuch as both are means to loving God, Who loves each person He has created in the same way), and removing from them the intentional motivation of concupiscence ("I love myself and others, ultimately, because God loves everyone in the same way"). In the next chapter, as we study the objective and subjective morality of human acts, we will see among other things that the primacy of God in natural human love is translated into the intentional primacy of the moral over the pleasurable good.

Chapter 3
"Lex" and "Lex Naturalis"

1. Introduction

It is well known that St. Thomas addresses the subject of law in a complete and systematic way in the *Summa theologiae* (1266–1273)—a late work, which was never completed, and in which he intended to "treat of whatever belongs to the Christian Religion, in such a way as may tend to the instruction of beginners," that is, "according to the order of the subject-matter" and "as briefly and clearly as the matter itself may allow."[1] The target audience and the author's pedagogical intent determine the main features of the work: not only its completeness, but also its systematicity, its terseness and its simplicity. In this work we do not, for the most part, find either the many arguments and objections of the *Quaestiones disputatae* or the critical apologetical style of the *Summa contra gentiles*.

In designing a complete didactic treatment of Christian doctrine, St. Thomas accomplishes a further synthesis of all of his thought, but he does not thereby intend to replace or devalue his other critical writings. Faced with the extreme clarity and systematicity of the *Summa theologiae*, the interpreter should therefore resist the temptation to consider the thought of Aquinas expressed there independently from his previous writings.[2] He should also be wary of the similar pitfall—pointed out also by

1 Aquinas, ST, *Prologue*.

2 Two authors who perhaps fall into this error are P. Hall, *Narrative and the Natural Law: An Interpretation of Thomistic Ethics*, p. 23; and D.M. Nelson, *The Priority of Prudence: Virtue and Natural Law in Thomas Aquinas and the Implications for Modern Ethics* (University Park, Pa.: Pennsylvania State University Press, 1992), p. 105.

MacIntyre[3]—of approaching individual arguments in such a way as to isolate them from one another.

The *Summa theologiae* is composed of three large parts, of which the second, in turn, is divided in two: the *prima secundae* and the *secunda secundae*. Each part is subdivided into questions, and each question into articles. In the prologue to each question, the author himself takes care to locate each particular subject within the overall order of the work and its parts. The structure of the argument is typical of the medieval *quaestiones*. Each article introduces a thesis expressing the opposite of the author's opinion (for example, I-II, q. 90, a. 1: "It would seem that law is not something pertaining to reason."); then several arguments or authoritative opinions favorable to this thesis are listed, and one or more against. There then follow the *respondeo*, that is, the author's own explanation, and solutions to the particular objections previously presented, beginning with the typical formulae: *Ad primum ergo dicendum quod . . .* , *Ad secundum dicendum quod . . .* , *Ad tertium . . .* , etc.

The *prima pars* deals with God, both in Himself (the divine essence and the Trinity of Persons) and in relation to creation (the procession of creatures from God). Here God is the Creator and the end or good of the whole universe, Who preserves it in being and *governs* it, directing it to its end (qq. 103–19). This part involves a study of the different types of creature, and in the discussion of that creature composed of body and soul we find an exposition of Aquinas's anthropology (qq. 75–102). The *secunda pars*, in St. Thomas's own words, concerns "the movement of the rational creature towards God." The subject of this part is the ultimate end of human life and the means for attaining it, which are human acts. After a general explanation of the ultimate end (I-II, qq. 1–5), there follow a general treatment of human acts—both in themselves (I-II, qq. 6–48) and in their intrinsic and extrinsic principles (I-II, qq. 49–114)—and a treatment of specific kinds of human acts (II-II, qq. 1–189). In the *prima secundae* Thomas deals with law and grace as extrinsic principles leading to the good (qq. 90–108), while in the *secunda secundae* he analyzes, among the cardinal virtues, justice, which has as its object the right (*ius*) (qq. 57–122). The *tertia pars* is strictly theological in character and regards Jesus Christ, "Who as man, is our way to God" (I, q. 2, prologue).

The treatment reserved for law in the *prima secundae* is subdivided into a general part, devoted to the nature (*De essentia legis*), divisions (*De*

3 A. MacIntyre, *Whose Justice? Which Rationality?*, p. 165.

legum diversitate), and effects of *lex* (*De effectibus legis*), and a special part, devoted to the particular types of *lex*: *lex aeterna*, *lex naturalis*, *lex humana*, *lex vetus* and *lex nova*. These particular types are placed in an analogical relationship with a single notion capable of embracing them all: "*quaedam rationis ordinatio ad bonum commune, ab eo qui curam communitatis habet, promulgata*."[4]

It is known that in St. Thomas, faith and reason contribute harmoniously to the attainment of a single truth. Nevertheless, it is always possible to distinguish clearly in his writings between the knowledge and arguments that rest solely on the acceptance by faith of truths revealed by God (that are based, in other words, on reason enlightened by faith), and the arguments that in and of themselves are within reach of natural reason alone. With regard to law, it should be pointed out that the first three types listed above generally fall under the second category, while the last two pertain intrinsically to the message of Christian Revelation.[5]

The subject of law appears in different parts of Aquinas's work. The writings preceding or contemporary to the *Summa theologiae* in which the subject is tackled most thoroughly include: the *Scriptum in quattuor libros Sententiarum magistri Petri Lombardi* (1254–56); the *Summa contra gentiles* (1259–64); the commentary on the *Nicomachean Ethics* (1271–72); and the commentary on the books of the *Politics* (1269–72).[6]

Among these writings, the most important is surely the *Summa contra gentiles*, not only because of its size, but also because it is the only writing, apart from the *Summa theologiae*, in which St. Thomas undertakes an overall synthesis of his thought. In this work, too, he is not constrained by the exegetical requirements of a commentary on other authors, and can freely pursue his own insights. In the *Contra gentiles*, including its discussion of law and related topics, we find an attempt at a theoretical

4 Aquinas, *ST*, I-II, q. 90, a. 4 c.

5 For a general introduction to Aquinas's concept of law, see J.-M. Aubert, *Loi de Dieu, lois des hommes* (Tournai: Desclée, 1964); O. Lottin, *Psychologie et morale aux XII et XIII siècles*, vol. II (Louvain-Gembloux: Abbaye du Mont César, 1948), ed. J. Duculot; R.G. De Haro, *La consciencia moral* (Madrid: RIALP, 1978); *La vida cristiana*; A.-D. Sertillanges, *La philosophie des lois* (Paris: Éditions Alsatia, 1946); T.E. Davitt, *The Nature of Law* (London: Herder Book, 1953); R. Jolivet, *Cours de philosophie* (Lyon-Paris: Emmanuel Vitte, 1948).

6 For the chronology of St. Thomas's works I use C. Fabro, *Introduzione a S. Tommaso: La metafisica tomista e il pensiero moderno* (Milan: Ares, 1983), pp. 47–54. For an introduction to his various works, see also A. Livi, *Tommaso d'Aquino: Il futuro del pensiero cristiano* (Milan: Mondadori, 1997).

synthesis coming not long before that of the *Summa theologiae*. Its hermeneutical importance for understanding the evolution of Aquinas's thought, as a key for reading and comparing differences and similarities, is evident; it is surprising that contemporary interpreters, for the most part, pay it no attention, limiting their interests exclusively to the systematic treatise of the *Summa theologiae*.[7] For this reason, I have decided in this chapter to explain St. Thomas's concept of *lex* precisely by starting with his treatment of it in the *Summa contra gentiles*. As a consequence, the discussion that follows can also be read as an in-depth interpretation of this work in relation to the subject under examination.

There is still a further reason, contingent but significant nonetheless, for undertaking a serious reexamination of the *Contra gentiles*. In his well-known essay, *Lex et virtus: Studi sull'evoluzione della dottrina morale di san Tommaso d'Aquino* (Rome: LAS, 1983), Giuseppe Abbà—one of the few authors who has recently tackled the subject of law in the work of St. Thomas with decisive competence—criticizes the "usual way of interpreting the second part [of the *Summa theologiae*] as if it were the systematic crowning of the preceding works."[8] Rather, he detects a real contradiction between the former and the latter. The "preceding works," according to Abbà, lack the central role assigned in the *Summa theologiae* to virtue, the fruit of Aquinas's deepening understanding of Aristotle's work. These works are invariably linked to a theology of law "in the Augustinian mold," focused on the *submission* of man to the divine government of the world, in which the function of virtue is only to "add firmness, delight and ease" to the observance of the law.[9]

Regarding the *Contra gentiles*, Abbà says that this work in particular "not only is of special interest" for his inquiry, "but has supplied one of its starting points." In chapters 113 through 138 of book III, there is a development of the law that is "quite bizarre, both because in the form in which it is elaborated . . . it does not have a counterpart in the other works . . . and because it has been drafted twice by St. Thomas."[10]

7 See, for example, A.J. Lisska, *Aquinas's Theory of Natural Law: An Analytic Reconstruction*; P. Hall, *Narrative and the Natural Law: An Interpretation of Thomistic Ethics*; D.M. Nelson, *The Priority of Prudence: Virtue and Natural Law in Thomas Aquinas and the Implications for Modern Ethics*.

8 G. Abbà, *Lex et virtus: Studi sull'evoluzione della dottrina morale di san Tommaso d'Aquino*, p. 86.

9 Ibid., p. 82.

10 Ibid., p. 73. Abbà has never abandoned the views expressed in *Lex et virtus*: see *Quale impostazione per la filosofia morale?*, p. 53 ff.

I believe that Abbà's interpretation is vitiated by an over-reaction to the legalism of the manualistic tradition and of modern third-person ethics, and that it embraces an unwarranted conflict between virtue and law, the only difference being that this time the latter, not the former, is defeated. In the interpretation I will offer of the *Contra gentiles*, my main concern will be to bring into relief its correspondence with, and similarity to, the *Summa theologiae*. Moreover, I will argue, taking up Abbà's specific objections in section 5, that the difference that he emphasizes between the first and second drafts is irrelevant as far as the overall sense of Aquinas's treatment of law is concerned.

What is more, a careful reading of the *Contra gentiles* will afford us the opportunity to outline the overall conceptual framework of St. Thomas's ethical vision and arguments. Only by starting from this framework is it possible to understand correctly the subsequent deepening, development, and clarification to be found at various points in the *Summa theologiae*.

The *Summa contra gentiles* is divided into four books, and each book into chapters. Like the *Summa theologiae*, it is intended as a complete compendium of Christian doctrine, but written in a more discursive and direct style (without the scholastic system of the *quaestiones*) for the apologetic purpose of "setting aside the errors that are opposed to it."[11] Apart from a number of local differences and a greater concern to distinguish truths accessible to natural reason alone from those attainable only through faith (which are grouped together in the last book), the overall arrangement of the subject-matter largely coincides with that of the *Summa theologiae*.

The first book contains the (philosophical) treatise on the existence and essence of God. The second contains the treatise on Creation (the procession of creatures from God). The third concerns the ordering of all creatures to God as their ultimate end (final cause). The fourth, finally, concerns some truths of the supernatural order, such as the mystery of the Trinity and the Incarnation of Christ.

The third book, in particular, is subdivided into three parts.[12] In the first part (chaps. 2–63), he explains how and why God is the ultimate end

11 Aquinas, *CG*, I, ch. 2.

12 Ibid., III, ch. 1. For the internal division of topics in the *Contra gentiles*, it is quite helpful to consult the *Indice rassuntivo e schematico*, included by T.S. Centi at the end of his translation of the *Summa contra gentiles* (Tommaso d'Aquino, *Somma contro i gentili* [Turin: UTET, 1975], pp. 1329–46).

of all things. In the second (chaps. 64–110), he addresses the theme of God's "universal government," that is, the way in which, whether in designing or in realizing an order, God directs everything to Himself (as the ultimate end) through His providence: in fact, nothing "escapes his rule, just as there is nothing that does not receive its being from Him."[13] In the third part (chaps. 111–63), St. Thomas dwells especially on the way in which God governs rational creatures—in other words, the way in which He directs them to their ultimate end. This way is twofold: guiding them by law (chaps. 111–46) and assisting them with grace (chaps. 147–63). This approach coincides perfectly with that adopted in the *prima secundae* of the *Summa theologiae* vis-à-vis the external principles of human acts: in fact, "the extrinsic principle moving to good is God, Who both instructs us by means of His Law, and assists us by His Grace."[14]

I should at this stage point out the order I will follow, along with the general order of correspondence—insofar as it bears on our subject—between the arguments of the *Contra gentiles* and those of the *Summa theologiae*:

1. The concept of providence, the main subject of book three, coincides with that of *lex aeterna*; we will deal with this in section 2, entitled "Providence and the Eternal Law."

2. Chapters 111–14 of book III concern the special way in which providence operates in relation to man, and explain why it was necessary for man to be given a law by God. The special relation of providence to rational creatures corresponds to the connection drawn in the *Summa theologiae* between the eternal law and the natural law; we will see this in section 3, "Freedom and Natural Law." There I will explain in what sense St. Thomas believes that God looks after man for his own sake and guides him with respect not only to acts of the species but also to those of the individual.

This last point is directly connected to "The Necessity of Law" for man, which is dealt with in subsection 3.1. This necessity, if referred to the natural orientation of man's freedom, pertains to the natural law, while if referred to the expediency of giving to man some further guidance for his actions, it pertains to the divine positive law, both old and new (I will discuss the peculiar function of divine law as *auxilium legis naturalis* later, in section 4.2, "Correspondence with the Natural Order"). Section 3 will also

13 Ibid.

14 Aquinas, *ST*, I-II, q. 90, *Prologue*.

provide the opportunity to set out a useful preliminary concept of law valid for both the *Summa contra gentiles* and the *Summa theologiae* (in subsection 3.2, "The concept of law"), and to clarify my position in relation to Maritain's well-known theory on the "knowledge of the natural law by inclination" (subsection 3.2.1, "Jacques Maritain: Natural Law and Inclinations").

3. Chapters 115–46 of book three of the *Contra gentiles* have as their subject-matter divine law, both old and new—which, as we will see, is constantly viewed in relation to the order of the natural law. More specifically, divine law is considered above all in relation to the precepts of the old law, especially those of the *Decalogue* (115–29); secondly, in relation to the counsels of perfection (130–38); and finally, in relation to the consequences of obedience and disobedience of the law, which are reward and punishment, and in fact moral good and evil (139–46). All this is followed, in the remaining chapters of book III (147–63), by the treatment of grace, which is nothing but the law of the New Covenant: the *lex nova.*

Both *lex vetus* and *lex nova* pertain to the field of theology because they are laws given by God to man through the Old and New Covenants, and their acceptance presupposes faith in the God of Israel and in Jesus Christ. In this book, I do not intend to enter into problems of a theological nature; consequently, I will not dwell specifically on either the old or the new law, or indeed on their mutual relation or their relation with other types of law. The divine law, however, is the authentic source of Thomistic speculation on the natural law, which by comparison always has an ancillary function in Aquinas's work. In fact, Aquinas is convinced that the law supernaturally[15] revealed by God is not extraneous to man such as he is, but fully corresponds to a natural order to whose aid it comes in order to sustain and perfect it. Divine law is thus paralleled by natural law, and the

15 Catholic theology traditionally distinguishes between supernatural and natural revelation: the former implies direct intervention by God in man's history in order to communicate some truth to him; the latter is creation itself which, manifesting God as its cause, may be considered the means by which He naturally reveals Himself to intelligent creatures. See for example M. Schmaus, *Dogmatica cattolica*, I, "Introduzione-Dio-Creazione," ed. N. Bussi (Turin: Marietti, 1959), pp. 14–26; and G. Falcon, *Manuale di apologetica* (Rome: Paolina, 1954), which defines natural revelation as "the manifestation of God and of His perfections through creatures and reason. In this sense it is sometimes said that God reveals Himself to our intelligence in the spectacle of created things and in the testimony of our conscience" (p. 62).

treatment of the latter is oriented principally toward furnishing a philosophical proof for the intrinsic reasonableness of the former.

If it is true that chapters 115–46 of book three of the *Contra gentiles* deal strictly with the divine law, it is equally true that their central goal is to give a rational defense thereof, and the result is a parallel and integrated treatment of divine and natural law. From this finely-tuned comparison St. Thomas's theoretical intentions with respect to natural law emerge clearly; this is the basic point of section 4, "Natural Law and Divine Law." Here, following the same order of treatment as Aquinas, the main concern of section 4.1, "Law as an Ordering to the Ultimate End," will be to bring into relief the deep meaning of divine law as the ordering of man to the love of God. In light of this end, I will also offer some clarifications regarding how we should understand man's subjection to the law, and regarding the relationship between law and virtue.

Subsection 4.2, "Correspondence with the Natural Order," will address directly the relationship delineated by Aquinas between natural law and divine law in regard to both the ultimate end and particular precepts. More specifically, I will discuss the three classes of precepts present in the *Contra gentiles*, and will bring out the natural reasonableness affirmed by St. Thomas of each class with regard to the ultimate end and the function of *auxilium* performed by the divine law for the natural. The second and third classes of precepts connect the pursuit of the ultimate end to respect for an objective natural order that reason is capable of knowing. Subsection 4.3, "Intention of the Ultimate End and the Order of Reason," seeks to explain how according to Aquinas these two aspects of the moral life are inseparable and mutually dependent.

The natural order, or the order of reason, is exemplified in the concepts of *proper end, natural measure*, and *hierarchy*. Subsection 4.4, devoted to these three concepts, may also be understood as a general introduction to the Thomistic doctrine of *natural ends*, in which resides St. Thomas's so-called "ethical naturalism." Subsection 4.5, "The Morality and Immorality of Acts," completes the preceding discussion, taking up the violation of the objective moral order and showing in what the ultimate subjective wickedness of moral evil resides, and how it is possible. This explanation will mainly require a sharpening of our understanding of the distinction between the moral good and the pleasurable good, and of the connection between this distinction and the doctrine of natural ends. Both 4.4 and 4.5 essentially provide the instruments necessary for a correct interpretation of the particular moral cases discussed by St. Thomas in relation to the second class of precepts. Subsection 4.6, "Fornication and Marriage," will round off nicely our analysis of *lex naturalis* in the *Contra gentiles*. Here, to be precise, we will work out in detail all the aspects of St. Thomas's ethical argument on this subject, in order to bring out more fully his realist approach and its consistency with the general philosophical principles previously described.

From the relation of natural law to providence set out in section 3, and its relation to divine law outlined in section 4, there will emerge from two different perspectives a *single concept of natural law* (accessible to philosophical reasoning) that is *inseparable from a transcendent point of reference*. In creating man, God places within his freedom a fundamental orientation. This orientation acts upon man's conscience, pointing to knowledge and love of God as the ultimate end and good of his existence and of his acts, and so demanding of him obedience to the divine will as manifested in the natural created order.

4. After the eternal law, the old and new divine law, and the natural law, the only remaining element in the design of the *Summa theologiae* is human law. It should be said in this regard that human law, although it makes a few appearances in the chapters of the *Contra gentiles*,[16] does not receive a specific treatment of its own. One reason for this might be that the work in question (unlike the *Summa theologiae*) is directed toward nonbelievers in order to convince them to embrace the *true faith*; it consequently gives more attention to those topics that bear directly upon Christian doctrine.

All the types of law present in the *Summa theologiae* appear in the *Contra gentiles*, even though from a systematic point of view the preferred topic of discussion is law as an action of God toward man. In general, St. Thomas's concept of law should be seen as a thorough synthesis of his entire doctrine of Creation, considered in view of the ultimate end to which Creation ordered. In fact, for St. Thomas law is above all the way in which the ordering of created realities to their ultimate end is *effectively* realized, and a main objective of the following discussion will be to bring this aspect of law to the fore. The synthetic function that the concept of law assumes in Thomas's work does not, however, preclude the need to address some particular topics separately, that is, outside the treatise on *lex*. This is why, for example, in the *Summa theologiae,* the explicit mention of *lex aeterna* does not preclude a generous treatment of providence

16 See for example Aquinas, *CG*, III, ch. 123.

in its own right, nor does the discussion of *lex nova* (or *evangelica*) preclude the treatise on grace.

2. Providence and the Eternal Law

The doctrine of law expounded in the *Summa contra gentiles* depends on the doctrine of providence, which is in turn nothing other than an aspect of God's causal action in the universe: God cannot have an end other than Himself, and He therefore wills all other things as means. Furthermore, His intellect and will are so perfect that through a single creative act He brings it about that things are, that they are maintained in being, that they move both individually and collectively toward the unique end (common good) for which they have been created, and that they attain this end. The ordering of all created things to the ultimate end and the concrete realization of such an ordering is exactly what St. Thomas calls providence.

God's causality extends to the total being of things. It is precisely because things are, and are in a particular way, and operate on the basis of their proper mode of being, that they resemble God and tend toward Him in a more or less mediated way as to their ultimate end. This ordering toward God as end can be analyzed in terms of a resemblance to God that depends, at bottom, on the doctrine of participation of being. "Resemblance to God" is thus "the ultimate end of things." "All created things are," in fact, "in a sense, images of the first agent, that is, of God, 'for the agent makes a product to his own likeness': Now, the function of a perfect image is to represent its prototype by likeness to it; this is why an image is made. Therefore, all things exist in order to attain to the divine likeness, as to their ultimate end. Furthermore, everything tends through its motion or action towards a good. . . . Now, a thing participates in the good precisely to the same extent that it becomes like the first goodness, which is God. So, all things tend through their movements and actions toward the divine likeness, as toward their ultimate end."[17]

When St. Thomas talks about the ordering of all created things to God, he does not have in mind the imposition of an extrinsic end, or an artificial theological superstructure, but the fact that each thing has a determinate way of being and acts according to its nature. It is precisely thus that, consciously or unconsciously, it tends toward God and contributes to the ordering of other things and of the whole universe to God. It is here that the doctrine of providence is united to that of the natural inclinations,

17 Aquinas, *CG*, III, ch. 19, and more generally, chs. 1–3, 16–23.

because the movement of things toward their proper ends,[18] the ends to which they are naturally inclined, is precisely what realizes on the natural plane (which does not preclude other interventions of a supernatural character[19]), the providential order established by God.

The being of created things is, at the same time, the *norm* of their operations, a norm whose efficacy rests on the movement imposed by their natural inclinations; and so providence (the creative act of God's intellect and will) can be described as the *law* by which He governs the world. Indeed, to govern is nothing other than to make use of "things by directing them to their end. . . . Hence it is that Sacred Scripture proclaims God as Lord and King . . . for it is the function of the king and lord to rule and govern those subject to their command. And so, Sacred Scripture attributes the course of things to divine decree."[20]

The notion of providence that we find in the *Summa contra gentiles* coincides perfectly with what is later identified in the *Summa theologiae* as *eternal law*: "the *ratio* of Divine Wisdom, as moving all things to their due end, bears the character of law. Accordingly the eternal law is nothing else than the *ratio* of Divine Wisdom, as directing all actions and movements."[21] This notion, scriptural corroboration aside, has essentially philosophical origins; and this is why the proof that St. Thomas offers for divine providence always ends up coinciding in his work with the proof for the existence of God given in the fifth way: the way of the natural finality of things.

Let us consider, in this regard, the following specific passages of the *Contra gentiles*: "[5] That natural bodies are moved and made to operate for an end, was proved [*CG*, III, ch. 3] by the fact that what happens to them is always, or often, for the best; and, if their workings resulted from art, they would not be done differently. But it is impossible for things that do not know their end to work for that end, and to reach that end in an orderly way, unless they are moved by someone possessing knowledge of the end, as in the case of the arrow directed to the target by the archer. So, the whole working of nature must be ordered by some sort of knowledge. And this, in fact, must lead back to God, either mediately or immediately, since every lower art and type of knowledge must get its principles from

18 Being itself is movement, act, the action of persisting in a certain nature.
19 See Aquinas, *CG*, III, ch. 98.
20 Ibid., III, ch. 64.
21 Aquinas, *ST*, I-II, q. 93, a. 1 c.

a higher one, as we also see in the speculative and operative sciences. Therefore, God governs the world by His providence. [6] Furthermore, things that are different in their natures do not come together into one order unless they are gathered into a unit by one ordering agent. But in the whole of reality things are distinct and possessed of contrary natures; yet all come together in one order, and while some things make use of the actions of others, some are also helped or commanded by others. Therefore, there must be one orderer and governor of the whole of things."[22]

3. Freedom and Natural Law

St. Thomas points to an essential difference, with respect to the operations of divine providence, between no-intelligent creatures and "intellectual and rational natures." It is necessary, he says, for divine providence to be exercised on the latter in a special manner because these surpass all other things both (a) in the order of natural perfection and (b) in the dignity of their end. In "the order of natural perfection," because "only the rational creature holds dominion over his acts, moving himself freely in order to perform his actions. Other creatures, in fact, are moved to their proper workings rather than being the active agents of these operations." And in "the dignity of their end," because "only the intellectual creature reaches the very ultimate end of the whole of things through his own operation, which is the knowing and loving of God; whereas other creatures cannot attain the ultimate end except by a participation in its likeness."[23]

In rational creatures (whether angelic or human) God has willed beings whose proper end is to direct themselves, freely and immediately, toward Him ("knowing and loving" Him); He must, therefore, by hypothetical necessity, attune the action of His providence to this end.

Man's freedom, that is, his having "dominion over his acts" and being "his own cause," is what accounts for his peculiar dignity among all creatures. It requires, as St. Thomas explains in chapter 112 of book three of the *Contra gentiles*, that providence look after him *for his own sake*, "while the way in which other things were created, things which have no dominion over their acts, shows this fact, that they are cared for, not for their own sake, but as subordinated to others."[24]

22 Aquinas, *CG*, III, ch. 64.
23 Ibid., III, ch. 111.
24 Ibid., III, ch. 112.

We should pay close attention here to the analogical language used by the Angelic Doctor. To be an instrument means to be willed not *for its own sake* but as a means to something else. As we have already seen, moreover, all creatures are instruments relative to God, because they all *are* for the sake of God. That is why Aquinas specifies that, when we say that "intelligent substances are guided by divine providence for their own sakes," we do not mean to deny "that they are . . . more ultimately referred to God and to the perfection of the universe. In fact, they are said to be providentially managed for their own sake, and other things for their sake, in the sense that the goods which they receive through divine goodness are not given them for the advantage of another being, but the things given to other beings must be turned over to the use of intellectual substances in accord with divine providence."[25]

The free agent is that which *uses* those things available to it. With respect to the goods that providence puts at its disposal, therefore, it is an end and they are means, because they are given to it precisely in order for it to make use of them. Obviously, all creatures can be qualified analogically as ends with respect to one thing and as means with respect to another. However, God moves nonrational creatures toward Himself directly, by means of their natural appetites (or inclinations). Without any awareness of it, they are constantly and inevitably moving toward Him. God, therefore, has no need to make use of anything else (any other means) to achieve this purpose. By the simple fact of *existing*, nonrational creatures realize the end for which they were created, independently of subsequent events. Man, on the other hand, realizes the designs of God only to a minimal extent by the simple fact of *existing*, that is, by the simple fact that he exists as a free creature. Rather, he must make good use of his freedom through the *upright use* of the goods available to him (that is, of all goods, even if only by contemplating or thinking of them). It is in this sense that one can say that God *makes use of* all other things for man's sake, in order to assist man's freedom without coercing it. And it is in this sense that St. Thomas can claim that man is willed (loved) for his own sake, whereas relative to man other things are willed only as means.

Let us once more consider Aquinas's own words: "That which is moved only by another being has the formal character of an instrument, but that which acts of itself has the essential character of a principal agent.

25 Ibid.

Now, an instrument is not valued for its own sake, but as useful to a principal agent. Hence it must be that all the careful work that is devoted to instruments is actually done for the sake of the agent, as for an end, but what is done for the principal agent, either by himself or by another, is for his own sake, because he is the principal agent. Therefore, intellectual creatures are so guided by God, as objects of care for their own sakes; while other creatures are subordinated, as it were, to the rational creatures."[26]

For our purposes it is important to stress that these conclusions, in St. Thomas's account, although they have a philosophical foundation, do not rest on the mere observation of man's freedom but on man's freedom *as willed by God* and *ordered to God*. The mere existence of a free being could not ground, *in absolute terms*—as Spaemann seems to suggest[27]—a value judgment ascribing a greater importance to this being than to other beings. But since it is God Who has willed and loved all that exists (and in relation to whom everything else is important), and since He confers a special importance on man as compared with other things, it makes sense to say that man is more important and that, compared with everything else, is loved *for his own sake* (it is clear that an expression like this can only make sense if it refers axiologically to God).

To put it another way, for Aquinas the peculiar dignity of man does not reside simply in the fact that he is free, but in the fact that he is *willed* to be free. This dignity, moreover, grounded in God, is in turn the ground, in absolute terms, of man's moral attitude toward others. This follows from what has already been said: we have seen that, in God's designs, the mere existence of freedom is not sufficient; rather, it needs to be exercised in a particular way, so that through his own personal choices, every human being can realize, in himself and in his environment, a more perfect resemblance to God. The limitations and obstacles inherent in the natural order are an integral part of God's plan and delimit the manner and the terms in which each person is called to develop his freedom. But free beings can recognize the ultimate meaning of freedom and they must therefore see it (in themselves and) in others as something sacred to be respected and, to the extent possible, to be assisted, promoted and properly directed. The end that gives value to man's freedom is thus God and not man.

26 Ibid.
27 R. Spaemann, *Basic Moral Concepts*; see especially ch. V.

Paradoxically, therefore, It is precisely because man *is not for his own sake* that others must respect him for his own sake. Here the heteronymous basis of Thomistic morality is especially evident.

From the peculiar dignity of rational creatures, St. Thomas goes on to draw another consequence in chapter 113, namely, that man is the only creature "directed by God to his actions, not only in accord with what is suitable to the species, but also in accord with what is suitable to the individual" ("for the sake of the individual").[28]

As we have just seen, individuals of nonrational species are not free and therefore are not called to do anything of their own to realize their resemblance to God and, in so doing, to bring about the greater perfection of the universe. Consequently, God deals with them in a generic way, moving them to the end by dint of necessity, through "the natural inclination common to the whole species."[29] God Himself, in His providential design, has planned for the unconscious activity of such creatures in such a way that, in any time and place, such activity always contributes to the ultimate end of the whole universe. In this sense, what matters to God is not the individual *per se* but that a certain generic mode of being and of acting be instantiated in a determinate situation. Free creatures, on the contrary, are called to recognize the ultimate end explicitly and to order their own acts to it voluntarily, in the various circumstances in which they find themselves. As far as rational individuals are concerned, therefore, it matters to God that *each one* of them turn to Him through free, unique and personal acts, and He arranges things in such a way that man has the possibility and opportunity of doing so.

The first way of providing for man in this way is to give each individual the requisite natural capacity. Thus, God has given to man "understanding and reason" so that he "can grasp in what different ways a thing may be good or bad, depending on its suitability for various individuals, times, and places."[30] And so, unlike other creatures, the human being is capable of distinguishing the "signs of the times" and, in the different circumstances in which he finds himself, he must recognize the true end toward which he is inclined, and choose the means for achieving it. This capacity somehow renders him similar to divine providence itself and is

28 Aquinas, *CG*, III, ch. 113.
29 Ibid.
30 Ibid.

the basis of his high calling to govern both himself and other creatures. As chapter 113 puts it: "The rational creature is subject to divine providence in such a way that he is not only governed thereby, but is also able to know the rational plan of providence in some way. Hence, it is appropriate for him to exercise providence and government over other things. This is not the case with other creatures, for they participate in providence only to the extent of being subordinated to it. Through this possession of the capacity to exercise providence one may also direct and govern his own acts. So, the rational creature participates in divine providence, not only by being governed passively, but also by governing actively, for he governs himself in his personal acts, and even others."[31]

By now it is evident that chapter 113 does nothing more than make explicit what was said in the preceding chapter. For man to be willed *for his own sake* means precisely: (a) that God has in mind not a generic freedom, but the exercise of freedom by each particular individual; and (b) that in His wisdom and omnipotence God not only gives man a nature *capable of freedom*, but also provides for each human individual a unique and unrepeatable plan in which everything else assumes the role of a *means* that simultaneously makes possible, orients and guides his choices.

Let us now move on to a comparison with the *Summa theologiae*. We noted earlier that the concept of providence in the *Contra gentiles* coincides with that of *lex aeterna* in the *Summa theologiae*. Then we saw that in the account of the *Contra gentiles*, man is distinguished from other creatures because in his case, "it is necessary that providence be exercised in a special manner." We can now say that from this point of view, the additional step taken in the *Summa theologiae* is simply to give a "special" name to this "special manner." Thus, while the being of all creatures can be described as the *eternal law* by which God governs them, directing them to the ultimate end of creation, the perfection and nobility of the being with which God has created man is described specifically as *natural law*. The "participation of the eternal law in the rational creature is called the natural law" because "among all others, the rational creature is subject to Divine providence in the most excellent way, in so far as it partakes of a share of providence, by being provident both for itself and for others."[32]

31 Ibid.
32 Aquinas, *ST*, I-II, q. 91, a. 2 c.

3.1. The Necessity of Law

Let us return to the *Summa contra gentiles*. In chapter 114 of book three, St. Thomas explicitly introduces the subject of law, and explains that "it was necessary for a law to be divinely given to man," once we grant the premise that, for the self-mastering rational creature, divine providence must concern itself (by hypothetical necessity), not only with directing the acts of the species, but also, and above all, with guiding the personal acts of the individual. Our goal in this section will be to clarify this passage: why, and in what sense, does the guidance of the individual require the existence of law?

I should say that this is perhaps the most difficult point in the interpretation of the treatise on law of the *Contra gentiles*, a point on which the supplementary elaboration to be found in the *Summa theologiae*—where natural law and divine law are clearly distinguished under various aspects—is sorely missed. In fact, in chapters 111 through 114, one notices a certain blending of the two types of law, which reaches a highly delicate point in precisely the chapter that we are currently examining. The philosophical unity of chapters 111–14 invites the interpreter to refer chapter 114, above all, to the necessity of the natural law, while the remainder of the treatise is more oriented toward the necessity of divine law.

I do believe that what we are dealing with here is not yet a perfectly defined analysis. Nonetheless, this analysis already presupposes a general concept of moral law, and should be referred, properly speaking, to both the natural and the divine law. The fact that St. Thomas concludes chapter 114 with a scriptural quotation typically associated with the natural law and another one typically associated with divine positive law lends significant support to this reading. "Hence it is said in Jeremias (31:33): 'I will write [my law] upon their hearts'; and in Hosea (8:12; Douay modified): 'I shall write my manifold laws for them.'" Here the inscription on the heart symbolizes the interiority of the natural law, and the multiplicity of precepts symbolizes the completeness and foresight of the revealed law.

Much more interesting support is to be found in the dialectic between law and the natural inclinations, which particularly dominates chapters 113 and 114. At first glance, one might easily be led to think that the natural inclinations constitute an as yet implicit reference to the natural law, and that *the law* is the divine law. This interpretation, however, does not survive a closer inspection. The natural inclinations emerge, rather, as the reign of universal necessity in actions of the species, by contrast with the circumstantial, personal action allowed by individual freedom. It is sufficient, in this context, to read the following passage from chapter 113: "divine providence extends to all singular things, even to the least. In the case of those beings, then, whose actions take place apart from the inclination appropriate to their species, it is necessary for them to be regulated in their acts by divine providence, over and above the direction which pertains to the species. But many actions are evident, in the case of the rational creature, for which the inclination of the species is not enough. The mark of this is that such actions are not alike in all, but differ in various cases. Therefore, the rational creature must be directed by God in his acts, not only specifically, but also individually."

This dialectic is taken up again at the beginning of chapter 114, precisely in order to establish the necessity of law. "Just as the acts of irrational creatures are directed by God through a rational plan which pertains to their species, so are the acts of men directed by God inasmuch as they pertain to the individual. . . . But the acts of irrational creatures, as pertaining to the species, are directed by God through natural inclination, which goes along with the nature of the species. Therefore, over and above this (*supra hoc*), something must be given to men whereby they may be directed in their own personal acts. And this we call law."[33] Freedom and law—in this discussion, which is more specific than the one on *lex aeterna*—are inseparable, and freedom is what makes the law necessary for man. Now since the concept of natural law (like that of human positive law) implies that man is free, it is evident that in the dialectic of chapter 114, natural law *too* must be situated, not on the side of the inclinations, but on the side of law. In the context of this comparison between necessity and freedom, chapter 114 can in fact be interpreted as dealing with the concept of law in general, inasmuch as this concept refers most properly to creatures that know "the 'why' of their action" (the end) and that, for this reason, have "the ability to act and not to act."[34]

33 Aquinas, *CG*, III, ch. 114: "Sicut enim actus irrationalium creaturarum diriguntur a Deo ea ratione qua ad speciem pertinent, ita actus hominum diriguntur a Deo secundum quod ad individuum pertinent [...] Sed actus creaturarum irrationalium, prout ad speciem pertinent, diriguntur a Deo quadam naturali inclinatione, quae naturam speciei consequitur. Ergo, supra hoc, dandum est aliquid hominibus quo in suis personalibus actibus dirigantur. Et hoc dicimus legem."

34 Ibid.

In light of these premises, the path we must follow in order to answer our initial question is quite clear: *law is necessary because man is free.* The first way of understanding this necessity is that one cannot command something of a subject that is not capable of obeying. St. Thomas speaks of this connection at two points in chapter 114, but correctly deduces from it not that law is necessary for freedom but that *freedom is necessary for law.* In the two passages in question he focuses first on the cognitive aspect of the connection and then on the volitional: "[3] Since law is simply a certain rational plan and rule of operation (*quaedam ratio et regula operandi*), it is fitting that law be given only to those beings who know the rational character of their work (*qui sui operis rationem cognoscunt*). Now, this is proper only to a rational creature. Therefore, it was appropriate that law was given to the rational creature only. [4] Moreover, law should be given to those having the power to act and not to act (*in quibus est agere et non agere*). Now, this is true to the rational creature only. Therefore, only the rational creature is capable of receiving law."

A second way of thinking about the necessity of law is in reference to the will of a superior who must direct or govern the will of an inferior. In this case, in fact, *freedom requires law*, but only in the relative sense that the freedom of an inferior requires that the superior use law. In chapter 114 we find this argument as well, obviously in relation to God and to man's ultimate end. Take, for example, the following passage: "Since law is nothing but a rational plan of operation (*ratio operis*), and since the rational plan of any kind of work is derived from the end, anyone capable of receiving the law receives it from him who shows the way to the end (*ad finem perducitur*). Thus does the lower artisan depend on the architect, and the soldier on the leader of the army. But the rational creature attains his ultimate end in God, and from God. . . . Therefore, it is appropriate for law to be given men by God."

Both the arguments that we have just outlined can legitimately provide some measure of support for the possibility and appropriateness of both human and divine law. However, not only are they incapable of explaining a hypothetical *absolute necessity of law* for man's freedom; they also run the risk of appealing to a purely external concept of law that is opposed to freedom. In brief, the meaning of law might be interpreted as follows: given the existence of a free being, if one wants him to adopt one mode of behavior rather than another, it is necessary to command it of him explicitly, and perhaps to punish him if he does not obey. It is obvious that in a model of this type, law would always be a ball and chain as far as freedom is concerned.

There is a third way, however, more radical than the others, to understand the necessity of law: *there cannot be freedom without law*. Here it is a question of focusing on the mode of being of free action, and of characterizing law as an essential part of that mode of being. The fundamental consideration in taking up the theme of natural law is, to use Yves Simon's expression,[35] that there be "a law immanent in free natures." It is clear that only a natural law of this kind can ground the nonexteriority of other laws (whether human or divine), which will not be mere impositions so long as they promote, rather than impede, *the law natural to freedom.*

I believe that this third explanation of the necessity of (natural) law, especially given its obvious centrality, is implicit in chapters 111–14. In 114 in particular, it conforms fully with the author's explicit theoretical intentions, namely, to demonstrate "that it was necessary for law to be divinely given to man (*quod necessarium fuit homini divinitus legem dari*)." Moreover, this explanation is connected more directly to the first point mentioned above, which sketches the transition from necessity to freedom, and which alone concludes not with a statement of mere appropriateness or possibility (as we saw for the first two ways of understanding law's necessity), but of strict necessity. "Therefore, over and above this (*supra hoc*), something must be given to men (*dandum est aliquid hominibus*) whereby they may be directed in their own personal acts. And this we call law." I will now try to show synthetically what type of argumentation this conclusion involves.

An individual's personal acts are objects of choices made possible by the capacity of discerning and of willing. In order to be able to choose whether to go right or left, one must be aware of his destination (or end) and want to reach it; only in view of the destination is it possible, subsequently, to judge the rationality of the choice carried out. This is not enough, however. There must also be a *primordial attraction* toward the end that permits the intelligence to know it as such and the will to desire it. This is how, as the neoclassical school (and this book, in ch. 2, section

35 Simon, Yves, *The Tradition of Natural Law: A Philosopher's Reflections*, pp. 60, 118–25. In the present context, Simon's reflections on the fact that freedom should not be thought of as an "event without a cause," and on the connection between the natural moral law and the natural inclinations or tendencies, are of particular interest.

4, "The Inclination to God") has emphasized, we should understand the Thomistic expressions that the good always has the nature of an end (*rationem finis*) and is the first notion of practical reason.[36] If, prior to the choice, everything were absolutely indifferent or of equal value for man, he could not even begin to move in any direction: he could not choose. As has already been emphasized, a man *does not choose* to be attracted to a woman (that is, to *know her as a good* or end), but because he is attracted, he *can* then *choose* whether or not to bring her to the cinema, whether or not to marry her, etc. And similarly for the other human goods.[37]

This line of reasoning about knowledge of good as a condition of the possibility of freedom extends even to the necessity of an ultimate good. In fact, even if one were to admit (entirely correctly, in my view) a plurality of human goods that determine and make possible the individual's freedom, choice would still be impossible if the attraction exercised by all these goods were objectively of equal value, that is, if all goods were encountered by the agent on the same level.

Herein, in my view, lies the error committed by the neoclassical authors. To begin to choose, there must always be an objective differentiation preceding the choice, and such differentiation can only be given, in the end, by the operation in the agent of a unique, ultimate end, or, to use a more classical language, by knowledge of all the ends *under a single* ratio *of goodness*. One can choose between two goods only for the sake of (in view of) a good prior to both, and one can choose among all the goods only for the sake of an ultimate good.[38] (I return to this theme from a different perspective, touching on the objection of the incommensurability of

36 See, for example, Aquinas, *ST*, I-II, q. 94, a. 2 c.

37 On this point see F. Amerio, *La dottrina della fede: Dogma, morale, spiritualità* (Milan: Ares, 1982), p. 279: "Proceeding with the analysis of the free act, we must make another observation: not all choices are equal; not all choices have the same value. Were it otherwise, there would be no reason for choosing; if the data were indifferent, all equivalent, the 'choice' would have no *raison d'etre*. In other words, the very possibility of choice—that is, of freedom—implies a difference in values, which, note carefully, precisely because they make the choice possible, are antecedent to it, preexist it somehow, and condition it. And not only do they condition it, but they qualify and differentiate it: some choices, some values, will more or less authenticate freedom; while other choices, other values, will more or less falsify freedom." Amerio's book is a good general introduction to Thomistic natural law and ethics.

38 St. Thomas fully develops this argument in the *Summa theologiae*'s treatise on the ultimate end (I-II, q. 1). See especially articles 4, "Whether there is one ultimate

values, in sections 4.4, "Proper End, Natural Measure, and Hierarchy," and 4.5, "The Morality and Immorality of Acts"). Furthermore, if, as I tried to show at the end of chapter 2, properly moral experience involves transcending love of self toward love of God, then in the ethical sphere the necessity of an ultimate end coincides with the necessity of loving God "before and more than oneself."

To summarize the third understanding of the necessity of law, one might say that reason and freedom cannot exist as "blank slates," without an end desired by the agent. An absolutely indeterminate freedom, or a freedom of total *indifference*, to use Ockham's terminology, cannot exist.[39] If God had created man free *simply*, man could not make even one choice, because it is only the actual desire of an end that makes the choice of means (or of other ends as means) psychologically possible. And it is clear that only in view of a single ultimate end, which transcends the love of concupiscence, is it possible to judge choices to be either *good* or *evil* (alternatively, *rational* or *irrational*) in an absolute sense: that is, to make an ethical judgment.

It is here that the subject of natural law comes in. For Aquinas the natural law is to be understood in the last analysis as the initial determination of freedom, or, to put it more fully, as the active presence in man's practical reasoning of the ultimate end and of the other human goods. Thus understood, it becomes the source, and a condition of the possibility, of both action and morality. Moreover, in this way natural law determines the content and ethical relevance of the other laws, both human and divine, whose commands, if they did not somehow make contact with what man *already* desires, would remain a matter of total indifference for him. The function of divine law as *auxilium legis naturalis*, which we will explore

end of human life"; 5, "Whether one man can have several ultimate ends"; and 6, "Whether man wills all, whatsoever he wills, for the ultimate end."

39 S. Pinckaers focuses particularly on the incompatibility between freedom and nature (or between freedom and the natural inclinations) created by Ockham's nominalism, as distinct from St. Thomas's naturalism: see *The Sources of Christian Ethics*, pp. 327–456 ("Part Three: Freedom and Natural Law"). "The most decisive point of Ockham's critique of St. Thomas's teaching on freedom was the breach between freedom and the natural inclinations, which were rejected from the essential core of freedom. According to St. Thomas, freedom was rooted in the soul's spontaneous inclinations to the true and the good. His entire moral doctrine was based on the natural human disposition toward beatitude and the perfection of good, as to an ultimate end. A person can never renounce this natural order of things, nor be prevented from desiring it" (pp. 332–33).

in more detail in section 4.2, "Correspondence with the Natural Order," suggests the need to provide some further assistance to man's freedom, but it also suggests that the divine law cannot be extraneous in content to the natural law, and cannot therefore be interpreted as a set of external commands that are imposed on man in order to subdue his will.

In the order of creation, the natural law was the means *necessary* in order to direct free creatures toward God—that is, in order to orient the "personal acts" of each individual human by inscribing in his being, as a *ratio operis* (norm of action), a primordial orientation to the ultimate end. The natural law thus arises as a necessary concomitant of freedom. The divine (old) law, on the other hand, was historically *appropriate* in order to assist human reason in its difficult journey toward knowledge of the good; and *necessary* (the new law) in order to disclose to man the knowledge of the ultimate perfection to which he is ordered, and to give him the capacity to reach it (namely, grace).

To conclude this section, it may be helpful to sketch a few key ideas on the Thomistic doctrine of natural law that should by now be evident, and will hopefully shed some light on the remainder of our discussion.

First of all, (a) the natural law pertains to the sphere of reason and not to any supposed inclinations of the nonrational part of human nature, as Luño seems to suggest.[40] (b) The natural law presupposes the capacity to know the ultimate end, but it does not refer to a purely theoretical sphere; rather, it refers to the *prescription* (*attraction*) of that end and the means necessary to attain it. Natural law, as an object of the intellect, can thus be defined, as it is in the *Summa theologiae*, as an act of reason "commanding something,"[41] and implies (c) the agent's awareness of the heteronymous origin of the prescription. In this sense, natural law can also be described, analogically, as the natural inclination (to the ultimate end) of human reason itself: an inclination that inclines by prescribing the good known (that is, by attracting the will of the agent toward it), and leaves the person subject to it free. As such, it should be seen as an aspect of the nature of the rational soul, and (d), notwithstanding its heteronymous character, it can by no means be understood as something external to man.

3.2. The Concept of Law

We can now attempt the following experiment: to formulate a general concept of law, albeit incomplete, by relating the data on providence and law

40 A.R. Luño, *Etica*, p. 215.

41 Aquinas, *ST*, I-II, q. 92, a. 2 c.

that we have found so far in the *Contra gentiles* to the more explicit account to be found in the *Summa theologiae*.[42] Such a concept will serve as an introduction to subsequent refinements that we will undertake in section 4, "Natural Law and Divine Law."

Law, then, appears as a *disposition of the intellect of a* (divine) *ruler who orders a multiplicity of things subject to Him* (all existing things), *directing them to a common end or good* (God Himself as the ultimate end). This definition, taken in its entirety, is only valid for the concept of eternal law. If, on the other hand, we eliminate the parenthetical terms, it becomes sufficiently broad to be equally valid for human law. Finally, if the content of the second parenthetical term is restricted to "all human things," the definition is adequate both for natural law and for (the old and new) divine positive law.

In the case of eternal law, the law imposes itself on and is evident to its intended subject because it coincides with their very being; in this way, the act of creation itself is its *promulgation*, and the creation of man is the promulgation of the natural law. The law given to man, then, whether divine or natural, is the particular way in which God's providence leads free creatures to their ultimate end. This implies that man can naturally come to know God as his own ultimate end and that of the whole universe, and recognize his *moral* duty to direct all his actions toward God. With regard to the natural inclinations, understood as the way in which the eternal law imprints its order onto things, the doctrine of law implies: (a) that there is a fundamental inclination of reason that impels man directly to God (natural inclination of the will to "love God before oneself and with a greater love"); and (b) that at least some inclinations (including the most fundamental one), even if their spark cannot be extinguished, leave man free to resist them, at least in part, thus acting in some way against his own nature (we will see how this is possible in section 4.5, "The Morality and Immorality of Human Acts"). In this way, the natural inclinations ground moral duty, inclining man toward the end without forcing him.

Here we find an outline, with all its potential implications, of the concept of natural inclinations in Thomistic philosophy. It is these inclinations that make the eternal law *efficacious* and *coercive*, with a necessitating

42 I have examined in depth the analogical nature of Aquinas's concept of law and of its elements, as they appear in the *Summa theologiae*, in my "Natural Law as Inclination to God" and "Law as 'Act of Reason' and 'Command.'"

efficacy in the case of creatures that lack freedom, and with a normative efficacy—the source of duties of conscience and natural punishment—in the case of creatures that are free. The natural inclinations will increasingly take center-stage in our account, because of the central role they assume in St. Thomas's treatment of the law. I will dwell on them especially in section 4.4, "Proper End, Natural Measure, and Hierarchy," in relation to the general doctrine of natural ends.

3.2.1. Jacques Maritain: Natural Law and Inclinations

The relation between law and the natural inclinations has been the object of a wide-ranging debate in recent times, particularly with respect to "connatural knowledge," or knowledge "by inclination," of which Maritain has spoken.[43] Without wishing to enter specifically into the merits of that debate, which would require a treatment of its own, it seems appropriate, nonetheless, to give at least some brief indication of the general thrust of my interpretation of St. Thomas with respect to Maritain's view.

When Maritain elaborates his theory of "knowledge of the natural law by inclination," he has in mind two principal goals of fundamental importance: (a) to defend the spontaneity and historicity of moral knowledge in the face of the prevailing rationalist interpretation of natural law, and (b) to oppose the idea of a total ethical autonomy in which it is man himself who creates the norms and principles of action.

In order to attain these goals, he distinguishes three elements in the discussion of natural law: an ontological element, an epistemological element, and a third element that is given by divine reason itself. The first element is simply human nature, i.e., the "normal functioning" of that particular being that belongs to the human species, and is therefore "grounded in the essence" of such a species. Natural law, in this first sense, is not to be understood merely as something already given, once and for all, but also as an "ideal order," whose concrete instantiations cannot be deduced

43 For a bibliography on the subject see G. Chalmeta, *Jacques Maritain: el elemento gnoseológico en la constitución de la ley moral natural*, extractum ex dissertatione ad Doctoratum in Facultate Philosophiae (Rome: Pontificia Universitas Urbaniana, 1989); and M. D'Avenia, *La conoscenza per connaturalità in S. Tommaso d'Aquino* (Bologna: ESD, 1992). By Maritain, see especially *Nove lezioni sulla legge naturale* (Milan: Jaca Book, 1985), ed. F. Viola; *Distinguish to Unite: The Degrees of Knowledge*, trans. Gerald B. Phelan; *Quattre essais sur l'esprit dans sa condition charnelle* (Paris: Desclée de Brouwer, 1956).

abstractly but "are something existential," which is developed in the course of the history of humanity and of every single man, in conjunction with the various circumstances of life. Thus, the prohibition of "genocide" can be said to pertain to the natural law, but only in regard to the particular historical circumstances in which some men are capable of "putting a whole human race or community to death."

"As an effective measure of practical reason," or "of human acts," on the other hand, the natural law should not be considered as grounded in nature, but "as known" by man, that is, in its epistemological dimension. This dimension is "fundamental," continues Maritain, because "law has the force of law" only "when it is promulgated," in other words, "when it is known and expressed in assertions of practical reason." In its epistemological dimension, each person's practical reason knows in an evident manner only that "we ought to do good and avoid evil," which is "the preamble and the principle of natural law rather than natural law itself"; all other knowledge is a product of successive "determinations," elaborated slowly and in relation to particular contexts.

It is at this point that Maritain proposes his concept of knowledge by inclination. In fact, he sees the danger of rationalism—and the consequent historicist and existentialist reactions—whenever the natural law is enclosed in *concepts* elaborated by human reason, which are always and only limited *ex post* determinations of the natural law rather than the natural law itself. Here, Maritain's own words are more eloquent than any commentary: "I believe," he writes, "that the teaching of St. Thomas, when he affirms that human reason discovers the rules of natural law under the guidance of the inclinations of human nature, should be understood in a much deeper way than is often the case. What I mean by this is that the way in which human reason knows the natural law is not the way of rational knowledge, but what is called knowledge by inclination."

And he goes on to say, "This notion of knowledge by inclination has been amply (though elsewhere) developed by St. Thomas. Knowledge by inclination or by connaturality is a kind of knowledge which is not as clear as the one obtained through concepts and conceptual judgments. Rather, it is obscure, unsystematic, a living knowledge, for the most part. It is knowledge by connaturality and sympathy, in which the intellect arrives at its judgments, consulting interior inclinations, the subject's interior perception, listening carefully to the interior melody, to the vibration of deep tendencies made conscious in the subjectivity. All of this culminates in a judgment not based on concepts, in a judgment that expresses nothing but the conformity of reason to those inclinations to which it accords itself."[44]

Precisely because knowledge by inclination does not depend on human reason (but on the inclinations), Maritain maintains that it is possible to preserve the heteronymous character of natural law: "if human reason were to interfere," he argues, "the law would only have the value of human authority." "The light of natural reason, which permits us to discern good and evil," is not that of "discursive reason, but that of reason which judges by connaturality on the basis of the properly human inclinations of our nature, inclinations derived from the eternal law." "It is not reason that makes us know the law, but the inclinations, and so, it is these, not the discursive faculty of reason, that are the formal element that makes the law known."[45]

Maritain's noble intentions regarding the defense of the natural law, while quite understandable given the time in which he wrote and his interlocutors, lead him to adopt certain overly poetic and insufficiently rigorous interpretations of Thomistic philosophy. Such interpretations seem to be based on a certain fear of intellectual—or conceptual—knowledge that attests to Maritain's unwitting and partial acceptance (at least in this specific area) of some rationalistic epistemological premises: in particular, the idea of *concepts* as *clear and distinct* units, and of *judgments* as equally clear and distinct deductions starting from those units. The result of his reaction is thus a *judgment not grounded in concepts* (where judgment is defined precisely as the union of two or more concepts), and a *nondiscursive reason* (where reason is defined, by contrast with intellectual knowledge, precisely by its discursiveness, that is, by the passage of its knowing from one concept to another and from one judgment to another).

From my point of view, the heteronymous character of the natural law rests on the natural knowledge of God and the natural inclination to love God "before oneself and with a greater love," as I explained in chapter 2. The spontaneity and historicity of the knowledge of natural law, on the other hand, depend at bottom on an accurate understanding of the *intentionality* of intellectual knowledge, which we also discussed in the second chapter. The concept and the judgment, for St. Thomas, are never stable, crystallized units, but are rather the knowledge that the intellect

44 J. Maritain, *Nove lezioni sulla legge naturale*, p. 49.
45 Ibid., p. 59.

possesses at a given moment of the reality with which, through the senses, it is in a continuous intentional relationship. It is this reality that the exercise of reason enables man to penetrate more deeply (on this point, see ch. 2, sections 3.2, "The Object of Human Knowledge," and 3.3, "Judgment and Reasoning").

It is certainly correct to distinguish the ontological aspect from the epistemological, but the ontological aspect of (eternal) law is given precisely by the natural inclinations inscribed by God in the being of created things—in other words, by their necessary movements toward the end. From this point of view, the fundamental natural inclination (the law) of human reason is to carry out the will of God in so far as this is manifest in the created order, of which man himself is a part.

When Aquinas speaks of the nature of law, or responds to the question, "*quid sit lex naturalis*," he is quite clear: law is not a virtue, nor a power, nor a passion. It is "*aliquid per rationem constitutum: sicut etiam propositio est quoddam opus rationis*"[46]; it is a "universal proposition of the practical intellect . . . directed to action"[47]; in the last analysis, it is an *act* of practical reason *commanding something*, just as "an assertion is a dictate of reason asserting something."[48] More particularly, law as a specific act is the *judgment* formulated by reason about what is good and what is evil to do.

Here, with respect to the being of human reason, it is easy to grasp the link between the ontological and epistemological aspects: the law of reason is, in fact, the natural inclination of the will to pursue the good known by the intellect, and this inclination is manifested precisely in the *dictate of reason commanding something*. The inclination of (practical) reason (reason is practical just in so far as it is primordially inclined to the good), then, is the *intellectual* (*intentional*) act by means of which man knows the nature of things in, broadly speaking, normative terms. Instead of practical reason, we could speak more figuratively of inclined or appetitive knowledge (or even of *knowledge by inclination*, on condition, however, that we do not exclude moral knowledge from the sphere of intellectual knowledge). Such knowledge is composed of some relatively universal judgments, which in the Thomistic tradition are referred to as the unchanging precepts of the natural law, and of other judgments that can be

46 Aquinas, *ST*, I-II, q. 94, a. 1.
47 Ibid., I-II, q. 90, a. 1 ad 2.
48 Ibid., I-II, q. 92, a. 2 c.; and q. 94, a. 2 ad 1.

derived through reasoning from the more universal precepts in the context of various historical contingencies.

As for the contribution to moral knowledge afforded by the virtue of prudence, it should be seen at a different level. Like a muscle that can be more or less well-trained, practical reason can be more or less perfected, through its *training*, to exercise spontaneously its cognitive operations and correctly formulate (*recta ratio agibilium*) its judgments and commands concerning good actions to be carried out.[49] This process of perfection reaches its highest point when the agent attains, in moral action, that "freedom for excellence" so aptly described by Pinckaers through the analogy of the art of piano-playing, and which is a manifestation of truly perfect knowledge and of the capacity for the spontaneous exercise of reason. And just as obtains in the theoretical sphere, the correct exercise of practical reason through good deliberation (in other words, correct moral-deliberative reasoning) constantly increases in the agent the *conceptual, intentional* knowledge of the moral good, or the desired end.

"Of course anyone is free to bang out notes haphazardly on the piano, as the fancy strikes him. But this is a rudimentary, savage sort of freedom. It cloaks an incapacity to play even the simplest pieces accurately and well. On the other hand, the person who really possesses the art of playing the piano has acquired a new freedom. He can play whatever he chooses, and also compose new pieces. His musical freedom could be described as the gradually acquired ability to execute works of his choice with perfection. It is based on natural dispositions and a talent developed and stabilized by means of regular, progressive exercises, or properly speaking, a *habitus*." Aristotle's and St. Thomas's prudent or good man in the moral sphere is like the good pianist in the artistic sphere; and is therefore the *truly* free man.[50]

4. Natural Law and Divine Law

In his speculations on law, St. Thomas is moved by several deep convictions that we must take into account if we wish to understand his writings. Revealing Himself to man, God has given him a law that encompasses a multiplicity of precepts and whose ultimate *ratio* is the love of God above

49 Ibid., II-II, q. 47.

50 See Servais Pinckaers *The Sources of Christian Ethics: Method, Content, History*, trans. Sr. Mary Thomas Noble, O.P. (Catholic University of America Press: Washington, D.C., 1995), pp. 354–74.

all things. God has even said explicitly that the way to love Him is to obey His will and His Commandments. Moreover, God's law is not opposed to reason and to human nature, but responds perfectly to their deepest essence: in obeying this law, man fulfils himself.

The fundamental concern that motivates Aquinas as he explicitly tackles the subject of law is to highlight (a) the ultimate end of loving God and, in view of this, (b) the intrinsic reasonableness of the particular precepts. With regard to human nature, then, the concern is to show the perfect correspondence between the *Decalogue* and the order imposed by the natural law, with regard to both the end and the content of the various precepts.[51] The divine law does not oppress man but discloses to him fully and with clarity the true needs of his heart; thus, from a moral perspective, it does not of itself add any precept to the natural law, not even the precept to acknowledge God, to love Him as one's ultimate end, and to obey His will. There is an indissoluble bond, according to Aquinas, that even at the natural level joins obedience to God, morality, and happiness (or beatitude): "*lex divina*," in fact, "*profertur homini in auxilium legis naturalis*."[52]

Since we are about to enter into the heart of the treatise on law found in the *Summa contra gentiles*, it is worth reviewing quickly the overall organization of this treatise, with regard to its typology of laws and to the basic order that it follows. As we have already seen, the proper object of the treatise is revealed divine law: its meaning and reasonableness. Providence completely replaces eternal law, while human law is mentioned only in passing. Not even the natural law receives a specific treatment, but its importance cannot be doubted because it is the permanent touchstone of divine law and its precepts.

Very roughly, one could think of Aquinas's whole discussion of law schematically by reducing it to three basic steps: (1) the necessity of law from the point of view of man's freedom; (2) law as prescription or order-

51 One of the best known and most important places in Sacred Scripture where the correspondence between divine revealed law and natural law is evinced is St. Paul's *Letter to the Romans*, in particular chapter 2, verses 12–16: "For as many as have sinned without law [given by God to the people of Israel] will also perish without law, and as many as have sinned in the law will be judged by the law. For not the hearers of the law are just in the sight of God, but the doers of the law will be justified. For when Gentiles, who do not have the law, by nature do the things in the law, these, although not having the law, are a law to themselves. They show the work of the law written in their hearts, their conscience also bearing witness, and between themselves their thoughts accusing or else excusing them."

52 Aquinas, *CG*, III, ch. 117.

ing to the ultimate end; (3) law as prescription of the means to attain the ultimate end.

These means to the ultimate end are indicated by the particular precepts of the law, of which the main ones discussed by Aquinas are those related to the *Decalogue*, following the traditional division between precepts of the first and those of the second Table of the Law. The first Table concerns human acts ordained directly to the love of God. This Table contains the first three Commandments, which prohibit polytheism and idolatry, and prescribe respect for the name of God and the performance of acts of worship: "I am the Lord your God: (1) Thou shalt not have strange gods before me" (2) "Thou shalt not take the name of God in vain" (3) "Remember that thou keep holy the Sabbath day."[53] The second Table concerns those human acts that are ordered to the love of God by way of respect for the creatures that He has loved for their own sake. Here we have the other seven Commandments: (4) "Honor thy father and mother," (5) "Thou shalt not kill," (6) "Thou shalt not commit adultery," (7) "Thou shalt not steal," (8) "Thou shalt not bear false witness against thy neighbor," (9) "Thou shalt not covet thy neighbor's spouse," (10) "Thou shalt not covet thy neighbor's goods."[54]

All of these precepts, expressed for the most part in a negative form, indicate a number of basic acts in the various spheres of action, without whose performance man cannot (at least, not fully) achieve his end. But the law's truth, its breadth, and its ultimate justification come from its openness to the ultimate end, not from the more or less general specification of its requirements with respect to various human contexts and goods. The main purpose of the following subsections will be to highlight the explicit centrality of the concept of ultimate end, and to show how St. Thomas understands, in relation to this concept, the correspondence between the precepts of divine law and the natural order (i.e., the order of the natural law).

4.1. Law as an Ordering to the Ultimate End

I have already mentioned several times that law, for the Angelic Doctor, is first of all an orientation, indication and prescription of the ultimate end. Indeed, after the introductory chapter on the necessity and concept of law (step one), chapter 115 of book III of the *Contra gentiles* immediately

53 Ibid., III, ch. 120.

54 Ibid., III, ch. 128. For the promulgation of the Ten Commandments, see *Exodus* 20, 2–17 and *Deuteronomy* 5, 6–21.

explains (step two) that "the divine law principally looks to the ordering of man toward God," because, among other reasons, "*the end for the human creature is to cling to God*, for his *felicity* consists in this. . . . So, the divine law primarily directs man to this end: that he may cling to God."[55] And the very next chapter explains that "the end of the divine law is the love of God" since "man adheres to God chiefly by love."[56] Here, by means of the contrast between adherence of the will *by love* and adherence of the will *by fear*, St. Thomas shows how man's subjection to the law ought to be understood.

Man, says, St. Thomas, can adhere to God with the intellect and with the will, but "the union which is effected through the intellect is completed by the union which pertains to the will, because through his will man in some way rests in that which the intellect apprehends. But the will adheres to a thing, either because of love or because of fear, but not in the same way. For, if one clings to something because of fear, he clings because of something else (*propter aliud*), for instance, to avoid an evil which threatens unless he clings to that thing. But, if one clings to a thing because of love, he does so for the sake of that thing (*propter seipsum*). Now, what is valued for its own sake is of greater importance than what is for the sake of something else (*Quod autem est propter se, principalius est eo quod est propter aliud*). Therefore, the adherence to God in love is the best possible way of clinging to Him. So, this is what is chiefly intended in the divine law."[57]

Aquinas later takes up this theme again, explaining that man can be impelled to observe the law by two motives. One is interior: when "man is voluntary in regard to observing what divine law prescribes. In fact, this is accomplished by man's love of God and his neighbor, for he who loves a person gives him his due spontaneously and joyfully, and he even adds something in excess by way of liberality."[58] The other is exterior: when "some people are not so disposed internally that they will do sponta-

55 Aquinas, *CG*, III, ch. 115: "*Finis autem humanae creaturae est adhaerere Deo*: in hoc enim felicitas eius consistit . . . Ad hoc igitur principaliter lex divina hominem dirigit, ut Deo adhaereat" (my italics).

56 Ibid., III, ch. 116: "homo autem potissime adhaeret Deo per amorem."

57 Ibid., III, ch. 116.

58 Ibid., III, ch. 128. The passage ends as follows: "So, the complete fulfillment of the law depends on love, according to the text of the Apostle: 'Love is the fulfilling of the law' (Rom. 13:10). And the Lord says that, 'on these two commandments,' that is, on the love of God and of neighbor, 'dependeth the whole law' (Matt. 22:40)."

neously what the law orders," and "they must be forced" to observe the law "from fear of punishments."[59]

This explanation of legal obligation is also relevant to human law and is much more realistic than it might at first appear to be. It overlaps, for instance, with recent developments in analytic jurisprudence that have brought into question traditional Austinian imperativism by showing that the existence of a legal system cannot be explained by the mere threat of sanctions. Rather, there must be an *acceptance* of the norms in the light of their justificatory *reasons*, at least on the part of the majority of the population and in regard to a considerable proportion of the rules. In other words, there must be some sort of *sharing* of the common end (or good), on which the rule depends. Only this sharing of a common good can lead to an observance of the rules that may be described as somehow *spontaneous*.[60]

It is true that, for St. Thomas, "the divinely given law derives its efficacy among men from the fact that man is subject to God, for no one is bound by the law of a ruler if he is not subject to him."[61] Nonetheless, although the law derives its force from divine authority, its end is not merely the subjection of creatures, as Abbà seems to suggest,[62] since obedience to the law out of fear is an "imperfect" obedience. When Aquinas says that the end of divine law is the subjection, or submission, of creatures, he is not referring to a sort of tyrannical control on God's part, or to the psychological motive that must guide the obedience of free creatures. He merely wants to underline the fact that the general function of law, according to the designs of Providence, is to ensure that every being is maintained in the order established by the Creator, and, in this sense, to ensure that every being is subject to Him.

The mode of subjection intended for man, however, is "perfect" obedience, which out of love for the Creator leads to a sharing of His End, and which comes about with "firmness and joy." It is worth noting that St. Thomas derives this last claim from the existence of an *ordering of law to*

59 Ibid.

60 On this question see especially J. Austin, *The Province of Jurisprudence Determined and the Uses of the Study of Jurisprudence* (London: Weidenfeld and Nicolson, 1971); H.L.A. Hart, *The Concept of Law*, as well as his "Introduction" to J. Austin, *The Province of Jurisprudence*; J. Raz, *Practical Reason and Norms*; Finnis, *Natural Law and Natural Rights*.

61 Aquinas, *CG*, III, ch. 115.

62 G. Abbà, *Lex et Virtus*, pp. 81–85.

virtue, based on the fact that acting with "firmness and joy" is one of the conditions of virtue and depends on doing things out of love.

It is surprising that Abbà, in claiming that virtue has, in the *Contra gentiles*, a merely subordinate role in relation to law,[63] neglects the *incipit* of this argument, in which it is law, if anything, that seems to be subordinate to virtue. Here is the entire passage: "Man's goodness stems from virtue, 'for virtue is what makes its possessor good'. [*Nic. Eth.*, II, 6, 1106a23]. Hence, law also intends to make men virtuous, and the precepts of law are concerned with acts of the virtues. But it is a condition of virtue that the virtuous man must act with firmness and joy. But love is the chief producer of this result, for we do a thing firmly, and with joy, as a result of love. Therefore, love of the good is the ultimate object intended in divine law."[64]

How can the ordering of the law to virtue be reconciled with its ordering to love of God? Virtue is an analogical concept indicating the quality of a subject in relation to an end. Drawing once again on Aristotle, St. Thomas further specifies: "that by which each thing is called good is the virtue that belongs to it; for 'the virtue of each thing is what makes its possessor and his work good.'"[65] A good ship is one that has the properties necessary to plough the waves speedily and safely: such properties are its virtues, which make it a good ship. *Absolutely speaking*, the virtue of a thing is that which makes it similar to God and therefore *good simpliciter*. For man, virtue is above all moral virtue: the result (acquired perfection) of the right (ultimate) orientation of his free acts; in other words, the actual capacity (disposition) to love God, to be charitable.

For men, to love God, to be like Him (*simpliciter*), and to be virtuous are concepts that coincide. If the end that God aims at through law is to bring man to love Him, then the law has as its object the virtuous man and

63 Ibid.

64 Aquinas, *CG*, III, ch. 116: "Bonitas hominis est per virtutem: *virtus enim est quae bonum facit habentem*. Unde et lex intendit homines facere virtuosos; et praecepta legis sunt de actibus virtutum. Sed de conditione virtutis est ut virtuosus *et firmiter et delectabiliter operetur*. Hoc autem maxime facit amor: nam ex amore aliquid firmiter et delectabiliter facimus. Amor igitur boni est ultimum intentum in lege divina."

65 Ibid., I, ch. 37. I am deliberately citing only from the *Contra gentiles* to bring out more forcefully the intrinsic coherence of this work with regard to the relations between the concepts of virtue and law. It is clear nonetheless that the concept of virtue expressed here is not altered in the *Summa theologiae*. See e.g. *ST*, II-II, q. 47, a. 4 c.

the acts that render him virtuous—and among these, those above all that order him directly to God. From man's point of view, however, the end always remains God and not his own perfection; otherwise, the quest for virtue would reduce the moral life exclusively to the love of concupiscence, precluding the love of God "before and more than oneself." The moral agent, in Thomistic ethics, wills his own virtue *first and foremost* because he knows that God wills it. In this way, virtue is (ought to be) intended by the agent only as a *fine effetto* (something we are happy to achieve as a secondary effect of our action), and the best education in virtue is the education that acknowledges and orients itself toward the authentic end.

Chapter 117, "That we are ordered by divine law to the love of neighbor," completes Aquinas's account of the *ratio legis*, suggesting that the love of God implies, as an immediate consequence, the love of man. The simplest explanation of this is that one cannot love God without loving what He loves: "Whoever loves a person must, as a consequence, also love those loved by that person and those related to him. Now, men are loved by God, for He has prearranged for them, as an ultimate end, the enjoyment of Himself. Therefore, it should be (*oportet igitur*) that, as a person becomes a lover of God, he also becomes a lover of his neighbor."[66] Here the most relevant point to notice for our purposes is that in Thomistic morality the *absolute* respect for (other) people depends on the fact that God *loves them for their own sakes;* in other words, absolute respect for others has a theological basis. *If there were no God*, we would lack the ethical demand for an absolute respect and inviolability. Here, as in chapter 115, Aquinas takes care to stress the correspondence between the supernatural order and the natural: "Divine law is offered to man as an aid to natural law," and "it is natural to all men to love each other."[67]

4.2. Correspondence with the Natural Order

Chapters 118 through 129, as already mentioned, are concerned with human acts commanded or prohibited by the various precepts of the Law. The discussion here is disjointed; one is left with the impression of a typical *ad hominem* argument. St. Thomas pays close attention only to several precepts relating to worship, sex, and food, trying always to bring out the general meaning, scope and reasonableness of divine law. It is not necessary at this point to enter in detail into the merits of particular prescrip-

66 Aquinas, *CG*, III, ch. 117.
67 Ibid.

tions (we will do this later on for fornication and marriage); it is important, on the other hand, to understand *how* and *why* St. Thomas discusses the correspondence of the divine law with the natural order.

The reason is expressed with greatest clarity in chapter 122: "We do not offend God except by doing something contrary to our own good."[68] The same point is put in different terms in chapter 126: "only those things that are opposed to reason are prohibited by divine law."[69] Chapter 129, the culmination and synthesis of the treatise on law, is entitled: "That some human acts are right according to nature and not merely because they are prescribed by positive law (*lege posita*)"[70] (where "positive law" means the law *posited* by God through Revelation. The concept of positivity applies analogically to both human and divine law).

The passages just cited clearly point to an inevitable convergence between the will of God and the human good, and this convergence is reflected in the relations between the divine law and the natural law. To offend God and to offend the natural good amount to the same thing, and the reason, in the end, is simple: *the natural order is the order that God has willed* in order to direct the whole of creation to Himself. The natural order is therefore important in an absolute sense (that is, in relation to God's will) both in its totality and in the individual elements of which it is composed. Respect for such an order is what leads both to man's (and other creatures') greatest good and to his greatest perfection and resemblance to God. This is why, for St. Thomas, the decisive proof of the reasonableness of the divine law is the human, or natural, reasonableness of the content of its precepts, as if to say that the proof of the reasonableness of divine law is the natural law.

This is how the natural law is always treated in Aquinas's work: not extensively and systematically, with a view to extracting ethical norms from it directly, but rather, in a residual and general way, with a view to showing the natural foundations of divine law. It would be a mistake to object, as one hears quite commonly today,[71] that St. Thomas's treatment of natural law is not very deep or elaborate. He had no need to probe the content of morality philosophically in a precise and detailed way, because

68 Aquinas, *CG*, III, ch. 122.

69 Ibid., III, ch. 126.

70 Ibid., III, ch. 129. The chapter begins thus: "From the foregoing it is apparent that things prescribed by divine law are right, not only because they are put forth by law, but also because they are in accord with nature."

71 See for example J. Finnis, *Natural Law and Natural Rights*; D.J. O'Connor, *Aquinas and Natural Law* (London: Macmillan, 1967).

this was already known to him through Revelation. Neither did he hope to find moral certainty in the arguments of natural reason alone. His only concern was to defend the divine law by bringing to light its natural foundation in a general way, and in the particular cases that were under dispute in his time.

(1) The conformity between divine and natural law is given first by the fact that, already in the natural order, God is man's ultimate good on which, in the last analysis, the morality and immorality of acts depend. In this regard, besides what has already been said, it is worth reading the absolutely unequivocal passage with which chapter 129 concludes: "those acts by which he inclines towards his natural end are naturally appropriate to an agent, but those that have the contrary effect are naturally inappropriate to the agent. Now . . . *man is naturally ordered to God as his end.* Therefore, the things by which man is brought to the knowledge and love of God are naturally right, but whatever things have the contrary effect are naturally evil for man. Therefore, it is clear that good and evil in human activities are based not on the prescription of law, but also on the natural order."[72]

(2) Given this axiological foundation for human acts, conformity to natural law next concerns the precepts of divine law inasmuch as they are directed toward the various human goods and their correct (hierarchical) ordering to man's ultimate end. (A bad act is, by definition, a *disordered* act: one directed toward a human good outside its objective ordering to the ultimate end.) As far as the agent's intention of the ultimate end is concerned, St. Thomas explains the natural reasonableness of the precepts of divine law: (a) in relation to the external acts through which man turns immediately toward God; (b) in relation to those acts that have as their object sensible goods; and (c) in relation to those acts that have as their object other human beings.

(a) The precepts that order human action directly to God are those that regard the worship of God, requiring the performance of certain gestures and external acts, such as sacrifices, genuflections, canticles, etc.[73] The reason for these precepts is not that God somehow needs such behavior

72 Aquinas, *CG*, III, ch. 129: "Unicuique naturaliter conveniunt ea quibus tendit in suum finem naturalem: quae autem e contrario se habent, sunt ei naturaliter inconvenientia. Ostensum est autem supra quod *homo naturaliter ordinatur in Deum sicut in finem.* Ea igitur quibus homo inducitur in cognitionem et amorem Dei, sunt naturaliter recta: quae autem e contrario se habent, sunt naturaliter homini mala" (my italics). For related passages, see chs. 17, 25.

73 Ibid., III, chs. 118–20.

from man. It is human nature itself, composed of body and soul, that requires the performance of such acts so that man may direct himself to God, so that man can be "recalled to divine matters," "so that our attention may be directed to God by these sensible deeds and that our love may be aroused. At the same time, then, we confess by these actions that God is the author of soul and body, to Whom we offer both spiritual and bodily acts of homage." It is good to bring out the logic of the ethical justification used by St. Thomas. From the natural normativity of the ultimate end (major premise), given the (partly) corporeal nature of the human being (minor premise), is derived the general duty, on the natural level, to performing sensible acts of worship (conclusion). The unity of body and soul, in Thomistic anthropology, is understood in such a radical way that the superior faculties of intellect and will cannot be exercised without the intervention of the senses, and are at once empowered and held back by them. Love and affection are nourished by sensible gestures and acts, and material things make up a part of what man offers as gifts to make known his feelings.[74] It is hardly necessary, then, to underline that in the sequence just described, the foundational normativity of the major premise preempts the charge of the naturalistic fallacy.

Let us now move on to the role of divine law. We are dealing here precisely with an aid (*auxilium legis naturalis*), which has a dual function: firstly, to bring properly into focus one's ethical duty; and secondly, to *specify it* in order to facilitate its performance by everyone. The duty to perform outward acts of worship, which depends on a synthesis of the ultimate end and bodily nature, is in itself universal and unchanging (here natural law and divine law coincide), while the specification of this duty (for example, the sacrifices prescribed by the Old Law) is particular and contingent (derived exclusively from divine positive law). The opening words of St. Thomas's justification of the precepts of worship of divine positive law are quite eloquent: "Since it is connatural for man to receive knowledge through his senses, and since it is very difficult to transcend sensible

74 The passage just cited continues as follows: "For this reason, it is not astonishing if heretics who deny that God is the author of our body condemn such manifestations. This condemnation shows that they have not remembered that they are men when they judge that the representation of sensible objects to themselves is not necessary for inner knowledge and for love. For it is evident from experience that the soul is stimulated to an act of knowledge or of love by bodily acts. Hence, it is obvious that we may quite appropriately use even bodily things to elevate our mind to God" (ibid. III, ch. 119).

objects, divine provision has been made for man so that a reminder of divine things might be made for him, even in the order of sensible things. The purpose of this is that the intention of man might be better recalled to divine matters, even in the case of the man whose mind is not strong enough to contemplate divine things in themselves. And it was for this reason that sensible sacrifices were instituted."[75] Therefore, God issues certain positive precepts historically to assist natural reason on a path that it finds "very difficult."

(b) Let us now move on to those precepts relating to the use of sensible things. Aquinas explains that "as man's mind may be raised up to God by means of corporeal and sensible things, if one uses them in a proper way to revere God, so, too, the improper use of them either completely distracts the mind from God, and so the end of the will is fixed in inferior things, or such abuse slows down the inclination of the mind toward God so that we become attached to things of this kind to an extent greater than is necessary."[76] Hence, it is necessary that "both the inner feelings and the use of corporeal things be regulated by reason"[77] so that they draw man closer rather than farther from God.

Acting *in accord with reason*, in Aquinas, is not an empty formula or an end in itself, since its ethical character rests on the fact that reason is ordered to God: it is the *means* by which man orders his acts, and therefore himself, to God. It is necessary that "all . . . things that are in man's power are ordered under reason" precisely because "man's mind is subordinated to God."[78] Here too, the order of ethical justification is quite clear: from the requirement to order (our) acts to the ultimate end (major premise), given that man acts by making use of sensible goods and that in this he can either draw nearer to or farther from God (minor premise), is derived the general duty to order sensible goods ultimately to God, i.e., to use them so that they bring one closer to Him (conclusion).[79] Here again, divine law intervenes as an *auxilium* in order to bring into focus and make specific man's moral duty in such a way that "his lower powers may be

75 Ibid.

76 Ibid., III, ch. 121.

77 Ibid.

78 Ibid., III, ch. 129.

79 The logical sequence of the syllogism can be clarified by expressing it more crudely: (a) all free acts must have God as their ultimate object; (b) some free acts have the use of sensible goods as their immediate object; (c) the use of sensible goods must have God as their ultimate object.

subject to reason, and his body to his soul, and . . . external things may subserve the needs of man."[80]

From the need to order the internal passions and the use of sensible goods to the ultimate end, Aquinas derives a very important consequence: namely, that the criterion of the morality or immorality of human acts is not constituted solely by the possibility of *offending one's neighbor*. In Thomistic ethics, even those precepts that pertain to the private, nonpublic sphere of the person are included within the scope of divine and natural law. Consequently, they can be interpreted *lato sensu* as legal precepts, since the ultimate *otherness* of justice is given by the relationship between man and God.[81]

(c) After the precepts regarding the worship of God and those regarding the use of sensible things, St. Thomas goes on to consider those regarding other human beings, because "among all those things which come within the use of man, the most important are other men," and more than in anything else, it is in his relations with other people that he can either approach or distance himself from God. In fact, man is a "social animal": he needs the other, and is helped by the other "both in regard to knowledge and to love. For men are of mutual assistance to each other in the knowing of truth, and one man may stimulate another toward the good, and also restrain him from evil." For this reason, especially in their reciprocal relations, men must behave "according to the order of reason," so that they do not impede, but assist one another "in the attaining of their common end."[82]

The rational justification of this class of precepts is parallel to that of the previous class. Given that human acts are ultimately to be ordered to God (major premise), and given that many human acts have as their object other men (minor premise), it follows that there is an ethical requirement to order relations with other men ultimately to God (conclusion). Within this field of justification come all the Commandments of the Second Table. Once again, finally, the divine law intervenes as an *auxilium*, because its end is "for man to cling to God," and it is therefore its task to guide man "to observe the order of reason in regard to all things that can come to his use," including other men. "It is necessary," then, "for man to

80 Aquinas, *CG*, III, ch. 121.

81 "Hereby is excluded the error of such as say that those acts alone are sinful, whereby our neighbor is either hurt or shocked" (ibid.).

82 Ibid., III, ch. 128.

be instructed by divine law, so that he may live in relation to other men, according to the order of reason."[83]

4.3. Intention of the Ultimate End and the Order of Reason

The foregoing treatment of the three classes of precepts of divine law discussed in the *Summa contra gentiles* has led us to conclude that for Aquinas, the various precepts of divine positive law are meant to sustain and support the natural order, which is inherently normative and has as its ultimate end the knowledge and love of God. In particular, the actual presence of the ultimate end in the intention of the agent emerges as the ultimate ethical truth of human action, rendering actions not only good and evil in an absolute sense, but *more or less good* and *more or less evil.*

Ultimate end, however, does not mean the *one and only end.* Aside from the first class of precepts, which, aiming directly at the worship of God, do not strictly speaking require the *use* of created goods but rather their *offering*, the justification of the other two classes requires a connection between the intention of the ultimate end, and respect for other ends according to some "rational order." These precepts, in the last analysis, imply a reference to something else: what they say is that, in order for the human soul to be able to turn to God, man needs to follow "the order of reason" in the various ends that shape his actions. This appears quite plainly in the explanation of the second class of precepts where, with regard to "sensible things," there is a "due" use (that is, a due *end*) that *may* draw man toward God, and an "improper" end or use that *may* either "slow down the journey" toward Him or "completely distance" the human soul from Him. Therefore, in order to realize the due end, one must regulate the use of sensible things with reason. But the same clearly holds for relations with other men, the object of the third class of precepts.

To understand the way in which St. Thomas conceives of human nature, we need to bear in mind not only (a) that it has a unique ultimate end and good that responds to the most basic demands and needs of reason and will, and that this ultimate end is the knowledge and love of God, but also (b) that human nature is not simple but composite, and consequently possesses, at different levels, a multiplicity of demands and needs linked to a multiplicity of goods capable of satisfying them according to a certain natural proportion; (c) that among the different needs and the

83 Ibid.

goods that satisfy them, we can recognize an order such that some goods are instrumental to others, and all are instrumental to man's ultimate end; and finally (d) that one can have objective knowledge of the ultimate end, of the variety of and differences between human needs and goods, and of the order that exists between them; such knowledge, however, like all human knowledge, is *intentional*, and though it may attain some certainties, taken as a whole it is always perfectible and gradual.

In Thomas's ethics and anthropology, therefore, man has a *natural* love for his ultimate end but also a *natural* love for every one of the partial ends that structure him as a being composed of soul and body. Natural love of partial ends depends intentionally on the love of self and, by itself, is not capable of transcending this love: in other words, natural love of partial ends cannot be separated from the love of concupiscence. Only love (of friendship) for God is capable of raising the pursuit of partial ends beyond the narrow dimension of concupiscence.

To follow the order of reason means to respect the proper good of each part of man, pursuing it according to a certain natural proportion, and according to its ordination to the other parts and to the whole (that is, to the unique end of the whole man). Hence, the key concepts for understanding the order of reason are: proper end or good, natural measure or proportion, and hierarchy. Before dwelling on these concepts, however, we need to turn briefly to the connection between the intention of the ultimate end and the order of reason (or the natural order).

In the first place, it should be pointed out that the expression "order of reason" may be misleading because it is susceptible to at least two different meanings. In its fullest sense, it encompasses the ordering of all things to God (or the natural love of God) as the ultimate end, while in another sense it encompasses only respect for partial ends. The sense relevant to our present discussion is the second. This is why respect for the order of reason in the use, for example, of sensible things, "*may*" draw us closer to God but does not *necessarily* do so. The order of reason, here, is only "the proper use" of certain human goods, not their ultimate intentional ordering: a man who stays in good physical health does not necessarily intend thereby to realize God's designs as well, or to order his energies and freedom ultimately to the end of giving glory to God. In short, the connection between the intention of the ultimate end and the order of reason in its second sense is not automatic.

The most important question for us, however, is why the intention of the ultimate end, for Aquinas, requires respect for a natural, objective order. How can one justify, on the basis of the pursuit of the ultimate end, the duty to follow "the order of reason" in the spheres of action pertinent to the various types of precepts? We have already touched on the ethical answer, which is simply that the natural order, in all its parts, is *willed by God* (which, as we saw in chapter two, man recognizes through natural or philosophic reason, in the tension of the ontological moment). In order to verify the soundness of this claim, it is sufficient to look at some of the central arguments that St. Thomas offers in chapter 126 to demonstrate that "carnal union" is not in itself morally evil. To demonstrate this, it is not enough merely to observe that it constitutes the "natural end of certain bodily members" or that it responds to a "natural inclination of the species." The decisive argument is, rather, that the nature of things responds to a precise divine disposition.

Let us consider the passages most directly involved: "[2] . . . the use of certain bodily organs is carnal union. So, carnal union is the end of certain bodily organs. But that which is the end of certain natural things (*finis aliquarum naturalium rerum*) cannot be evil in itself, because things that exist naturally (*ea quae naturaliter sunt*) are ordered to their end by divine providence. . . . Therefore, it is impossible for carnal union to be evil in itself. [3] Besides, natural inclinations (*naturales inclinationes*) are present in things from God, Who moves all things. So, it is impossible for the natural inclination of a species to be toward what is evil in itself. But there is in all perfect animals a natural inclination toward carnal union. Therefore, it is impossible for carnal union to be evil in itself."[84]

These arguments are taken up again at the beginning of the next chapter, where St. Thomas proposes to demonstrate "that the use of food is not a sin in itself." The argument goes like this: "Just as the exercise of sexual capacities is without sin, provided it be carried on with reason, so also in the case of the use of food. Now, any action is performed in accord with reason when it is ordered in keeping with what befits its proper end. But the proper end (*finis debitus*) of taking food is the preservation of the body by nutrition. So, whatever food can contribute to this end may be taken without sin. Therefore, the taking of food is not in itself a sin."[85]

The theonomic basis for the rectitude of the natural inclinations is expressed in no uncertain terms in the *Summa theologiae* with regard to the natural love of men and of angels: "As natural knowledge [that is, the intellectual knowledge that does not depend on reason's discursive process] is always true (*vera*), so is natural love well regulated (*recta*);

84 Aquinas, *CG*, III, ch. 126.
85 Ibid., III, ch. 127.

because natural love is nothing else than the inclination implanted in nature by its Author. To say that a natural inclination is not well regulated (*recta*), is to derogate from the Author of nature."[86]

Objective knowledge of natural ends and inclinations is not, by itself, sufficient to ground morality; on the other hand, the appeal to the will of God is not in St. Thomas a voluntaristic assertion, since it is by natural love that man "loves the will of God before himself and with a greater love," and also because man recognizes that *God wills* what in His wisdom He has planned in the most perfect way possible. The ordering of every part of human nature is thus what most perfectly realizes the good of the whole man, and, at the same time, constitutes the set of conditions in which he can come to recognize God and acknowledge Him as his own end, without "setting the end of his will in inferior things" or "attaching himself to them more than is necessary."

The doctrine of natural ends ceases to have a factualistic or voluntaristic flavor within an anthropology that, like Thomas's, shuns even the most minimal dualism between body and soul, to the point of positing a necessary connection between actions—even the most material ones—and the intentions of the person who chooses them. Given this connection, a person's actions can lead him, in the last analysis either to a closed search for himself or toward an attitude of openness to reality, and ultimately, to God. Respect for natural ends, according to Aquinas, shapes our intentions in such a way that it disposes us to accept our creaturely condition and opens us to God. In other words, a right natural love for the various human goods (that is, a love in conformity with God's created order) in itself directs man's intention toward a right love for the Creator of the whole universe. This is a certainty that undoubtedly comes to St. Thomas from faith, but it is also entirely consistent with that part of his metaphysics in which he explains the creation of things and the existence of God.

If the *proper* (*debitus*) use of human things of itself directs man's intention toward the love of God, the reverse is also true: if one's ultimate intention rests in God, this of itself leads one to respect the natural order. In the things around him, man may ultimately see only opportunities for realizing himself, and this leads toward an attitude of arbitrary manipulation. Alternatively, he may see in these things the reflection of a will that transcends himself and is the repository of his own true good and that of

86 Aquinas, *ST*, I, q. 60, a. 1 ad 3.

the whole universe, and this leads him toward an attitude of understanding, care, and respect.

In Thomistic philosophy, then, it is possible to know objectively the goods and properties of the human being independently of a consideration of God; on this point I agree, for example, with Anthony Lisska's recent observations.[87] According to this same philosophy, however, we can also objectively know God, human nature is made ultimately for Him, and a strictly ethical, i.e., absolute, respect for the order of reason comes from an awareness, whether spontaneous (common sense) or reflexive, of the creatureliness of this order and of its ordering to God.[88] For these reasons, I can agree neither with Lisska nor with any other interpretation of St. Thomas that attempts, in any way, to derive from his thought the idea of an ethics without God. At this point, however, I would like to consider in greater detail the problem of the content of the order of reason, in the second sense that we have distinguished: that is as concerning not the ordering of things to God, but only respect for partial ends.

4.4. Proper End, Natural Measure, and Hierarchy

The principal goal of the present section is to illustrate the method by which St. Thomas in the *Contra gentiles* shows the goodness and badness of certain acts, starting from the observation of one or more natural ends of the human being. We already know that the path to follow in this regard is connected to the intention of the ultimate end and to the way in which the order of reason influences this intention. More particularly, we know that the wickedness of the *improper use* of human things formally consists in the removal of man's intention from God, causing him *to set the end of his will in inferior things* or *to attach himself to them more than is necessary*. We also know that the notion of the order of reason or natural order can be understood through the concepts of proper end, natural measure, and hierarchy. I will now attempt to contextualize and to deepen our understanding of these concepts so that we can subsequently proceed directly to the particular cases discussed by Aquinas.

87 A. Lisska, *Aquinas's Theory of Natural Law: An Analytic Reconstruction*, esp. ch. V.

88 Among contemporary interpreters of St. Thomas, Simon decisively maintains the necessity of recourse to God as the basis for the normativity of the natural order: Y. Simon, *The Tradition of Natural Law: A Philosopher's Reflections*, pp. 62–63, 136–45. It seems to me, however, that Simon does not sufficiently emphasize the practical, or ethical aspect of reference to God.

Let us begin with a deeper clarification of several points regarding the general doctrine of natural ends. This doctrine can be summed up as follows: reality, as the object of a free, creative act, is intrinsically purposeful both in its totality and in each of its parts, because each and every free act cannot but be performed in view of a given end. For the same reason, within each created thing the end of any part is ordered to the end of the whole, because the part is willed by the agent precisely as a part. This ordering of reality is objectively revealed in the necessary movement of things toward determinate ends (in other words, in their rational movement), on account of which we say that they possess natural inclinations toward these ends. The end of each thing, then, is said to be its good, because good is an analogical concept indicating that toward which something or someone tends, that which is sought or desired: "When we say that good is what all desire, it is not to be understood that every kind of good thing is desired by all; but that whatever is desired has the nature of good (*ratio boni*)."[89] The ends of natural inclinations are thus the natural or ontological goods of things.

In man, the natural inclinations basically act in two ways:

(1) Some involve necessary movements that occur independently of the exercise of freedom—for example, the circulation of blood or the growth of hair (or the growth of the organism in general), as well as most other biological functions. In these both the specific end of the individual parts and their reciprocal ordering and harmony are evident (think, for example, of the coordinated action of the organs of the digestive system).

(2) Other inclinations depend on free choices, in the sense that their operation is filtered through the exercise of rational action, either (a) *normally but not necessarily*, as occurs with nutrition or sexual union (a man decides to eat or to have sexual intercourse with a woman, but he can realize either function unconsciously, under the influence of medical treatment or purely by the operation of instinct, as is noted in the behavior of some madmen); or (b) *of necessity*, as in artistic contemplation or friendship in its various forms (as distinct from mere *sociabilitas*, which is common to other animals as well). These last inclinations cannot be separated from the exercise of freedom because they always have as their object the good as *universal*, i.e., rational, or as *chosen*. Consequently, they presuppose a state of consciousness on the part of the agent, and in this way they can properly be described as inclinations of the rational or spiritual part of the human being.

89 Aquinas, *ST*, I, q. 6, a. 2 ad 2.

Usually, these distinctions are made in relation not to the inclinations but to the acts that spring from them in view of their natural ends. Thus, the distinction just explained corresponds perfectly to the classical distinction in ethics between "acts of man" and "human acts," which we discussed in chapter 2, section 4.3, "The Formal Object of Ethics."[90] By putting the emphasis on the inclinations, we can bring home more forcefully the fact that the movement of things toward their ends should always be understood as an act that is necessary and basic, even when, as in the case of man, freedom enters the picture.

The twofold mode of operation of human inclinations should not be absolutized, for there are some inclinations that are more difficult to interpret—think, for example, of the relation between mere play (which can perhaps, in some cases at least, take place without rational awareness) and joking or irony (which seem invariably to require rational awareness). Similarly, there can be other inclinations of a biological character, normally independent of the use of reason, that are partly subject to it some of the time—for example, breathing or the beating of the heart (which some people, it seems, do manage to control partially in certain conditions). In any case, what matters is that in normal conditions, a series of inclinations exert pressure on man's free actions, making themselves felt as needs to be satisfied and pointing to their proper ends as goods to be attained (to put it more vividly, one might say that man does not choose his proper goods but is subject to them).

All these inclinations flow, as a matter of necessity, from the unique inclination of man's volitional faculty to pursue in every deliberation the good known by the intellect (the so-called *voluntas ut natura*). Moreover, the intellect always knows the good in its rationality: it knows, for example, the objective reason for eating, and that there is a way of eating proportionate to that reason; and it always knows the good of the parts as a function of the good of the whole, which on some occasions requires eating, on others playing, sleeping, praying, etc., according to a certain order and hierarchy (the so-called *voluntas ut ratio*).

From the point of view of rational knowledge of the good, which controls free choices, the order of intention of individual goods is always encompassed and controlled by the intention of the ultimate good (this is true not only for natural self-love in the ontic moment, but also for natural love of God in the ontological moment), and this solves the problem of

90 On this distinction see especially A.R. Luño, *Etica*, pp. 6–9. See also Y. Simon, *The Tradition of Natural Law: A Philosopher's Reflections*, pp. 78–82.

the mutual incommensurability of ends.[91] I can choose, for example, to play football instead of eating a sandwich because I believe that *for me, now, it is good* to play football (or that God prefers that I play football now). This is not an absolute and abstract judgment that football is a good for me and sandwiches are not, but a contextualized ordering of particular ends in view of the good of the whole. This good, insofar as it is my ultimate end, relativizes all partial goods as *means* (*voluntas ut ratio*).

Choosing particular goods in view of the ultimate end is like choosing, in view of the good overall condition of a car, whether this is the best time to change the tires or to check the oil. Although tires and oil are in themselves different and incommensurable things, they nonetheless fall under a single criterion of choice, given the objective and partial functions that they fulfill in the car. The term "good" is always relative to something or someone (in the sense that something is always good for something or someone). For this reason, simply to speak of several goods already entails relativizing and comparing them with respect to the single unified good of a composite entity. In this context, the opening of Aristotle's *Nicomachean Ethics* is especially helpful:

> . . . as there are numerous pursuits and arts and sciences, it follows that their ends are correspondingly numerous: for instance, the end of the science of medicine is health, that of the art of shipbuilding a vessel, that of strategy victory, that of domestic economy wealth. Now in cases where several such pursuits are subordinate to some single faculty—as bridle-making and the other trades concerned with horses' harness are subordinate to horsemanship, and this and every other military pursuit to the science of strategy, and similarly other arts to different arts again—in all these cases, I say, the ends of the master

91 I have already mentioned that the exponents of the neoclassical school of natural law have denied the existence of an ultimate end in human action, attempting to gain leverage from the concept of the incommensurability of different human goods. They used to maintain that this is the only way to offer a radical critique of consequentialism because, with no measuring stick common to all goods, there cannot logically be a calculation of the greater good or lesser evil. This neoclassical position is well-represented by Finnis, *Fundamentals of Ethics*; and Grisez, "Against Consequentialism," *American Journal of Jurisprudence*, 23 (1978). For an interesting critique of this position, see M.J. Perry, "Some Notes on Absolutism, Consequentialism, and Incommensurability," *North Western University Law Review*, 79 (1985). As mentioned in the Introduction, I have developed my own critique of the neoclassical position on incommensurability in my article, "I valori fondamentali nella teoria neoclassica della legge naturale."

> arts are things more to be desired than all those of the arts subordinate to them; since the latter ends are only pursued for the sake of the former. (And it makes no difference whether the ends of the pursuits are the activities themselves or some other thing beside these, as in the case of the sciences mentioned.)
>
> If therefore among the ends at which our actions aim there be one which we wish for its own sake, while we wish the others only for the sake of this, and if we do not choose everything for the sake of something else (which would obviously result in a process ad infinitum, so that all desire would be futile and vain), it is clear that this one ultimate End must be the Good, and indeed the Supreme Good.[92]

And again:

> Are we then to suppose that, while the carpenter and the shoemaker have definite functions or businesses belonging to them, man as such has none, and is not designed by nature to fulfil any function? Must we not rather assume that, just as the eye, the hand, the foot and each of the various members of the body manifestly has a certain function of its own, so a human being also has a certain function over and above all the functions of his particular members?[93]

The fallibility of a concrete choice (due to the difficulty of determining what the good of the whole requires here and now), or its apparent irrationality (I choose a sandwich because right now, I prefer to eat a sandwich) does not take away in the slightest from the fact that the condition of its possibility is the intentional reference to the good of the whole (even the criterion of pleasure transcends the individual, partial good by treating it as a means to the complete good).

It is hardly necessary to repeat that man's ultimate good (the good of the whole), which corresponds to the most fundamental inclination of the soul, is neither some sort of material well-being, understood as the maximal satisfaction of all the other inclinations, nor simply an Aristotelian "living in accord with reason," but rather a good that in its fullness goes beyond all the finitude and contingency of this world and responds to man's deepest aspirations to eternity and happiness; for Aquinas, the ultimate good is "the knowledge and the love of God." Man understands that

92 Aristotle, *Nicomachean Ethics*, I, 1, 1094a6–22.

93 Ibid., I, 6, 1097b29–34. On this relation between the ultimate end and the plurality of goods, see H. Veatch, *Human Rights: Fact or Fancy?*, pp. 79–81.

to this good, a good fully proportionate to our free choices, all other things are subordinate. Obviously, man's knowledge of the ultimate good is intentional, and therefore admits of various degrees.

Let us now move on to the concept of natural measure. Among the needs relating to the inclinations and the goods that satisfy them, there is a certain natural proportion without which man is left more or less frustrated, and as Maritain would put it does not "function" well.[94] Such proportionality responds to the order established by God, and at the same time determines man's greatest good, his greatest perfection and likeness to God. For Aquinas, the most obvious example has to do with food: "man has this natural endowment, he may use lower things for the needs of his life. Now, there is a definite measure according to which the use of the aforesaid things is proper to human life, and if this measure is set aside the result is harmful to man, as is evident in the immoderate eating of food. Therefore, there are some human acts that are naturally fitting and others that are naturally unfitting."[95] The existence of a natural proportion can easily be verified not only with regard to the example of food, but with regard to all human goods, even spiritual goods, which if enjoyed insufficiently leave man in a state of need and desire, and if pursued out excessively create boredom, fatigue, and even nausea.

Finally, a brief remark on hierarchy. It has already clearly emerged that besides the natural measure applicable to individual goods, St. Thomas maintains that there is among the various needs or goods a hierarchy or objective order that maintains the importance of particular goods while at the same time relativizing them in view of a higher exigency. Aquinas is very clear on this point: "since our nature is composed of the spiritual and the corporeal, there are several goods for us. Our good in regard to understanding is indeed different from what it is according to sensation, or even according to the body. Now, there is a certain order of these various things that are man's goods, based on the fact that what is less primary is subordinated to what is more primary."[96]

The activities of the mouth, the stomach and the intestines, for example, are secondary compared to the entire digestive system, and the digestive system is secondary compared to the preservation of the organism. St.

94 I am referring, of course, to his "ontological element of the natural law": the "normality of functioning." See J. Maritain, *Nove lezioni sulla legge naturale*, pp. 43–48.

95 Aquinas, *CG*, III, ch. 129.

96 Ibid., III, ch. 108.

Thomas expresses this succinctly, saying that "the proper end of taking food is the preservation of the body by nutrition."[97] Where necessary, what is secondary can be sacrificed—all medical ethics is based on this principle. Even the preservation of the organism, though necessary in itself, is secondary relative to its functioning; in the case of a human being, it is secondary, above all, relative to the exercise of freedom. This is why in extreme cases, the sacrifice of life for the sake of a higher value is not seen by common sense to be something immoral.

As I pointed out earlier, the concept of hierarchy characteristic of Thomistically-inspired classical ethics has recently been questioned by certain interpretations, particularly those of John Finnis and Germain Grisez, on the basis of their analysis of the basic values of human existence.[98] The ensuing debate has given rise to numerous criticisms of this sort of interpretation, including, among the more authoritative, those of Ralph McInerny, Richard McCormick and Russell Hittinger.[99]

In addition to the observations already made, and aside from the serious problems of consistency in the theory of Finnis and Grisez, on which I cannot dwell here,[100] I believe that a large part of the difficulty associated with this particular issue arises from an approach typical of contemporary analytic philosophy which, concentrating excessively on the analysis of reasoning, easily loses sight of the objective reality of the human being who is the repository of that reasoning activity. Particularly illuminating in this regard are Veatch's reflections on the "transcendental" [or, we might add, "immanentistic,"] turn" that has characterized modern thought from Descartes on, and which gives rise to the "linguistic turn" in contemporary philosophy.[101] It is not a matter of underestimating the impor-

97 Ibid., III, ch. 127.

98 See especially, G. Grisez, *The Way of the Lord Jesus*, vol. I, "Christian Moral Principles," p. 156; J. Finnis, *Natural Law and Natural Rights*, pp. 92–93.

99 See R. McInerny, "The Principles of Natural Law," pp. 10–11; R.A. McCormick, *Notes on Moral Theology: 1981–1984* (Lanham, Md.: University Press of America, 1985), p. 136; R. Hittinger, *A Critique of the New Natural Law Theory*, pp. 23–24, 74–79.

100 For an examination of these problems see my article, "I valori fondamentali nella teoria neoclassica della legge naturale."

101 See especially Veatch's *For an Ontology of Morals*; and *Human Rights: Fact or Fancy?* For an explicit critique by Veatch of Finnis and Grisez, see also "Natural Law and the 'Is-Ought' Question: Queries to Finnis and Grisez"; and (with Rautenberg) "Does the Grisez-Finnis-Boyle Moral Philosophy Rest on a Mistake?" On the linguistic turn in contemporary philosophy, see M. Jori (ed.),

tance of logical coherence in moral reasoning, but of taking care to avoid a reductive attitude or vision when one sets about reflecting on the human being and his behavior.

4.5. The Morality and Immorality of Acts

The clarifications we have made concerning the meaning of proper end, natural measure, and hierarchy should convey more precisely how, for St. Thomas, to offend God is at the same time to act against one's own good. Moral evil, or sin,[102] must always in one way or another be the violation of one or more of these three elements. This is the so-called *objective morality* (or the objective aspect of the morality) of human acts.

Moral evil, however, should never be understood as a sort of material violation but always as "a disorder of the will."[103] A simple mistake about the goodness of a food can cause death but not necessarily sin; and a mistake about a moral norm (concerning order and proportion in the pursuit of the good) can also be inculpable and may entail no responsibility for an evil act; indeed, it may even merit praise for (the intention of) the one who carried it out. Sin always comes about when "we desire what is only relatively good for us, in opposition to what is absolutely good."[104] This is the *subjective morality* of human acts, which depends on the intention of the agent.

The distinction between objective and subjective morality is very important in classical ethics, but it should obviously be understood in an analogical sense, without absolutizing it. From a comprehensive point of view, such as to include also the inclinations of the intellect and the will, and thus the natural ordering of free human acts, even a disorder in the will should be seen as an objective violation of the moral order.

I must now show how, as far as the intentionality of the agent is concerned, moral evil is always characterized in the Thomistic doctrine as an error concerning the ultimate end, which normally leads to further errors concerning other objective aspects of the morality of acts.

We have seen that to every natural inclination there corresponds an

Ermeneutica e filosofia analitica: Due concezioni del diritto a confronto (Turin: Giappichelli, 1994), especially M. Jori's introduction and the essays by F. Viola, "La critica dell'ermeneutica alla filosofia analitica italiana del diritto," and G. Zaccaria, "Tra ermeneutica ed analitica: dal contrasto alla collaborazione."

102 The two concepts coincide to the extent that violation of the order willed by God is considered to be the root of moral evil.

103 Aquinas, *CG*, III, ch. 127.

104 Ibid., ch. 108.

objective end or good whose satisfaction, according to a certain order and a certain measure, contributes to the good of the whole. We can take a further step by saying that the satisfaction of any inclination necessarily has a subjective element, pleasure, which can be anything from mere physical well-being due to the proper functioning of the organism, or the amusement of play, to the rational satisfaction of scientific, personal or professional achievement, or the interior peace that comes from acting in accord with one's conscience.

In Aristotelian-Thomistic philosophy, it is not objectively possible to separate pleasure from the ends of the natural inclinations, because pleasure is precisely the subjective side of the objective satisfaction of a need or potentiality of the human being. Anyone who experiences pleasure experiences it by virtue of some objective feature, whether bodily or spiritual, of human nature. To every proper end there thus corresponds a certain pleasure, which increases or decreases depending on one's respect for the natural measure or the order between goods. Thus sin, for St. Thomas, besides violating the human good, also diminishes pleasure, which is not in itself evil but an intrinsic aspect of the good.

The objective end of the inclinations, with the measure and order that characterize it, is the *moral good* (*bonum honestum*). Pleasure is the *pleasurable good* (*bonum delectabile*). The moral good and the pleasurable good are the two basic forms under which the good presents itself to human consciousness; the *useful good* is only "the means by which." In the *Summa theologiae*, the moral good is defined in relation to the "movement of the appetite," as that which is "sought after as the last thing absolutely terminating the movement of the appetite, as a thing towards which for its own sake the appetite (*appetitus*) tends." The pleasurable good, on the other hand, is "that which terminates the movement of the appetite in the form of rest in the thing desired." And the useful good is "the thing desired that terminates the movement of the appetite relatively, as a means by which something tends toward another."[105]

The moral good and the pleasurable good are not in themselves opposed. On the contrary, they are bound up with each other: the maximum of one corresponds to the maximum of the other. Man, however, is capable of artificially separating the two (according to Catholic theology, especially because of the disorder introduced by original sin), distorting the objective good for the sake of the ultimate pursuit of pleasure (broad-

105 Aquinas, *ST*, I, q. 5, a. 6 c.

ly understood) alone. It is this separation that is the source of the moral evil of a fundamentally egoistic intentionality, expressed by St. Thomas, as we have seen, in terms of "setting the end of the will in lower things" or "attaching oneself to them more than is necessary." The evil of this intentional act ultimately resides in the fact that one ultimately seeks in such an act oneself alone and not God (*aversio a Deo et conversio ad creaturam*).[106] The argument described earlier concerning the second class of precepts is, in this sense, general in scope, as suggested by the reference not only to "sensible things" but to "interior sentiments," and to the acts of the third class aimed at other men.

Thus understood—as an unnatural separation between moral good and pleasurable good and the pursuit of the latter to the detriment of the former—moral evil may be characterized as an *error* concerning the ultimate end; provided, that is, that we are speaking of a *culpable* error, i.e., an error committed by someone who, in one way or another, has ignored or silenced a demand of his conscience to the effect that a given action, though attractive/unattractive (pleasant/less pleasant), should/should not be done, or done in this or that way, because it is objectively good/evil. In light of the dimension of error and moral reasoning, one can more easily and adequately grasp the meaning of the expression used to indicate morally upright action, *recta ratio agibilium*.

One might nevertheless wonder how all of this is possible. That is, how is it possible, given the action of the inclinations—in itself ordered—and given the objectivity of the good and its coextensiveness with pleasure, that man, in the pursuit of pleasure, should intentionally cut himself off from the moral good? In fact, he cannot help pursuing the good that presents itself as such to his consciousness, and the action of the inclinations should lead him, by itself, to knowledge of his genuine good. The answer to this question rests on the interaction between two cardinal principles of Thomistic philosophy: the non-self-evidence of God's existence

106 One can easily glimpse in this rational explanation the heart of the Christian moral tradition, expressed admirably by St. Augustine through the metaphor of the two loves generated by the terrestrial and heavenly cities respectively: "two cities have been formed by two loves: the earthly by the love of self, even to the contempt of God; the heavenly by the love of God, even to the contempt of self. The former, in a word, glories in itself, the latter in the Lord. For the one seeks glory from men; but the greatest glory of the other is God, the witness of conscience" (St. Augustine, *City of God*, trans. Marcus Dods, D.D. [New York: The Modern Library, 1950], book 14, ch. 28).

for the human mind; and the existence in man of a principle of disorder (evil) that is easy to encounter in experience but whose existence remains, in itself, philosophically inexplicable.

For Aquinas, man does not know God directly in this life, but can know Him only through created reality, in a veiled, imperfect, and confused way (the "direct vision" of God is supernatural beatitude, which is, by definition, beyond the reach of human capacities). Now the fact that the ultimate good in itself (what it is exactly) is not to be found among the immediate conceptions of the human intellect, but necessarily requires reasoning, makes it objectively possible for the intellect to be mistaken in its understanding of the good or in treating as the ultimate end something that is not the ultimate end. And the will, although it is ultimately ordered to God, cannot help pursuing as the ultimate good whatever is presented to it as such by the intellect. In the Catholic tradition, this mistake is often expressed through the scriptural metaphor of *idols*. Man cannot do without God, and his mistake leads him to *idolize* something, that is, to treat as an absolute end something that is not an absolute end: one's profession, study or some other passion, or even one's wife, one's house, a humanitarian cause, etc.

St. Thomas stresses in the *Summa theologiae* that the non-self-evidence of God's existence is the basis for the possibility of moral evil, explaining that the natural tendency to "love God before oneself and with a greater love" is also retained in the sinner. "Since God's substance and universal goodness are one and the same, all who behold God's essence are by the same movement of love moved toward the Divine essence as it is distinct from other things, and according as it is the universal good. And because He is naturally loved by all so far as He is the universal good, it is impossible that whoever sees Him in His essence should not love Him. But such as do not behold His essence, know Him by some particular effects, which are sometimes opposed to their will. So in this way they are said to hate God; yet nevertheless, so far as He is the universal good of all, every thing naturally loves God more than itself."[107] Moreover, in the treatise on the ultimate end, while explaining that all men have the same ultimate end, he says that "those who sin turn from that in which their ultimate end really consists," but "they do not turn away from the intention of the ultimate end, which intention they mistakenly seek in other things."[108]

The non-self-evidence of God's existence thus functions as the objec-

107 Aquinas, *ST*, I, q. 60, a. 5 ad 5.
108 Ibid., I-II, q. 1, a. 7 ad 1.

tive condition of possibility of moral evil, but the fact remains that it would be difficult for an ideally *perfect* human to err since his inclinations would, of themselves, lead him toward the ordered exercise of his powers, including those of the intellect and the will. The possibility of mistaking the objective good is, however, facilitated by the operation in man (and in all things) of a *principle of disorder* that sometimes separates, in the short term, the moral good from the pleasurable (just as, due to disease, eating may be unpleasant even if it is good, or due to the scarcity of material resources the good of one person can appear bad for another) and always removes harmony and proportion from the action of the various human powers. In this condition the intellect reasons with difficulty, easily substituting pleasure for the true good and thereby suffering the influence of the disorder that affects the passions and other inclinations—above all the will, which discovers within itself a perverse tendency to desire the good for its own benefit (pleasure) rather than turning to what is good in itself.

In this situation of objective disorder, rectitude of action requires effort and sacrifice to restrain the disordered impulse toward pleasure, redirecting it toward the quest for the moral good—which at the same time automatically implies a better knowledge of and quest for God.

In light of this brief synthesis, one can also intuitively grasp the consistency between Aquinas's philosophical view and his theological approach to heavenly beatitude. Once in possession of a perfect vision of God, unmediated by creatures and freed from the disorder caused by sin, man *will no longer be able to sin*, receiving thereby not a privation but a perfection of freedom. In fact, freedom consists formally in choosing (in willing) the known good, and evil is always an error concerning the good, that is, a lack of freedom in relation to the true good. The person who knows perfectly cannot but always choose perfectly, enjoying perfectly the chosen good.

Given the clarifications provided in the last few sections regarding the natural order and its complexity and ethical relevance, and also regarding the intentionality of the moral agent, we can now move on to analyze directly some specific cases discussed by Aquinas.

4.6. Fornication and Marriage

The cases I have in mind are taken up by St. Thomas as examples of the second class of precepts of the divine law, which concerns sensible goods (the first and third classes concern acts of worship and acts toward one's fellow human beings). This class takes on a central importance in our discussion not only because Aquinas himself, as already mentioned, includes in it both sensible things and interior feelings, but also because he explicitly presents the third class as an application of the principle enunciated in the second. The third class arises out of the observation that "among all those things which come within the use of man, the most important are other men." As we shall see in a moment, the second class of precepts contains the idea, fundamental for Aquinas, that morality resides essentially not in man's will but in God's, and that respect for the will of God presupposes respect for the nature of created things, that is, for their natural ends.

In chapter 122 of book III of the *Contra gentiles*, St. Thomas addresses the following bipartite question: "The reason why simple fornication is a sin according to divine law, and that matrimony is natural." By way of introduction, we can condense the overall structure of the argument into two denials and two affirmations: (1) Aquinas denies that the wickedness of fornication resides in the offense or scandal given to other people; (2) he denies that it resides *simply* in the offense against the will of God; (3) he affirms that fornication is bad because it is contrary to the natural end of the emission of semen; (4) he affirms that marriage is natural because necessary for the education of offspring. Faced with this very rough sketch of the argument, however, it is essential to avoid the risk of any depreciation or trivialization of the theses involved in it. To this end, we must proceed by connecting them with the conclusions already reached in the preceding sections.

First of all, with regard to what we saw in section 4.2, "Correspondence with the Natural Order," it should be pointed out that we are dealing here with a typical Thomistic treatment of *natural law*, understood as a reasoned defense of *divine law*. One should not be deceived by the reference in the title to divine law. This reference entails two things: (a) that the existence of precepts of divine positive law prohibiting fornication and affirming the good of marriage is undisputed; and (b) that the chapter is meant to supply the *reason* for such precepts according to the natural order.

In addition, I should clarify that Aquinas does not have in mind, with regard to fornication, the emission of semen, or marriage, a merely material or factual understanding of human acts. The concept of a human act implies intentionality: if an act is not done "on purpose," consciously and voluntarily, it cannot be a sin, simply because it is not a human act.

Fornication is the consensual act in which two people, free of other bonds, decide to have sexual intercourse without mutually committing themselves to a marital relationship; thus, cases both of violence and of adultery are excluded from the present discussion. The emission of semen is the human act that voluntarily brings about this effect; consequently, events associated with states of unconsciousness such as dreams, drunkenness and madness are excluded. Marriage, finally, is the act by which two persons of opposite sexes give themselves to each other for their whole lives, accepting all the consequences of their union. Human acts are defined (specified) by the intention with which they are done, so that if two free persons engage in a complete sexual act with the intention of giving themselves totally, we must not consider them fornicators but, to all intents and purposes, spouses. It may be useful to recall that in St. Thomas's time, absent modern legal provisions on the form of marriage (which are morally relevant because they affect the intention), marriages could legitimately be contracted—not only according to natural law but also to human law—*re*: not, that is, *verbis vel scriptis* but *per facta concludentia.*[109]

These clarifications allow us to grasp the meaning and the scope of chapter 122. The opening of the chapter ("From the foregoing we can see the futility of the argument of certain people who say that simple fornication is not a sin") is a reminder, a continuation, and a conclusion of the previous chapter, in which the *raison d'etre* of the second class of precepts was explained. This *incipit* suggests that, whatever the specific argument to be presented, the wickedness of the act of fornication depends on its involving an *improper use* of things, such that man's intention is drawn away from God, *leading him to set the end of his will in lower things* or *to attach himself to them more than is necessary.*

(1) Let us now turn to the first of the four steps listed above: the denial that the wickedness of fornication lies in the offense given to other persons. To be precise, St. Thomas denies that consensual fornication either constitutes an injustice toward the partner (or toward his or her guardian), or an injury toward some third party who might be scandalized by the behavior. In this way, he replies to those who deny the illicitness of fornication by appealing to the argument from consent, or by pointing out the weakness of the argument from scandal: he simply accepts the validity of their objections. Let us read, in this regard, the first and third steps of chapter 122:

109 See F. Finocchiaro, *Il matrimonio nel diritto canonico* (Bologna: Il Mulino, 1989), pp. 54–55.

From the foregoing we can see the futility of the argument of certain people who say that simple fornication is not a sin. For they say: Suppose there is a woman who is not married, or under the control of any man, either her father or another man. Now, if a man performs the sexual act with her, and she is willing, he does not injure her, because she favors the action and she has control over her own body. Nor does he injure any other person, because she is understood to be under no other person's control. So, this does not seem to be a sin. . . .

Likewise, it also would seem an inadequate answer to say that some injury is done to one's neighbor by this action, inasmuch as he may be scandalized. Indeed, it is possible for him to be scandalized by something which is not in itself a sin. In this event, the act would be accidentally sinful. But our problem is not whether simple fornication is accidentally (*per accidens*) a sin, but whether it is so essentially (*per se*).[110]

One cannot fail to appreciate the clarity with which St. Thomas lays out his intentions—which suggests that we should avoid making superfluous comments. Precisely because in the case in question an injustice—in the form of a violation of the freedom of the partner—cannot be maintained, Aquinas looks for another objective cause for the wickedness of the act. And precisely because this other cause must be objective, it cannot reside merely in people's beliefs. This is, without a doubt, the simplest and most comprehensible interpretation of the passage. For our purposes it is nonetheless important to stress that behind Aquinas's every reference to an objective order of human good, there are always (a) the idea that the goodness or evil of actions is not based merely on man's will, and (b) the immediate appeal to a transcendent ethical foundation.

Here it is important not to misunderstand the opening words of the passage quoted above. The absence of injustice (due to the consensual nature of the act) in simple fornication does not mean that in the order of justice, the morality of behavior depends on the arbitrary will of the parties, but only that in this order, evil presupposes the unjustified violation of another person's freedom. Therefore, when St. Thomas turns soon afterwards (in chapter 128) to the precepts of the third class, pertaining to the order of justice, he does not base them ultimately on the violation of the will of another. Rather, the order of justice, which makes possible

110 Aquinas, *CG*, III, ch. 122.

"among men . . . an ordered concord, or peace," is identified as the natural order (of reason) of human relations, *willed by God* for the "attainment of the common end" by all. Man's freedom, in other words, is willed by God and is the natural (objective) aspect of the order of justice; the axiological foundation of this order, however, remains the will of God.

From this point of view, the ethical justification of the third class of precepts is identical to that of the second. The only qualification is that two different types of natural order need to be explained for the two different classes of precepts: the natural order of social relations, on the one hand, and that based on various constitutive aspects of individual human beings, on the other. Without God, neither order could generate a requirement of absolute respect. For acts prohibited by the second class of precepts, moreover, because there is no violation of the natural order of social relations, we must look for a different type of objective violation of the natural order.

There is another way of bringing to light, still at the *incipit* of St. Thomas's argument, the necessity of a transcendent ethical foundation. Given that the consent of the partner implies the absence of any violation of justice, and given that the scandal of third parties may be unfounded, the path that Aquinas takes—as we already know—is to explain that fornication is contrary to the human good independently of the order of justice. Yet why should this be so important as to entail a moral duty?

Let us admit for the sake of argument that fornication, besides the pleasure it gives, does cause some sort of harm. Now if both parties are willing to accept this harm for the sake of the pleasure, why should they not do so? To whom else must they answer in evaluating their own good? And even if they fail to understand fully what their greatest good is, why should they be considered bad? As a matter of choosing one's own *greatest good*, the intention not to fornicate would be identical with the intention to fornicate. If there were no God, even in the presence of an objective order of human good, the individual will would remain the ultimate ethical criterion. However, since the objective order *is* the will of God, and the intentional attitude toward the natural order determines man's attitude toward God, it makes sense for Aquinas to undertake an in-depth study of that order and to propose it as a criterion of morality.

We must now make a further qualification concerning St. Thomas's intentions. If in fact, as we have seen so far, he does not consider simple fornication an injustice toward the consenting partner, it is also true that he does not consider it an injustice toward possible future offspring. This mere eventuality, were it to occur, would certainly give rise to a moral responsibility of justice toward the children, but it could not ground the intrinsic injustice of the initial extramarital act. We should recall that the form of argument common to the second class of precepts is in no way connected to the offense or harm of other persons but only to individual morality. To dispel any doubt on this point, it is enough to reread the closing words of chapter 121: "Now, by this conclusion we refute the error of some who say that those acts only are sinful whereby one's neighbor is offended or scandalized." Whatever evil Aquinas perceives behind simple fornication, it must lie not in the possible consequences of the act, but *intrinsically* in the objective meaning of the act and in the intention of the person who performs it.

This apparent indifference toward harm done to other persons might understandably give rise to some perplexity. Would not the most obvious argument, for someone who wants to condemn fornication morally, be to demonstrate that even with mutual consent it objectively harms one's partner (and oneself)—for example, by treating him or her not as a person but as an object of pleasure? Moreover, why should we not consider the negative consequences: future children deprived of a family, poorly brought up, or abandoned (or even thrown away); the abortion of unwanted babies; hasty marriages and unhappy families? In discussions bearing on this subject, such arguments are too frequent to be ignored, and the hypothetical nature of some of these negative consequences should not be overemphasized, as if it were a strong objection. As a matter of fact, the consequences for children and families have always been so significant—even in St. Thomas's time (consider the use of the medieval wheel, which is today being reconsidered, interestingly, in certain Italian cities)—that fornication, even if not intrinsically evil, should at least be considered, like the use of firearms, a *dangerous activity*—perhaps not so grave as to merit punishment, but certainly grave enough to be somehow discouraged.

Nevertheless, Aquinas is interested in finding a proof of the intrinsic wickedness of fornication, not of its dangers, however numerous. From this perspective, the first argument just mentioned (moral harm of one's partner and oneself) is different from the others, insofar as it does not involve a mere possibility. On the other hand, why should this harm be relevant? In reality, to affirm a principle of responsibility for one's own good and for that of others, independently of and even against the relevant persons' wills, necessarily entails the acceptance of: (a) the existence of an objective order of human good, and (b) a significance (of this good) transcending the individual will. This is precisely what St. Thomas sets out to establish by examining, *not the only* way to reach the required conclusions, but the way that seems to him simplest and most direct. We might add that the agent's ethical concern for (what he holds to be) the objective good of human beings is precisely what leads him to assume an attitude of responsible attentiveness toward all the foreseeable consequences of his acts, even consequences for as yet nonexistent and hypothetical persons and situations. This is how the discussion of possible consequences fits into Aquinas's ethical foundation.

(2) Equipped with the foregoing premises, it is now easy to grasp the meaning of the second negative thesis distinguished above: namely, the denial that the wickedness of fornication lies *exclusively* in the will of God. The second step in the text of chapter 122 (previously omitted) is thus an eloquent endorsement of what I have already said about the transcendent basis for ethics and the connection between the will of God and the objective order of nature. It runs as follows:

> Now, to say that he injures God would not seem to be an adequate answer. For we do not offend God except by doing something contrary to our own good, as has been said. But this does not appear contrary to man's good. Hence, on this basis, no injury seems to be done to God.[111]

These words are a perfect declaration of intent, signaling the transition to the constructive phase of St. Thomas's argument, in which he seeks to show that fornication is "contrary to the good of man," and that consequently through fornication one "does injury to God."

(3) We are now entering the most delicate part of the argument, concerning the natural end of the emission of semen. Now, more than ever, it is essential not to misunderstand St. Thomas's intentions. We need therefore to touch immediately upon the *open structure* of his argument and, at the same time, to understand his reference to the emission of semen in its proper context.

In Thomistic ethics, in order to qualify an act as intrinsically evil—once the axiological foundation of the natural order has been clarified—it is sufficient to show that it necessarily involves rejecting the objective meaning of the natural structure of human beings. This assertion does not require further qualifications, because when we speak of objective mean-

111 Aquinas, *CG*, III, ch. 122.

ing we include the hierarchical relation to the whole and to the ultimate end. Faced with an act that rejects the good of some part of the human being, one must ask oneself whether or not that rejection is required by the objective good of the whole. If it is so required, then the sacrifice of the part is only an apparent rejection, because through this sacrifice one actually *affirms*, in a state of necessity, the objective meaning of the *part as such*. The sacrifice of a leg can thus be morally licit. Likewise, to take a less tired example, it may also be licit to undertake an intense and burdensome task for the good of one's family or one's country. Moral reasoning focuses in both cases on: (a) a prudential evaluation of the hierarchical relation; and (b) a prudential evaluation of the necessity of the sacrifice to be undertaken.

Now if it is true that fornication irremediably negates the meaning of some aspect of man's natural structure (by hypothesis, the emission of semen), this already provides sufficient grounds for deducing its objective immorality. This does not mean, however, that other negations cannot be exposed. Rather, given the context in which the emission of semen assumes its meaning (as a human act), the denial of the objective meaning of that whole context—i.e. the context of sexual intercourse and interpersonal love—is necessarily implicit in the act of fornication. St. Thomas is extremely succinct, and as we have said before, he chooses the argumentative approach that appears simplest to him. One finds implicit within his approach, nonetheless, an openness to further refinement and expansion of his reflections on the natural order that may be violated by fornication, including those reflections we find in recent developments in the phenomenology of human love and sexual union.

With these clarifications behind us, we can finally enter *in medias res*. How should the Thomistic argument on the natural end of the emission of semen be approached? Human semen, says Aquinas, "is necessary for the propagation of the species," and in order to attain this goal it must be emitted from the man. But this is not enough. It is also necessary "that it be emitted for generation, to which the sexual act is directed." Generation, on the other hand, "would be frustrated unless it were followed by proper nutrition" and " appropriate upbringing."

> [But our problem is not whether simple fornication is accidentally a sin, but whether it is so essentially]. Hence, we must look for a solution in our earlier considerations. We have said that God exercises care over every person on the basis of what is good for him. Now, it is good for each person to attain his end, whereas it is bad for him to

> swerve away from his proper end. Now, this should be considered applicable to the parts, just as it is to the whole being; for instance, each and every part of man, and every one of his acts, should attain the proper end. Now, though the male semen is superfluous in regard to the preservation of the individual, it is nevertheless necessary in regard to the propagation of the species. Other superfluous things, such as excrement, urine, sweat, and such things, are not at all necessary; hence, their emission contributes to man's good. Now, this is not what is sought in the case of semen, but, rather, to emit it for the generation (*ad generationis utilitatem*), to which the sexual act is directed. But man's generative process would be frustrated unless it were followed by proper nutrition, because the offspring would not survive if proper nutrition were withheld. Therefore, the emission of semen ought to be so ordered that both the generation and the upbringing of offspring could follow from it (*ut sequi possit et generatio conveniens, et geniti educatio*).[112]

St. Thomas has in mind a natural order that transcends and determines particular organs and particular individuals, and which is ordered to the end of the "preservation of the [human] species." Within this order, the inclination to sexual union between man and woman and the inclination to care for offspring take on their full meaning—not to mention the whole complex, complementary structure of man and woman (physical, psychic, biological, emotional, affective, sentimental, rational, moral, etc.) that leads from the couple's union to the generation, education, and upbringing of children. Within this natural order, the family has a fundamental role because, through the stable union between husband and wife (marriage), it is the point where different generations meet: the place most appropriate to human nature, in which the past, present, and future of the species are conjoined.

Semen does have an intrinsic finality that is absolutely univocal (it is directed to the generation of another being of the same species) and that everyone is capable of recognizing. This finality is realized during sexual intercourse and constitutes its objective meaning (the emission of semen into the woman's vagina).[113]

112 Aquinas, *CG*, III, ch. 122.

113 The best contemporary, Thomistically-inspired interpretation of the natural order of sexual and marital relations is that of K. Wojtyla, *Love and Responsibility* (New York: Farrar Straus & Giroux Inc., 1981), trans. H. T. Willetts. For the purposes of my discussion, see in particular chapter I, "The Person and the Sexual Urge"; and the section entitled "Marriage" in chapter IV, "Justice Towards the Creator."

At this point, I should clarify that St. Thomas divides his discussion of the immorality of fornication into two stages, which is also why he links this discussion to the question of the naturalness of marriage.

(a) First of all, Aquinas thinks of the case in which the agents explicitly intend to exclude generation. In a situation like this, in light of what has already been said, the intentional separation of the moral good (the natural end of the emission of semen, or of sexual intercourse, or of sexual relations in general, etc.) from the pleasurable good (the pleasure associated with the sexual act) is evident. In their choice, the man and woman resist God's designs, going against the order given by Him; and they *remove their intention from God, placing their wills in inferior things.* Obviously, intentionality can vary widely from subject to subject depending on the agent's concept of God, and the allocation of responsibility presupposes at least some awareness on the part of the subject, however vague, that for the sake of his own pleasure he is violating an objective order that transcends himself.

To grasp the immorality of the act more clearly, it may be helpful to add a few brief specifications concerning evaluations based both on hierarchy and necessity, and concerning subjective responsibility. On the one hand, even if one were to argue (and this is clearly not what St. Thomas thinks) for the existence, within sexual relations, of a moral good hierarchically superior to generation—say, the consolidation of interpersonal love—the necessity of sacrificing the inferior good would still be absent. In fact, *it is possible to abstain* from sexual relations, even if only occasionally, without thereby *necessarily* impeding the former good; and this is the case because there are so many possible ways (including, at times, abstention itself) to express and consolidate a genuine love. On the other hand, if the subjects are engaged in a sincere search for the moral good, and not merely for sexual enjoyment, but suffer from an erroneous evaluation of the criteria of hierarchy and necessity, there may well be an absence of subjective responsibility for the act of fornication. There is nonetheless inevitably an objective impoverishment of the human good associated with unitive relations between a man and a woman.

(4) (b) Then there is the other case, decidedly more rare, in which the fornicators are not concerned to exclude the possibility that their relationship give rise to the generation of offspring. Here, evidently, the immorality of the act cannot reside in an intentional injury to the moral good of generation, and so St. Thomas broadens his perspective to include the natural end of marriage. As regards the end of the "propagation of the

species," he maintains, "it must . . . be contrary to the good for man if the semen be emitted under conditions such that generation could result but the proper upbringing would be prevented."[114]

Marriage, for Aquinas, is natural because in the human species the female, by herself, is not sufficient to nurture and educate the offspring. For this reason, men and women have the "natural instinct" (the inclination) to form together "a society," "over no short period of time." For the same reason, the particular relationship that brings with it the possibility (even if, at times, this is very remote) of having a child, should occur within the context of that natural society between man and woman. Only such a society, which in the natural order constitutes the context suited to the generation, upbringing, and education of children, *justifies*—that is, renders morally just before everyone—(complete) sexual relations, which by their nature must, consequently, always be *conjugal relations*.

If one correctly frames the context of justification in which the natural order takes on ethical relevance, and if one understands St. Thomas's practical, terse style, as well as the "sensibilities of his time," his attentive and penetrating study of natural finality will be found to be intellectually satisfying and stimulating. For a correct interpretation and critical rereading, I believe it is useful to review the entire passage in which he connects the naturalness of marriage with the evil of fornication.

> Likewise, it must also be contrary to the good for man if the semen be emitted under conditions such that generation could result but the proper upbringing would be prevented. We should take into consideration the fact that, among some animals where the female is able to take care of the upbringing of offspring, male and female do not remain together for any time after the act of generation. This is obviously the case with dogs. But in the case of animals of which the female is not able to provide for the upbringing of offspring, the male and female do stay together after the act of generation as long as is necessary for the upbringing and instruction of the offspring. Examples are found among certain species of birds whose young are not able to seek out food for themselves immediately after hatching. In fact, since a bird does not nourish its young with milk, made available by nature as it were, as occurs in the case of quadrupeds, but the bird must look elsewhere for food for its young, and since besides

114 Aquinas, *CG*, III, ch. 122.

this it must protect them by sitting on them, the female is not able to do this by herself. So, as a result of divine providence, there is naturally implanted in the male of these animals a tendency to remain with the female in order to bring up the young. Now, it is abundantly evident that the female in the human species is not at all able to take care of the upbringing of offspring by herself, since the needs of human life demand many things which cannot be provided by one person alone. Therefore, it is appropriate to human nature that a man remain together with a woman after the generative act, and not leave her immediately to have such relations with another woman, as is the practice with fornicators.

Nor, indeed, is the fact that a woman may be able by means of her own wealth to care for the child by herself an obstacle to this argument. For natural rectitude in human acts is not dependent on things accidentally possible in the case of one individual, but, rather, on those conditions which accompany the entire species.

Again, we must consider that in the human species offspring require not only nourishment for the body, as in the case of other animals, but also education for the soul. For other animals naturally possess their own kinds of prudence whereby they are enabled to take care of themselves. But a man lives by reason, which he must develop by lengthy, temporal experience so that he may achieve prudence. Hence, children must be instructed by parents who are already experienced people. Nor are they able to receive such instruction as soon as they are born, but after a long time, and especially after they have reached the age of discretion. Moreover, a long time is needed for this instruction. Then, too, because of the impulsion of the passions, through which prudent judgment is vitiated, they require not merely instruction but correction. Now, a woman alone is not adequate to this task; rather, this demands the work of a husband, in whom reason is more developed for giving instruction and strength is more available for giving punishment. Therefore, in the human species, it is not enough, as in the case of birds, to devote a small amount of time to bringing up offspring, for a long period of life is required. Hence, since among all animals it is necessary for male and female to remain together as long as the work of the father is needed by the offspring, it is natural to the human being for the man to establish a lasting association with a designated woman, over no short period of time. Now,

> we call this society *matrimony*. Therefore, matrimony is natural for man, and promiscuous performance of the sexual act, outside matrimony, is contrary to man's good. For this reason, it must be a sin.[115]

Concerning marriage too, we must keep in mind the open structure of St. Thomas's argument. For his purposes, it is enough to bring out as many points as are sufficient to highlight the fittingness, for the education of offspring, that the man and woman should form a stable society, thus explaining the reason for their "natural instinct" to do so.

It is interesting, in order to capture the rigor with which Aquinas attends to the data of the natural order, to note that he does not claim to have demonstrated here the indissolubility of marriage, but only the *necessity* that conjugal partners remain together on a stable basis, "for a long time." The indissolubility of marriage, and its other properties of being "one man with one woman" and of being "not between relatives," call for other observations about human nature to which he devotes the subsequent chapters, 123–25. My goal here—namely, to bring into relief the typical structure of ethical justification in his treatment of specific moral cases, does not require me to address these other issues. Rather, it may be helpful to dwell briefly on the lines immediately following the long passage of chapter 122 just cited. There, St. Thomas focuses on the objective gravity of simple fornication in both of the forms he has highlighted:

> Nor, in fact, should it be deemed a slight sin for a man to arrange for the emission of semen apart from the proper purpose of generating and bringing up children, on the argument that it is either a slight sin, or none at all, for a person to use a part of the body for a different use than that to which it is directed by nature (say, for instance, one chose to walk on his hands, or to use his feet for something usually done with the hands) because man's good is not much opposed by such inordinate use. However, the inordinate emission of semen is incompatible with the natural good; namely, the preservation of the species. Hence, after the sin of homicide whereby a human nature already in existence is destroyed, this type of sin appears to take next place, for by it the generation of human nature is precluded.[116]

First of all, the air of gravity in Aquinas's words should come as no

115 Aquinas, *CG*, III, ch. 122.
116 Aquinas, *CG*, III, ch. 122.

surprise. He has in mind the objective wickedness of the act, not the subjective responsibility of those involved, which always depends on the degree of their awareness and their consent. Nor does he intend to make a direct comparison between the gravity of murder and that of any fornicatory or masturbatory act. Rather, in relation to God, Who wills the existence of human nature, not only acts aimed at destroying human nature, but also those aimed at impeding its continuation in history as He has ordained it, should be seen as offenses of no small account, in other words, as mortal sins. Aquinas is also guided in this evaluation by the Ten Commandments, which are interpreted by the Judeo-Christian tradition in hierarchical order, and in which the fifth, on the taking of life, precedes the sixth, on impure acts. So as not to exaggerate the comparison with murder, we can also recall that the ultimate goal of chapter 122 is not to set up a comparison between various grave acts but rather to refute "the error of those who say that there is no more sin in the emission of semen than in the emission of any other superfluous matter, and also of those who state that fornication is not a sin."[117]

What is more interesting for us, however, is the comparison with the other natural ends, and the examples related above. To criticize the Thomistic doctrine by adducing examples of this type, all too easily comparing them, for instance, with the end of sexual relations, would be to mistake Aquinas's argument by improperly assuming a flat and rationalistic view of natural ends. Faced with a potentially immoral act, the structure of the argument involves a serious and painstaking reflection on all aspects of the natural order: proper end, measure, and hierarchy. As regards hands and feet, for example, it is understood that such organs *serve* the purpose of (human) external action *in several ways*. For example, they allow people to play, to work and to exercise. Among these activities, there is obviously one that pertains in a strict sense to the feet and legs. However, given the potentiality of the hands and arms for external action, there is nothing to stop one from trying, every so often—and for whatever reason (amusement, sport, or work)—to walk on one's hands. Here the limited physical ability of human beings, more than any moral disorder, prevents a defect in measure or hierarchy from turning into an ethical problem worthy of note.

117 Ibid.

5. A Response to Abbà

Let us turn in conclusion to Abbà's critical observations, with which we opened our discussion. These observations, as already mentioned, hinge on the idea of a conflict between the ethical doctrine of the *Contra gentiles*, based on a theology of law in the "Augustinian mold," and that of the *Summa theologiae*, characterized by the primacy of the virtues. The fact that Aquinas apparently drafted the treatise on law of the *Contra gentiles* twice (the text that we have considered being clearly the second version) is, according to Abbà, further evidence of such a conflict.

As far as the concept of law and the typology of laws are concerned, I believe I have already shown that there is no conflict, but rather a substantial agreement, between the *Summa contra gentiles* and the *Summa theologiae*. I would here add a minor observation, perhaps obvious but nonetheless worth keeping in mind: the treatment of law that appears in the second *Summa* is much more extensive and elaborate than that which appears in the *Contra gentiles*. The development that undoubtedly takes place between these two works, therefore, involves not only the concept of virtue, but also a definite advance in Aquinas's understanding of law.

But what exactly does Abbà mean when he speaks of a "theology of law in the Augustinian mold"? He means a concept of law as purely exterior, to which we alluded to in section 3.1, "The Necessity of Law," and which involves the subordination of the individual's freedom through the threat of punishment. This is a legalistic model, closely analogous to that current in modern thought, in which the only motive accompanying obligation is a threat, and the only thing that matters is to verify the agent's guilt by comparing his behavior with the relevant legal provisions.

At this stage, it is hardly necessary to point out that such a model is sharply opposed not only (1) to what St. Thomas explicitly says in chapter 115 of book III of the *Contra gentiles* regarding how we should understand man's "submission" to the law (see 4.1, "Law as an Ordering to the Ultimate End"); but also (2) to the entire argument extending from that chapter at least as far as chapter 129, according to which law is fundamentally an ordering to the ultimate end, and the morality of actions depends on the agent's intention being qualified by love for that end (see sections 4.2 and following).

In the *Summa theologiae*, as in the *Contra gentiles*, (eternal) law remains for St. Thomas the indispensable ethical foundation pointing to the transcendent source of the moral order and determining, by means of the natural inclinations, its immanent end. For man, law consists in the first place of practical reason's intrinsic dynamism toward the known good (which always presents itself, naturally, as good both morally and pleasurably), and in the second place of the obligatory character of the means for attaining this good. The first aspect is radical: if there were no law (as a rational inclination), there would be no practical reason, because there could be no *known good* (here too, see especially section 3.1, "The Necessity of Law"). In fact, when we say that good is the first notion of practical reason, we already refer implicitly to the natural law. Human law and divine positive law have ethical relevance, moreover, and are not merely violent impositions, insofar as they are ordered more or less mediately to the good to which man is naturally inclined, directing us—at various moments and in various contexts—to certain actions as means to that end.

Certainly, the *Summa theologiae* contains a generous treatment of virtue that is not to be found in the *Contra gentiles*. This is undoubtedly an advance, and a completion of Aquinas's ethical doctrine, which rightly requires the moral philosopher to shift his attention from the highly abstract data yielded by reflection on the rational foundation of the moral order, and to focus on the concrete ethical existence of the individual, the formation of his personality, and the gradual development of his knowledge of and love for of the good. It thus also opens up new perspectives for the correct evaluation of subjective responsibility. In no way, however, is this enrichment opposed to the role of law and the *necessary* interaction between law and virtue.

Law, as I have said, is what always determines for the moral agent the normativity (broadly speaking) of the known good and the means for attaining it: it is always the intentional *act* of reason "commanding something." The "rational powers," however, explains Aquinas, are not necessarily directed to one thing only, like the natural powers, and they therefore need a *habit* to perfect and coordinate their orientation toward the natural end: this habit is moral virtue.[118]

Let us now consider that moral virtue, as a habit perfecting the orientation of practical reason, determines within practical reason the extent of one's knowledge of and love for the good, and also the extent of one's

118 See in particular Aquinas, *ST*, I-II, q. 49, a. 4; q. 55, a. 1; q. 57, a. 5; II-II, q. 47.

knowledge of the means for attaining it. Moral virtue, therefore, determines also the intensity with which the agent recognizes to the normativity of the law, and, indeed, the level of knowledge that he possesses of the law. The fundamental act of our inclination toward the good pertains to law, and every ethical choice has law as its principle in that law is the specific *act* (that is, the normative means-to-end judgment) formulated by reason in the concrete situation. However, every ethical choice also depends on the operation of the moral *habit* that orients or *inclines* the rational power toward the right end and the right judgment. The distinction between act and habit shapes the distinction and relationship between law and virtue throughout St. Thomas's work, and explains why *one cannot know and observe the law without being virtuous, and vice versa.*

Let us now move on to the problem of the two drafts. The modification introduced in the second draft pertains to the chapters of the third book coming after 111, "Intelligent creatures are subject to divine providence in a special way," and 112, "That rational creatures are governed by Providence for their own sakes, and other creatures in reference to them." Indeed, chapters 113–18, according to Abbà, are "completely new" and "develop the argument along entirely different lines" as compared to the first version, of which, as he sees it, "there is not a trace to be found."[119]

What did the first version do, according to Abbà? It derived from man's freedom his possible *guilt* before the law, but it did not explain "why human acts must be governed according to a law." In the first draft, the law "imposes on man those actions that are naturally right"—as chapter 129 ("That some human acts are right according to nature and not merely because they are prescribed by positive law"), which is "substantially identical in the two drafts," testifies. In the first version, however, "the concept of law itself is not explained, nor are reasons given why the divine government must be accomplished through law": law, in the first draft, is only the "criterion according to which human acts are judged by God."[120]

This gap will be filled in by the second version, especially in chapters 113, "That the rational creature is directed by God to his actions not only for the sake of the species, but also according to what befits the individual," and 114, "That laws are divinely given to man." In these chapters, law is defined as the appropriate way, given the natural inclinations, to

119 Abbà, *Lex et virtus*, pp. 78–84.
120 Ibid.

guide human beings to their end. In fact, law is an act of reason pertaining to divine providence, and rational creatures are capable of understanding it as such. As before, however, the function of the law remains "to enunciate the order conforming to reason" and "to induce man to observe it" through "the subordination" of his will.[121]

Abbà's goal in this comparative study is to show that in the second version, albeit against the backdrop of an unchanged legalistic and externalist account, we find a certain germinal attention to the interior aspect of the human being's freedom as "source of his own actions," "capable of governing himself."[122] To this conclusion he adds only that the insight in question, left undeveloped in the *Contra gentiles*, is nonetheless a prelude to the path of the virtues later taken in the *Summa theologiae*.

By all means. However, in light of such explanations I cannot but conclude that Abbà's insistence on the difference between the two versions is exaggerated, and probably results from a hasty enthusiasm for the possibility of an additional argument for his basic thesis on the relationship between virtue and law. "It is significant," he concludes, "that St. Thomas proceeded to a second draft, thoroughly revising the order of chapters, eliminating some and introducing others. A careful comparison of the two versions would lead to more than one surprise. . . . But the very existence of two versions ought already to cause some disquiet. St. Thomas is not such a peaceful, straightforward thinker as is often believed. The handwriting . . . shows that he revises his positions, corrects himself, tries one path and then abandons it, opens new paths, tosses around suggestions."[123]

Faced with these claims, one naturally wonders what is so strange or "disquieting" about Aquinas's manner of proceeding? Anyone who has tried to write even a short book knows well how often one finds oneself changing the initial structure, correcting individual arguments, eliminating parts already written and introducing new parts, etc. Imagine how it must have been for someone who wrote more than one *Summa*, even more so when there were no computers. But let us look at the issue on its merits: the impression one gets from the words of Abbà is that between the two versions, there is no difference worth highlighting that bears on his discussion of the meaning of law. Abbà himself tells us that the function of law is the same in both versions: to enunciate the order of reason and to

121 Ibid.
122 Ibid., p. 83.
123 Ibid.

induce one to observe it by subjecting him to it, or—what amounts to the same thing—by threatening punishment in the case of disobedience. It is clear, then, that if law is in both cases a vehicle for the order of reason, the fact that only the second version concentrates on a definition explicitly connected to the reason of the legislator cannot amount to a substantial difference.

If the second version is also associated, for Abbà, with a legalistic model within an "Augustinian mold"—and he states this explicitly—then it is evident that my contrary interpretation of the *Contra gentiles*, based on *this* version, cannot be undermined by the existence of a first and different version, even if it were legalistic. In fact, however, Abbà does not seem to have paused for a critical reading of the entire treatise on law, but only of some elements in the first chapters. If he had, he would have noticed, as we have, that chapters 119 through 129—which deal with the second and third classes of precepts and are *identical in the two versions*—embody the same concept of law that dominates chapters 113–18, added in the second version, and that the concept in question is not legalistic. This observation alone is sufficient to conclude that the first version does not embody a legalistic philosophy. However, something more can be said on this question.

Abbà repeatedly insists that the first version does not explain the "reason for the necessity of a law to govern man"; it does not explain, in other words, "why human acts must be governed according to a law." According to Abbà's own words, however, this is not explained by the second version either, whose only advance as compared to the first is that it places greater emphasis on the rational character of law. As far as I can see, Abbà simply fails to recognize the *third way* of understanding the necessity of law (see 3.1, "The Necessity of Law"), which is bound up with the existence of a natural law and can alone ground the nonexteriority of any law. It is extremely significant, in this regard, that this *third way* can easily be found in the longest passage to which Abbà refers among those that were *eliminated* from the second version. This passage, he tells us, is the "fifth argument" by which the first version of the chapter coming after 112 seeks to demonstrate the possibility of guilt in human acts. Let us read it in its entirety, and in its original language, just as Abbà himself presents it:

> Item. Quaecumque divina providentia gubernantur, ex ea sortiuntur principia convenientium operationum. Differenter tamen. Quaedam namque consequuntur formas naturales ex quibus inclinantur in pro-

> prias operationes, sicut plantae et inanimata. Animalia vero irrationalia accipiunt naturalem aestimationem, per quam aguntur ad suos actos. Homines vero naturale iudicium rationis habent a Deo, per quod conveniens ab inconvenienti distinguere possunt. Id autem quod secundum huiusmodi iudicium naturale rationis rectum apparet, dicitur lex naturalis. Hoc tamen interest, quod quadam naturali necessitate sequuntur plantae et inanimata inclinationes formarum et virtutum naturalium; et similiter animalia irrationalia motum naturalis aestimationis; sed homines iudicium naturale rationis possunt sequi et non sequi. Sic igitur homini ex divina providentia imposita est lex quam potest sequi et non sequi. Manifestum est autem quod ad legislatorem pertinet praemiare vel punire eos qui legem ab eo positam servant vel transgrediuntur: unde consuetum est quod legislatores suis legibus poenas adiungunt et praemia. Ad Deum igitur pertinet homines pro suis actibus punire vel praemiare, quod oportet iudicio quodam fieri. Sunt igitur hominum actus divino iudicio subiecti.[124]

The beginning of this passage is of fundamental importance. It immediately refers us to the radical sense in which the government of divine providence should be understood—namely, as inscribed in the very being of created things, and as working through their natural inclinations (see 2, "Providence and the Eternal Law"). The entire discussion therefore focuses on showing the distinctive ways in which different creatures have received from God, within their very being, their "*principia convenientium operationum*": animals, plants, and inanimate objects through natural inclinations that they cannot help following, but men through the "*iudicium naturale rationis*" that "*possunt sequi et non sequi,*" and which is the "*lex naturalis.*" "*Sic igitur homini ex divina providentia imposita est lex quam potest sequi et non sequi.*" It is precisely *in this way and in this sense*—"*sic igitur*"—that divine providence has imposed the natural law upon human beings: not as an external imposition, but as a principle that acts internally, and that they can "*sequi et non sequi.*"

Man can thus incur guilt, but reward and punishment are not inflicted from the outside. Rather, they are the necessary natural consequences, whether positive or negative—as the chapters of book III on this subject (not altered in the second version) explain[125]—for man's good and happiness. In the same (internal) sense in which we can say that God the

124 Abbà, *Lex et virtus*, p. 79.

125 See in particular Aquinas, *CG*, III, chs. 139–41.

Legislator imposes the natural law upon man, we can also say that God the Judge imposes on him the good and the evil that naturally follow the fulfillment or violation of that law.

This passage from the first version, cited by Abbà, fully confirms my interpretation of the second version. As I have repeatedly underlined, there is a deep philosophical unity that links chapters 111 and 112 (on the special way in which providence concerns itself with rational creatures) both backward, to the entire third book, and forward, to the remaining chapters of the treatise on law—and among the latter, especially to chapters 113 and 114 (the only chapters to which Abbà really pays close attention), whose new version should be seen, from this perspective, as nothing more than a further refinement of a preexisting doctrine.

Conclusion

Thomas Aquinas is unanimously considered the greatest natural law theorist of all time, and his thought, both metaphysical and ethical, is today enjoying a newfound popularity, especially on account of the attention it has received from various contemporary thinkers in the analytic school. More specifically, Aquinas's thought has been the most important influence on the current revival, in the fields of ethics, politics, and law, of philosophical positions explicitly or substantively grounded in natural law. In my extensive Introduction and in Chapter One, "The Neoclassical Critique of Conventional Natural Law Theory," I set out to indicate the principal elements and motives of the current rediscovery of St. Thomas, particularly with regard to the natural law ethics.

The overall purpose of this work, on the other hand, has been to demonstrate that the Thomistic concept of the natural law is based on the interaction of the two basic notions of nature and the will of God; in particular, I have argued that the will of God grounds the axiological importance of the natural order. For St. Thomas, man, by means of natural *reason* alone, reaches an intentional and spontaneous knowledge of God and of the natural order as created (that is, *willed*) by God. With his *will*, he then naturally loves God before himself and with a greater love, and so also in the same way he loves both the will of God and the natural order.

The love of God as ultimate end ensures that nature takes on a transcendent (and thus properly ethical) importance in man's eyes, giving rise—with respect to the reasons of fittingness, utility and necessity detectable in nature—to the absolute judgment of good and evil proper to moral conscience. Morality, in fact, rests upon the moral subject's transcendence of self-love (love of concupiscence), understood as the ultimate formality of the upright pursuit of the various human goods. Self-love cannot, by itself, bring one to the genuine experience of moral duty or obligation, since the latter involves a sincere sacrifice, or gift, of one's own good out of love for something greater. Whoever undertakes such a sacrifice, even without fully realizing it, is in some measure loving the will of God before and more than his own.

This metaphysical and ethical approach is summed up by Aquinas in the doctrine of natural law, which I have laid out fully in the third chapter, "Lex and Lex Naturalis." This law is, above all, the act of Divine Wisdom that creates man, ordering him (inclining him) to know and love God Himself more than anything else. Natural law thus exists in man as the act, or judgment, of practical reason (*per modum praecipiendi*: commanding something) that, in the different circumstances of his life, indicates to him what is good and what is evil in an absolute sense, independently of his own interests, desires, or pleasures.

The reference to the will of God and to natural ends inherent in Thomistic ethics has often given rise, in difference historical periods, to rationalist and voluntarist tendencies in interpreting the natural law. Moreover, the positivist thought of the past two centuries, based on the neat separation of facts from values and on the logical impossibility of moving from the former to the latter, has caused a general skepticism toward all forms of ethical naturalism. It is in this context that one should read both the analytic attempt of the neoclassical school to delineate an objective natural-law ethics not based on the knowledge of nature, and the more general tendency of several interpreters of St. Thomas (including some outside the analytic camp) to ground moral norms and requirements without appealing to God.

Given the theonomic and naturalistic outcome of my investigation of St. Thomas's ethical thought, I have made a special effort in Chapter Two, "The Presupposition of *Lex Naturalis:* Man as *Capax Dei*," to bring out the breadth and depth of his thought concerning human knowledge of the will of God. I then went on to argue that if the order of nature acquires ethical relevance for man by virtue of the will of God, this reference to the will of God nevertheless escapes the naturalistic fallacy by relying on a particular interpretation of moral experience: that is, of the primordial knowledge of the good upon which human action depends. Here, the problem is no longer Hume's law but the validity of this interpretation.

Finally, I have sought to emphasize that St. Thomas's ethics escapes the charge of rationalism, above all through its understanding of the intentionality of human knowledge and the complexity of the elements that make up the natural order (proper ends, hierarchy, and natural measure). Aquinas's ethics also escapes the charge of voluntarism, mainly because obedience to the will of God depends not on fear of punishment, but on love and a sharing of the end, and because the will of God manifests itself to human consciousness precisely in the reasons, or ends, of created things.

Bibliography

This bibliography includes several works that are not cited directly, but which proved very useful in studying and understanding the problems dealt with in this book. References in square brackets indicate either the original editions of the works cited or the Italian editions I originally used.

Abbà, G. *Lex et virtus: Studi sull'evoluzione della dottrina morale di san Tommaso d'Aquino*. Rome: LAS, 1983.

————. *Felicità, vita buona e virtù: Saggio di filosofia morale*. Rome: LAS, 1989.

————. *Quale impostazione per la filosofia morale?* Rome: LAS, 1996.

Ackerman, B. A. *Social Justice in the Liberal State*. New Haven: Yale University Press, 1980.

Alvira, T., L. Clavell and T. Melendo. *Metafisica*. Pamplona, S.A.: Ediciones Universidad de Navarra, 1982.

Ambrosetti, G. *La filosofia delle leggi di Suárez*. Roma, 1948.

————. *Il diritto naturale della riforma cattolica: Una giustificazione storica del sistema di Suárez*. Milan: Giuffrè, 1951.

Amerio, F. *La dottrina della fede: Dogma, morale, spiritualità*. Milan: Edizioni Ares, 1982.

Anscombe, E. M. "Modern Moral Philosophy." *Philosophy*, 33 (1958).

Aristotle. *Opere [Collected Works]*. Bari: Universale Laterza, 1973–.

————. *La Metafisica*. Ed. G. Reale. Naples: Loffredo, 1968.

————. *Etica Nicomachea*. Critical edition. Translation, introduction, and comments by M. Zanatta. Milan: Biblioteca Universale Rizzoli, 1986.

————. *The Complete Works of Aristotle*. Revised Oxford translation. Ed. Jonathan Barnes. Princeton, NJ: Princeton University Press, 1984.

————. *Nichomachean Ethics*. Trans. H. Rackham. Cambridge, Massachusetts and London: Harvard University Press, 1934.

Artigas, M. and J. J. Sanguineti. *Filosofia della natura*. Florence: Le Monnier, 1989.

Ashley, B.M. "What is the End of the Human Person? The Vision of God and Integral Human Fulfillment." In L. Gormally, ed., *Moral Truth and Moral Tradition: Essays in Honor of Peter Geach and Elizabeth Anscombe*. Dublin: Four Courts, 1994.

Aubert, J.-M. *Loi de Dieu, lois des hommes*. Tournai: Desclée, 1968.

(St.) Augustine. *Contra Faustum Manichaeum libri triginta tres*.

————. *Confessions*. Trans. John K. Ryan. New York: Image Books, 1960. [*Le confessioni*. Trans. A. Landi. Rome, Edizioni Paoline, 1978].

————. *City of God*. Trans. Marcus Dods, D.D. New York: The Modern Library, 1950. [*La città di Dio*. Ed. M. C. Borgogno. Rome, F.S.P. Edizioni Paoline, 1952].

Austin, J. *The Province of Jurisprudence Determined and the Uses of the Study of Jurisprudence*. London: Weidenfeld and Nicolson, 1971.

Basti. G. *Filosofia dell'uomo*. Bologna: ESD, 1995.

Battaglia, F., *Le carte dei diritti*. Florence: Sansoni, 1946.

Beyleveld, D., and R. Brownsword. "The Practical Difference between Natural Law Theory and Legal Positivism." *Oxford Journal of Legal Studies*, 5 (1985).

Bix, B. "Natural Law Theory." In D. Patterson, ed., *A Companion to Philosophy of Law and Legal Theory*. Oxford: Oxford University Press, 1996.

Bobbio, N. *Giusnaturalismo e positivismo giuridico*. Milan: Edizioni di Comunità, 1977.

————. *Il positivismo giuridico*. Turin: Giappichelli, 1979.

————. *L'età dei diritti*. Turin: Einaudi, 1990.

Bourke, V. J. "Two Approaches to Natural Law." *Natural Law Forum*, 1 (1956).

————. "Natural Law, Thomism — and Professor Nielsen." *Natural Law Forum*, 5 (1960).

Boyle, J., G. Grisez., and Tollefsen. *Free Choice: A Self-Referential Argument*. Notre Dame: University of Notre Dame Press, 1976.

————. "That the Fetus Should Be Considered a Legal Person." *The American Journal of Jurisprudence*, 24 (1979).

————. "Practical Reasoning and Moral Judgment." *Proceedings of the American Catholic Philosophical Association*, 58 (1984).

————. "Natural Law and the Ethics of Traditions." In R. P. George, ed., *Natural Law Theory: Contemporary Essays*. Oxford: Oxford University Press, 1992.

————. "The Personal Responsibility Required for Mortal Sin." In L. Gormally, ed., *Moral Truth and Moral Tradition: Essays in Honor of Peter Geach and Elizabeth Anscombe*. Dublin: Four Courts, 1994.

Bradley, G. V. "Response to Hittinger." *The American Journal of Jurisprudence*, 39 (1994).

————. Bradley and R. P. George. "The New Natural Law Theory: A Reply to Jean Porter." *The American Journal of Jurisprudence*, 39 (1994).

————. Bradley and R. P. George. "Marriage and the Liberal Imagination." *The Georgetown Law Journal*, 2 (1995).

Broderick, A. "The Radical Middle: Natural Right of Property in Aquinas and the Popes." *Solicitor Quarterly*, 3 (1964).

Brown, J., ed. *Selections from Three Works of Francisco Suárez, S.J.*, trans. Gwladys L. Williams, Ammi Brown and John Waldron, with certain revisions by Henry Davis, S.J. Oxford: Clarendon Press, 1944.

Calhoun, R.L. "Democracy and Natural Law." *Natural Law Forum*, 5 (1960).

Carcaterra, G. "Per una fondazione dei valori." In F. D'Agostino, ed., *Ontologia e fenomenologia del giuridico: Studi in onore di Sergio Cotta*. Turin: Giappichelli, 1995.

Cattaneo, M. A. "Il diritto naturale nel pensiero di H. L. Hart." *Rivista internazionale di Filosofia del Diritto*, XLII, 4 (1965).

————. "Introduzione a H. L. A. Hart." In H. L. A. Hart, *Il Concetto di Diritto* (trans.). Turin: Einaudi, 1965.

Cavanna, A. *Storia del Diritto Moderno in Europa: Le fonti e il pensiero giuridico 1*, Milan: Giuffrè, 1979.

Celano, B. "Giustificazione di norme e procedure ideali." *Analisi e diritto* (1992).

———. *Dialettica della giustificazione pratica: Saggio sulla legge di Hume*. Turin: Giappichelli, 1994.

Chalmeta, G. *Jacques Maritain: el elemento gnoseológico en la constitución de la ley moral natural.* Extractum ex dissertatione ad Doctoratum in Facultate Philosophiae. Rome: Pontificia Universitas Urbaniana, 1989.

———. Ed., *Crisi di senso e pensiero metafisico*. Rome: Armando, 1993.

———. "La fondazione postmoderna della giustizia politica. Dall'utilitarismo alla neutralità e... ritorno." *La Società*, 2 (1995).

Choza, J. *Manual de antropología filosófica.* Madrid: Ediciones Rialp, S. A., 1988.

Constable, G. W. "Who Can Determine What the Natural Law Is?" *Natural Law Forum*, 7 (1962).

Copleston, F. *History of Philosophy*. Westminster, Maryland: The Newman Press, 1963.

Cotta, S. *Il concetto di legge nella Summa Theologiae di San Tommaso d'Aquino*. Turin: Giapichelli, 1955.

———. "Diritto naturale: ideale o vigente?" In AA.VV. *Diritto naturale: Verso nuove prospettive*. Rome: Giuffrè, 1977.

———. *Diritto persona mondo umano*. Turin: Giappichelli, 1989.

Covell, C. *The Defence of Natural Law (A Study of the Ideas of Law and Justice in the Writings of Lon Fuller, Michael Oakeshot, F. A. Hayek, Ronald Dworkin and John Finnis)*. New York: St. Martin Press, 1992.

D'Agostino, ed. *Pluralità delle culture e universalità dei diritti*. Turin: Giappichelli, 1996.

———. *Il diritto come problema teologico*. Turin: Giappichelli, 1997.

D'Avenia, M. *La conoscenza per connaturalità in S. Tommaso d'Aquino*. Bologna: ESD, 1992.

D'Entrèves, A. P. *Natural Law: An Introduction to Legal Philosophy*. London: Hutchinson University Library, 1951.

———. "The case for Natural Law Re-Examined." *Natural Law Forum*, 1 (1956).

Dan-Cohen, M. *Rights, Persons, and Organizations: A Legal Theory for Bureaucratic Society*. Berkeley: University of California Press, 1986.

David, W. "The Immutability of Natural Law according to Suarez." *The Thomist*, 1 (1998).

Davies, B. *How is God Love?* In L. Gormally, ed., *Moral Truth and Moral Tradition: Essays in Honor of Peter Geach and Elizabeth Anscombe*. Dublin: Four Courts, 1994.

———. "Aquinas, God, and Being." *The Monist*, 4 (1997).

Davitt, T. E. *The Nature of Law*. St. Louis: Herder, 1951.

———. "Law as Means to End. Thomas Aquinas." *Vanderbilt Law Review*, 14 (1960).

De Finance, J. *An Ethical Inquiry*. Trans. Michael O'Brien S.J. Rome: Editrice Pontificia Università Gregoriana, 1991. [*Éthique Générale*. Rome: Presses de l'Université Grégorienne, 1967].

De Haro, R. G. *Legge, coscienza e libertà*. Trans. M. Di Palma. Milan: Edizioni Ares, 1984 [*La consciencia moral*. Madrid: Ediciones RIALP, 1978]

———. *La vita cristiana: Corso di teologia morale fondamentale*. With the assistance of I. de Celaya, W. May, and J. M. Yanguas. Milan: Edizioni Ares, 1995 [*La vida cristiana*. Pamplona: EUNSA, 1982].

Del Vecchio, G. *Storia della filosofia del diritto*. Milano: Giuffrè, 1958.

Di Blasi, F. *La teoria della legge naturale nel pensiero di John Mitchell Finnis*. Doctoral thesis directed by M. Jori. Milan: Università degli studi di Milano, 1994.

———. "La conoscenza naturale di Dio in Tommaso d'Aquino." *Aquinas*, 2 (1999).

———. "I valori fondamentali nella teoria neoclassica della legge naturale." *Rivista Internazionale di Filosofia del Diritto*, 2 (1999).

———. "Legge Naturale e Volontà di Dio: Finnis, Grisez, Suárez e la Teoria Convenzionale." *Iustitia*, 3 (2000).

———. "The Concept of Truth and the Object of Human Knowledge." In F. T. Arecchi (ed.), *The Scientific and Philosophical Challenge of Complexity*. Milan: ASRui, 2000.

———. Review of J. Finnis, *Aquinas: Moral, Political, and Legal Theory* (Oxford University Press: New York 1998). *Journal of Law & Religion* 16 (2001).

———. "Ultimate End, Human Freedom, and Beatitude: A Critique of Germain Grisez." *American Journal of Jurisprudence* 46 (2001).

———. "Rapporti Prematrimoniali o Rapporti Anti-Matrimoniali?" *Studi Cattolici* (Oct. 2001).

————. "Natural Law as Inclination to God." In J. Goyette, M. S. Latkovic, and R. Myers, eds., *St. Thomas Aquinas and the Natural Law Tradition*. Washington, D.C.: Catholic University of America Press, forthcoming.

————. "What Nature? Whose Nature? Reflecting on Some Recent Arguments in Natural Law Ethics." In M. Waddell, ed., *Reclaiming Nature: Essays in Thomistic Philosophy and Theology*. St. Augustine's Press: South Bend, IN, 2002 [with an introduction by Ralph McInerny].

————. "Practical Syllogism, *Proairesis*, and the Virtues: Toward a Reconciliation of Virtue Ethics and Natural Law Ethics," *New Things & Old Things*, 3 (2004).

————. "Law as 'Act of Reason' and 'Command,'" Forthcoming.

Dietze, G. "Natural Law in the Modern European Constitutions." *Natural Law Forum* 1 (1956).

Donagan, A. *The Theory of Morality*. Chicago: University of Chicago Press, 1977.

Dworkin, R. A. *Taking Rights Seriously*. Cambridge, MA: Harvard University Press, 1977.

————. "Natural Law Revisited." *University of Florida Law Review*, 34 (1982).

————. *Law's Empire*. London: Fontana Press, 1986.

————. "La fonte di ogni libertà." In *Il Sole-24 Ore* (10 March 1996).

Fabro C. *Dio: Introduzione al problema teologico*. Rome: Studium, 1953.

————. *La nozione metafisica di partecipazione (secondo S. Tommaso d'Aquino)*. 3rd revised edition. Turin: Società editrice internazionale, 1963.

————. *Dall'essere all'esistente*. Brescia: Morcelliana, 1965.

————. *L'uomo e il rischio di Dio*. Rome: Studium, 1967.

————. *Introduzione a S. Tommaso: La metafisica tomista e il pensiero moderno*. Milan: Edizioni Ares, 1983.

Falcon, G. *Manuale di apologetica*. Rome: Edizioni Paoline, 1954.

Fassò, G. "Natural Law in Italy in the Past Ten Years." *Natural Law Forum*, 1 (1956).

————. *Storia della filosofia del diritto*. Bologna: Il Mulino, 1966.

Fay, C. "Toward a Thomistic-Anthropological View of the Evolution of Obligation." *Natural Law Forum*, 7 (1962).

Fay, T. A. "La teoria della legge naturale di San Tommaso. Alcune recenti interpretazioni." *Divus Thomas*, 2 (1994).

Finnis, J. M. "Blackstone's Theoretical Intentions." *Natural Law Forum*, 12 (1967).

———. *Scepticism Self-Refutation, and the Good of Truth*. In Hacker and Raz, eds., *Law, Morality and Society: Essays in Honour of H.L.A. Hart*. Oxford: Clarendon Press, 1977.

———. *Natural Law and Natural Rights*. Oxford: Clarendon Press, 1980.

———. Finnis and G. Grisez, "The Basic Principles of Natural Law: A Reply to Ralph McInerny." *The American Journal of Jurisprudence*, 26 (1981).

———. "Natural Law and the 'Is'-'Ought' Question: An Invitation to Professor Veatch." *Catholic Lawyer*, 26 (1981).

———. *Fundamentals of Ethics*. Oxford: Clarendon Press, 1983.

———. "Human Good(s) and Practical Reasoning." *Proceedings of the American Catholic Philosophical Association*, 58 (1984).

———. "The Authority of Law in the Predicament of Contemporary Social Theory." *Notre Dame Journal of Law, Ethics and Public Policy*, 1 (1984).

———. "On 'Positivism' and 'Legal Rational Authority'." *Oxford Journal of Legal Studies*, 5 (1985).

———. "On 'The Critical Legal Studies Movement'." *American Journal of Jurisprudence*, 30 (1985).

———. "On Reason and Authority in *Law's Empire*." *Law and Philosophy*, 6 (1987).

———. Finnis, G. Grisez, and J. Boyle, Jr. "Practical Principles, Moral Truth, and Ultimate Ends." *American Journal of Jurisprudence*, 32 (1987).

———. Finnis, G. Grisez, and J. Boyle, Jr. *Nuclear Deterrence, Morality and Realism*. Oxford: Clarendon Press, 1987.

———. Finnis, G. Grisez, J. Boyle, W. May, and J. Ford. *The Teaching of Humanae Vitae: A Defense*. San Francisco: Ignatius Press, 1988.

———. Finnis, G. Grisez, J. Boyle, W. May, "Every Marital Act Ought to Be Open to New Life: Toward a Clearer Understanding." *The Thomist*, 52 (1988).

———. "Law as Co-ordination." *Ratio Juris*, 2 (1989).

———. Finnis, G. Grisez, and J. Boyle. "Incoherence and

Consequentialism (or Proportionalism): A Rejoinder." *American Catholic Philosophical Quarterly* 64 (1990).

————. Ed., *Natural Law.* Vol. I. Aldershot: Dartmouth, 1991.

————. Ed., *Natural Law.* Vol. II. Aldershot: Dartmouth, 1991.

————. *Moral Absolutes: Tradition, Revision, and Truth.* Washington, D.C.: The Catholic University of America Press, 1991.

————. "Natural Law and Legal Reasoning." In R. P. George, ed., *Natural Law Theory: Contemporary Essays.* Oxford: Oxford University Press, 1992.

————. "On Conditional Intentions and Preparatory Intentions." In L. Gormally, ed., *Moral Truth and Moral Tradition: Essays in Honor of Peter Geach and Elizabeth Anscombe.* Dublin: Four Courts, 1994.

————. "The Truth in Legal Positivism." In R. P. George, ed., *The Autonomy of Law: Essays on Legal Positivism.* Oxford: Oxford University Press, 1995.

————. "Is Natural Law Theory Compatible with Limited Government?" In R. P. George, ed., *Natural Law, Liberalism, and Morality: Contemporary Essays.* Oxford: Clarendon Press, 1996.

————. *Aquinas. Moral, Political, and Legal Theory.* Oxford: Oxford University Press, 1998.

Finocchiaro, F. *Il matrimonio nel diritto canonico.* Bologna: Il Mulino, 1989.

Frey, R. G., ed. *Utility and Rights.* Oxford: Basil Blackwell, 1985.

Fuller, L. L. "Positivism and Fidelity to Law: A Reply to Professor Hart." *Harvard Law Review*, 71 (1958).

————. "Human Purpose and Natural Law." *Natural Law Forum*, 3 (1958).

————. "A Rejoinder to Professor Nagel." *Natural Law Forum*, 3 (1958).

————. *The Morality of Law* (1964). New Haven: Yale University Press, 1969.

Gahl, R. A., Jr. *Practical Reason in the Foundation of Natural Law according to Germain Grisez, John Finnis and Joseph Boyle, Jr.* Doctoral dissertation directed by Prof. Gabriel Chalmeta, Roman Athenaeum of the Holy Cross. Rome: Faculty of Philosophy, 1991.

————. "From the Virtue of a Fragile Good to a Narrative Account of Natural Law." *International Philosophical Quarterly*, 37, 4 (1997).

García-Huidobro, J. *Razón práctica y derecho natural. El iusnaturalismo de Tomás de Aquino*. Valparaíso: EDEVAL, 1993.

Garcia, J. L. A. "'*Deus sive Natura*': Must Natural Lawyers Choose?" In R. P. George, ed., *Natural Law, Liberalism, and Morality: Contemporary Essays*. Oxford: Clarendon Press, 1996.

Garcia López, J. *Nuestra sabiduria racional de Dios*. Madrid: Institution 'San José de Calasanz' de Pedagogía, 1950.

Garrigou-Lagrange, O.P., *God: His Existene and His Nature*. St. Louis, MO.: B. Herder Book & Co., 1934.

Geach, P. *The Virtues*. Cambridge: CUP, 1977.

Gelinas, E. T. "'*Ius*' and '*Lex*' in Thomas Aquinas." *The American Journal of Jurisprudence*, 15 (1970).

George, R. P., "Recent Criticism of Natural Law Theory." *University of Chicago Law Review*, 55 (1988).

————. "Human Flourishing as a Criterion of Morality: A Critique of Perry's Naturalism." *Tulane Law Review*, 63 (1989).

————. "Individual Rights, Collective Interests, Public Law, and American Politics." *Law and Philosophy*, 8 (1989).

————. Ed., *Natural Law Theory: Contemporary Essays*. Oxford: Oxford University Press, 1992.

————. *Making Men Moral: Civil Liberties and Public Morality*. Oxford: Oxford University Press, 1993.

————. Ed., *The Autonomy of Law: Essays on Legal Positivism*. Oxford: Oxford University Press, 1995.

————. Ed., *Natural Law, Liberalism, and Morality: Contemporary Essays*. Oxford: Clarendon Press, 1996.

————. *In Defense of Natural Law*. Oxford: Clarendon Press, 1999.

Gewirth, A. "Can Any Final Ends Be Rational?" *Ethics*, 1 (1991).

Gilson, E. *God and Philosophy*. New Haven: Yale University Press, 1941.

————. *Le philosophe et la théologie*. Paris: Librairie Arthème Fayard, 1960.

————. *Christian Philosophy: An Introduction*. Trans. Armand Maurer. Toronto: Pontifical Institute of Mediaeval Studies, 1993. [*Introduction à la philosophie chrétienne*. Paris: Librairie philosophique J. Vrin, 1960].

————. *Elements of Christian Philosophy*. New York: Doubleday & Company, 1960.

Goldsworthy, J. D. "God or Mackie: The Dilemma of Secular Moral Philosophy." *American Journal of Jurisprudence*, 30 (1985).

Gonzalez, A. L. *Teología natural.* Pampona: Ediciones Universidad de Navarra, S.A., 1982.

Gormally, L., ed. *Moral Truth and Moral Tradition: Essays in Honor of Peter Geach and Elizabeth Anscombe*. Dublin: Four Courts, 1994.

Grasso, K. L., G. V. Bradley, and R. P. Hunt, eds. *Catholicism, Liberalism and Communitarianism: The Catholic Tradition and the Moral Foundations of Democracy*. Maryland: Rowman & Littlefield Publishers, 1995.

Grisez, G. "Kant and Aquinas: Ethical Theory." *Thomist*, 21 (1958).

————. "The Logic of Moral Judgment." *Proceedings of the American Catholic Philosophical Association*, 36 (1962).

————. "Sketch of a Future Metaphysics." *The New Scholasticism*, 38 (1964).

————. *Contraception and the Natural Law*. Milwaukee: The Bruce Publishing Company, 1964.

————. "The First Principle of Practical Reason: A Commentary on the Summa theologiae, 1–2, Question 94, Article 2." *Natural Law Forum*, 10 (1965).

————. "A New Formulation of Natural Law against Contraception." *Thomist* 30 (1966).

————. "Methods of Ethical Inquiry." *Proceedings of the American Catholic Philosophical Association*, 41 (1967).

————. "Man, Natural End of." In *New Catholic Encyclopedia*. New York: McGraw-Hill, 1967.

————. *Abortion: The Myths, the Realities, and the Arguments*. New York: Corpus Book, 1970.

————. "Toward a Consistent Natural-Law Ethics of Killing." *The American Journal of Jurisprudence*, 15 (1970).

————. "Choice and Consequentialism." *Proceedings of the American Catholic Philosophical Association* 51 (1977).

————. Grisez and R. Shaw. *Beyond the New Morality. The Responsibilities of Freedom* (1974). 3rd Revised Edition. Notre Dame: University of Notre Dame Press, 1988.

————. *Beyond the New Theism. A Philosophy of Religion*. Notre Dame: University of Notre Dame Press, 1975.

————. "Against Consequentialism." *American Journal of Jurisprudence*, 23 (1978).

————. Grisez and J. Boyle. *Life and Death with Liberty and Justice*. Notre Dame: University of Notre Dame Press, 1979.

———. *The Way of the Lord Jesus. Volume One: Christian Moral Principles*. Chicago: Franciscan Herald Press, 1983.

———. "Practical Reasoning and Christian Faith." *Proceedings of the American Catholic Philosophical Association*, 58 (1984).

———. "Moral Absolutes: A Critique of the View of Josef Fuchs, S.J." *Anthropotes*, 2 (1985).

———. "The Structures of Practical Reason: Some Comments and Clarifications." *Thomist*, 52 (1988).

———. Grisez and R. Shaw. *Fulfillment in Christ: A Summary of Christian Moral Principles*. Notre Dame: University of Notre Dame Press, 1991.

———. *The Way of the Lord Jesus. Volume Two: Living a Christian Life*. Quincy, Illinois: Franciscan Press, 1993.

Grison, M. *Corso di filosofia tomista, VI: Teologia naturale o teodicea.* Brescia: Paideia, 1967.

Grotius, H. *Prolegomenti al diritto della Guerra e della pace (1625).* Trans. G. Fassò. Naples: Morano, 1979 [*De iure belli ac pacis* (1625), Prolegomena]

Guastini, R. "Diritti." In P. Comanducci and R. Guastini, eds., *Analisi e diritto: Ricerche di giurisprudenza analitica*. Torino: Giappichelli, 1994.

Guerra, M. *Storia delle religioni*. Brescia: La Scuola, 1989.

Haldane, J. "Analytical Thomism." In *Oxford Companion to Philosophy.* Oxford: Oxford University Press, 1995.

———. "Analytical Thomism: A Brief Introduction." *The Monist*, 4 (1997).

———. "Tomismo analitico." *Il Sole-24 Ore* (2 August 1998).

Hall, P. M. *Narrative and the Natural Law: An Interpretation of Thomistic Ethics*. Notre Dame and London: University of Notre Dame Press, 1994.

Hare, R. M. *The Language of Morals*. Oxford: Oxford University Press, 1954.

Hart, H. L. A. "Are There any Natural Rights?" *The Philosophical Review*, 64 (1955).

———. "Positivism and the Separation of Law and Morals." *Harvard Law Review*, 71 (1958).

———. *The Concept of Law*. Oxford: Clarendon Press, 1961.

———. *Law, Liberty and Morality*. London: Oxford University Press, 1963.

————. Introduction to J. Austin, *The Province of Jurisprudence Determined and the Uses of the Study of Jurisprudence*. London: Weidenfeld and Nicolson, 1971.

Hervada, J. *Introduzione critica al diritto naturale*. Milan: Giuffrè, 1990 [*Introducción crítica al Derecho Natural*. Pamplona: Ediciones Universidad de Navarra, S.A., 1981].

Hibbs T. "Divine Irony and the Natural Law: Speculation and Edification in Aquinas." *International Philosophical Quarterly*, 30 (1990).

Higgins, T. J. *Man as Man: The Science and Art of Ethics*. Revised Edition. Milwaukee: The Bruce Publishing Co., 1958.

Hittinger, R. *A Critique of the New Natural Law Theory*. Notre Dame: University of Notre Dame Press, 1987.

————. "After MacIntyre: Natural Law Theory, Virtue Ethics, and Eudaimonia." *International Philosophical Quarterly*, 29 (1989).

————. "Varieties of Minimalist Natural Law Theory." *The American Journal of Jurisprudence*, 34 (1989).

————. "Natural Law and Virtue: Theories at Cross Purposes." In R. P. George, ed., *Natural Law Theory: Contemporary Essays*. Oxford: Oxford University Press, 1992.

————. "Natural Law as 'Law.' Reflections on the Occasion of 'Veritatis Splendor'." *The American Journal of Jurisprudence*, 39 (1994).

Jaffa, H. V. *Thomism and Aristotelianism*. Chicago: University of Chicago Press, 1952.

Johnstone, B. V. "The Structures of Practical Reason: Traditional Theories and Contemporary Questions." *Thomist*, 50 (1986).

Jolivet, R. *Trattato di filosofia*, V, *Morale*. Brescia: Morcelliana, 1959.

John Paul II. *Catechism of the Catholic Church*. Dublin: Veritas, 1995.

————. *Veritatis Splendor* (1993) (encyclical letter on the foundations of moral philosophy and moral theology). Vatican Translation. Boston, MA: Pauline Books & Media, 1993.

————. *Crossing the Threshold of Hope*. Trans. Jenny McPhee and Martha McPhee. New York: Alfred A. Knopf, 1994.

————. *Tertio Millennio Adveniente* (Apostolic letter). Vatican Translation. Boston, MA: Pauline Books & Media, 1994.

————. *Evangelium Vitae* (1995) (encyclical letter on the value and inviolability of human life). Vatican Translation. Boston, MA: Pauline Books & Media, 1995.

———. *Fides et Ratio* (encyclical letter on the relationship between faith and reason). Vatican Translation. Boston, MA: Pauline Books & Media, 1998.

Jonas, H. *Il principio responsabilità*. Ed. P.P. Portinaro. Turin: Einaudi, 1990 [*Das Prinzip Verantwortung*. Frankfurt and Main: Insel Verlag, 1979].

Jori, M., ed. *Ermeneutica e filosofia analitica: Due concezioni del diritto a confronto*. Turin: Giappichelli, 1994.

Kelsen, H. "Foundation of the Natural Law Doctrine." *Anglo-American Law Review*, 2 (1973).

Kretzmann, N. "*Lex Iniusta non Est Lex*: Laws On Trial in Aquinas' Court of Conscience." *American Journal of Jurisprudence*, 33 (1988).

Leclercq, J. "Suggestions for Clarifying Natural Law." *Natural Law Forum*, 2 (1957).

———. "Natural Law the Unknown." *Natural Law Forum*, 7 (1962).

Lee, P. "Permanence of the Ten Commandments: St. Thomas and His Modern Commentators." *Theol. St.*, 42 (1981).

Lisska A. J. *Aquinas's Theory of Natural Law. An Analytic Reconstruction*. Oxford: Clarendon Press, 1996.

Livi, A. *Il punto di partenza della filosofia secondo Gilson*. Rome: Pontificia Università Lateranense, 1960.

———. *Filosofia del senso comune*. Milan: Edizioni Ares, 1990.

———. *Tommaso d'Aquino: Il futuro del pensiero cristiano*. Milan: Mondadori, 1997.

Lottin, O. *Psychologie et morale aux XII et XIII siècles*, II. Louvain-Gembloux: Abbaye du Mont César-J. Duculot Éditeur, 1948.

Lucas Lucas, R. *L'uomo spirito incarnato: Compendio di filosofia dell'uomo*. Milan: Edizioni Paoline, 1993.

Luño, A. R. *Etica*. Florence: Le Monnier, 1992 [*Etica general*. Pamplona: Ediciones Universidad de Navarra, S.A., 1991].

MacCormick, N. "Natural Law Reconsidered." In *Oxford Journal of Legal Studies*, 1 (1981).

———. "Natural Law and the Separation of Law and Morals." In R. P. George, ed., *Natural Law Theory. Contemporary Essays*. Oxford: Oxford University Press, 1992.

———. "The Ideal and the Actual of Law and Society." In J. Tasioulas, ed., *Law, Values and Social Practices*. Aldershot: Dartmouth Publishing Co., 1997.

Macedo, S. *Against the Old Sexual Morality of the New Natural Law Theory*. In R. P. George, ed., *Natural Law, Liberalism, and Morality: Contemporary Essays*. Oxford: Clarendon Press, 1996.

Machan, T.R. "A Reconsideration of Natural Rights Theory." *American Philosophical Quarterly*, 1 (1982).

MacIntyre, A. *After Virtue. A Study in Moral Theory*. Notre Dame: University of Notre Dame Press, 1981.

————. *Whose Justice? Which Rationality?* Notre Dame: University of Notre Dame Press, 1988.

————. *Three Rival Versions of Moral Enquiry (Encyclopaedia, Genealogy and Tradition)*. Notre Dame: University of Notre Dame Press, 1990.

————. "Moral Dilemmas." *Philosophy and Phenomenological Research*, 50 (1990).

————. "Moral Relativism, Truth and Justification." In L. Gormally, ed., *Moral Truth and Moral Tradition: Essays in Honor of Peter Geach and Elizabeth Anscombe*. Dublin: Four Courts, 1994.

Mackie, J. L. *Ethics: Inventing Right and Wrong*. London: Penguin, 1977.

————. "Rights, Utility, and Universalization." In R.G. Frey, ed., *Utility and Rights*. Oxford: Basil Blackwell, 1985.

Maritain, J. *Distinguish to Unite: The Degrees of Knowledge*. Trans. Gerald B. Phelan. Notre Dame: University of Notre Dame Press, 1995. [*Distinguer pour unir: ou les degrés du savoir*. Paris: Desclée de Brouwer, 1932–59].

————. *Sept leçons sur l'être et les premiers principes de la raison speculative*. Paris: Téqui, 1934.

————. *Les droits de l'homme et la loi naturelle*. New York: Editions de la Maison Française, 1942.

————. *Court traité de l'existence et de l'existant*. Paris: Hartmann, 1947.

————. *Nove lezioni sulla legge naturale*. Ed. F. Viola. Milan: Jaca Book, 1985 [The Italian edition was published before the original French edition, *Neuf leçons sur la loi naturelle* (1950)].

————. *Approches de Dieu*. In J. Maritain, *Ateismo e ricerca di Dio*, trans. M. Barattini. Paris: Alsace, 1953.

————. *Quattre essais sur l'esprit dans sa condition charnelle*. Paris: Desclée de Brouwer, 1956.

Martin, C. "Virtues, Motivation and the End of Life." In L. Gormally, ed., *Moral Truth and Moral Tradition: Essays in Honor of Peter Geach and Elizabeth Anscombe*. Dublin: Four Courts, 1994.

May, W. E., ed. *Principles of Catholic Moral Life*. Chicago: Franciscan Herald Press, 1981.

———. "Aquinas and Janssens on the Moral Meaning of Human Acts." *The Thomist*, 48 (1984).

McCormick, R. A. *Notes on Moral Theology 1965 through 1980*. Washington DC: University Press of America, 1981.

———. *Notes on Moral Theology: 1981–1984*. Lanham, Md.: University Press of America, 1985.

McInerny, R. "The Principles of Natural Law." *The American Journal of Jurisprudence*, 25 (1980).

———. *Ethica Thomistica*. Notre Dame: University of Notre Dame Press, 1982.

———. *Aquinas and Analogy*. Washington, D.C.: The Catholic University of America Press, 1996.

———. "Grisez and Thomism." In N. Biggar-R. Black, eds., *The Revival of Natural Law*. Aldershot: Ashgate, 2000.

McKim, R. and P. Simpson. "On the Alleged Incoherence of Consequentialism." *New Scholasticism*, 62 (1988).

Mead, M. "Some Anthropological Considerations Concerning Natural Law." *Natural Law Forum*, 6 (1961).

Melina, L. *Morale: tra crisi e rinnovamento*. Milan: Edizioni Ares, 1993.

Modica, G. *Fede libertà peccato: Figure ed esiti della 'prova' in Kierkegaard*. Palermo: Palumbo, 1992.

Molina, E. *La moral entre la convicción y la utilidad: La evolución de la moral desde la manualística al proporcionalismo y al pensamiento de Grisez-Finnis*. Pamplona: Ediciones Eunate, Servicio de Publicaciones de la Universidad de Navarra, 1996.

Mondin, B. *Il sistema filosofico di Tommaso d'Aquino:. Per una lettura attuale della filosofia tomista*. 2nd Revised Edition. Milan: Massimo, 1992.

Moore, M. S. "Causation and the Excuses." *California Law Review*, 4 (1985).

———. "Law as a Functional Kind." In R. P. George, ed., *Natural Law Theory: Contemporary Essays*. Oxford: Oxford University Press, 1992.

————. "Good without God." In R. P. George, ed., *Natural Law, Liberalism, and Morality: Contemporary Essays*. Oxford: Clarendon Press, 1996.

Nagel, E. "On the Fusion of Fact and Value: A Reply to Professor Fuller." *Natural Law Forum*, 3 (1958).

————. "Fact, Value, and Human Purpose." *Natural Law Forum*, 4 (1959).

Nelson, D. M. *The Priority of Prudence: Virtue and Natural Law in Thomas Aquinas and the Implications for Modern Ethics*. University Park, Pa.: Pennsylvania State University Press, 1992.

Nielsen, K. "The Myth of Natural Law." In S. Hook, ed., *Law and Philosophy*. New York: New York University Press, 1958.

————. "An Examination of the Thomistic Theory of Natural Moral Law." *Natural Law Forum*, 4 (1959).

Noonan, J. T., Jr. "Indissolubility of Marriage and Natural Law." *The American Journal of Jurisprudence*, 14 (1969).

Nozick, R. *Anarchy, State, and Utopia*. New York: Basic Books, 1974.

Nussbaum, M. *The Fragility of Goodness: Luck and Ethics in Greek Tragedy and Philosophy*. New York: Cambridge University Press, 1986.

————. *Love's Knowledge*. Oxford: Oxford University Press, 1990.

O'Connor, D. J. *Aquinas and Natural Law*. London: Macmillan, 1967.

Owen H. P. *The Moral Argument for Christian Theism*. London: Allen and Unwin, 1965.

(St.) Paul, *Letter to the Romans*.

Perry, M. J. "Some Notes on Absolutism, Consequentialism, and Incommensurability." *North Western University Law Review*, 79 (1985).

Pinckaers, S. *The Sources of Christian Morality* (1985). Trans. Sr. Mary Thomas Noble, O.P. Washington, D.C.: Catholic University of America Press, 1995. [*Les sources de la morale chrétienne (Sa méthode, son contenu, son histoire)*. Fribourg: Editions Universitaires Fribourg Suisse, 1985.

Plato. *Tutti gli scritti [Collected Works]*. Ed. G. Reale. Milan: Rusconi, 1991.

Plattel, M. G. "Personal Response and the Natural Law." *Natural Law Forum*, 7 (1962).

Polo L. *Quien es el hombre*. Madrid: Ediciones Rialp, 1991.

Porter, J. "Basic Goods and the Human Good in Recent Catholic Moral Theology." *The Thomist*, 47 (1993).

Possenti, V. *La buona società: Sulla ricostruzione della filosofia politica*. Milan: Vita e Pensiero, 1983.

———. *Terza navigazione. Nichilismo e metafisica*. Rome: Armando Editore, 1998.

Pound, R. "Natural Natural Law and Positive Natural Law." *Natural Law Forum*, 5 (1960).

Putnam, H., "Thoughts Addressed to an Analytical Thomist." *The Monist*, 4 (1997).

Rawls, J. *A Theory of Justice*. Cambridge, MA: The Belknap Press of Harvard University Press, 1971.

Raz, J. *Practical Reason and Norms*. London: Hutchinson, 1975.

———. "The Obligation to Obey: Revision and Tradition." *Notre Dame Journal of Law, Ethics and Public Policy*, 1 (1984).

———. *The Morality of Freedom*. Oxford: Clarendon Press, 1986.

Recasens S. L. *La filosofia del Derecho de Francisco Suárez*. México: Editorial Jus, 1947.

Rescher, N. *The Coherence Theory of Truth*. Oxford: Oxford University Press, 1973.

Rhonheimer, M. *La prospettiva della morale: Fondamenti dell'etica filosofica*. Trans. A. Jappe. Rome: Armando Editore, 1994 [Original manuscript: *Die Perspektive der Moral: Grundlagen der philosophischen Ethik*].

Ricoeur, P., *Oneself as Another*. Trans. Kathleen Blamey. Chicago: University of Chicago Press, 1992.

Robinson, D.N. "Lloyd Weinreb's Problems with Natural Law." In R. P. George, ed., *Natural Law, Liberalism, and Morality: Contemporary Essays*. Oxford: Clarendon Press, 1996.

Rommen, H. *Die Staatslehre des F. Suárez*. München: M. Gladbach, 1926.

———. "Natural Law in Decisions of the Federal Supreme Court and of the Constitutional Courts in Germany." *Natural Law Forum*, 4 (1959).

———. *The Natural Law. A Study in Legal and Social History and Philosophy*. Trans. T. R. Hanley. St. Louis: Herder Book, 1947. [*Die ewige Wiederkehr des Naturrechts*. Munich: Kösel, 1936].

Rousseau, J.-J. *On the Social Contract*. Trans. D.A. Cress. Indianapolis: Hackett, 1987.

Sandel, M. J. *Liberalism and the Limits of Justice*. Cambridge: Cambridge University Press, 1982.

Sanguineti, J. J. *Lógica*. Pamplona: Ediciones Universidad de Navarra, S.A., 1984.

Schiavello, A. *Diritto come integrità: incubo o nobile sogno? Saggio su Ronald Dworkin*. Turin: Giappichelli, 1998.

Schmaus, M. *Dogmatica cattolica. Volume I (Introduzione-Dio-Creazione)*. Turin: Marietti, 1959.

Selznick, P. "Sociology and Natural Law." *Natural Law Forum*, 6 (1961).

Sertillanges, A.-D. *La philosophie des lois*. Paris: Éditions Alsatia, 1946.

Shanley, B. J. "Analytical Thomism." *The Thomist*, 1 (1999).

Shellens, S. M. "Aristotle on Natural Law." *Natural Law Forum*, 4 (1959).

Silving, H. "Positive Natural Law." *Natural Law Forum*, 3 (1958).

Simmonds, N. E. *Central Issues in Jurisprudence: Justice, Law and Rights*. London: Sweet & Maxwell, 1986.

Simon, Y. *The Tradition of Natural Law: A Philosopher's Reflections*. New York: Fordham University Press, 1965.

Simonds, R. T. "The 'Natural Law' Controversy: Three Basic Logical Issues." *Natural Law Forum*, 5 (1960).

Spaemann, R. *Basic Moral Concepts*. Trans. T. J. Armstrong. London and New York: Routledge, 1989. [*Moralische Grundbegriffe*. Munich: 1986].

————. "Christian Ethics of Responsibility." In L. Gormally, ed., *Moral Truth and Moral Tradition: Essays in Honor of Peter Geach and Elizabeth Anscombe*. Dublin: Four Courts, 1994.

Stout, J. "Truth, Natural Law, and Ethical Theory." In R. P. George, ed., *Natural Law Theory: Contemporary Essays*. Oxford: Oxford University Press, 1992.

Strauss, L. *Natural Right and History*. Chicago and London: The University of Chicago Press, 1953.

Suárez, F. *De bonitate et malitia actuum humanorum* (1582). In F. Suarez, *Opera Omnia*. Vol. IV. Ed. D.M. André. Paris: Bibliopolam, 1856.

————. *Tractatus De Legibus ac Deo Legislatore* (1612). Madrid: C.S.I.C., 1974. [for the English translation see James Brown].

Suñer, P. "Teocentrismo de la ley natural." In F. Suárez, *De Legibus*. Vol. III. Madrid: C.S.I.C., 1974, pp. XXXVIII-LV.

Taliaferro, C. "God's Natural Laws." In R. P. George, ed., *Natural Law, Liberalism, and Morality: Contemporary Essays*. Oxford: Clarendon Press, 1996.

Taylor, C. *The Malaise of Modernity*. Concord (Ont.): Anansi, 1991.

Theron, S., "The Resistance of Thomism to Analytical and Other Patronage." *The Monist*, 4 (1997).

Thomas Aquinas. *Scriptum in quattuor libros Sententiarum magistri Petri Lombardi* (1254–56).

————. *Truth*, vol. 3, Questions XXI–XXIX (1256–59). Translated from the definitive Leonine text (*Quaestiones Disputatae de Veritate*) by Robert W. Schmidt, S.J. Chicago: Henry Regnery Company, 1954. [*Le questioni disputate. La verità*. Critical Edition. Ed. P. R. Coggi O.P. Bologna: ESD, 1992–93].

————. *Summa Contra Gentiles* (1259–64). Trans. A. C. Pegis (Book I), James F. Anderson (Books II and III), and C. J. O'Neill (Book IV. Notre Dame and London: University of Notre Dame Press, 1956. [*Somma contro i gentili*. Translation, introduction, and comments by T.S. Centi. Turin: Utet, 1975].

————. *Liber de Veritate Catholicae Fidei contra errores Infidelium seu Summa contra Gentiles*. Rome: Marietti, 1961.

————. *Quaestiones Quodlibetales* (1256–73). Ed. R. M. Spiazzi O.P. Rome: Marietti, 1949.

————. *On the Power of God* (1265–67). Translated by the English Dominican Fathers. Westminster, Maryland: The Newman Press, 1952. [*Quaestio disputata De Potentia*] [For qq. I–VII, cf. *La potenza di Dio*. Trans. A. Campodonico. Florence: Nordini Editore, 1991].

————. *Summa Theologiae* (1266–73). Translated by the Fathers of the English Dominical Province. [*La Somma teologica*. Critical Edition. Translated and commented by the Domenicani italiani. Florence: Salani, 1967].

————. *Expositio in Evangelium sancti Ioannis* (1269–72). In Tommaso d'Aquino, *Catena Aurea in Quattuor Evangelia*, ed. A. Guarienti O.P. Rome: Marietti, 1953.

————. *In libros Politicorum Aristotelis expositio* (1269–72). Ed. R.M. Spiazzi O.P. Rome: Marietti, 1951.

————. *In decem libros Ethicorum Aristotelis ad Nicomachum expositio* (1271–72). Ed. R.M. Spiazzi O.P. Rome: Marietti, 1949.

————. *Compendium Theologiae ad fratrem Reginaldum socium suum carissimum* (1272–73). In Tommaso d'Aquino, *Opuscola Theologica*, ed. R. A. Verardo O.P. Rome: Marietti, 1954.

Toddington, S. *Rationality, Social Action and Moral Judgment*. Edinburgh: Edinburgh University Press, 1993.

————. "Method, Morality and the Impossibility of Legal Positivism." *Ratio Juris*, 9 (1996).

Tribe, L. H. "Constitutional Calculus: Equal Justice or Economic Efficiency?" *Harvard Law Review*, 3 (1985).

Triolo, L. *Primato del diritto e giustizia: Diritti fondamentali e Costituzione*. Turin: Giappichelli, 1996.

Utz, A. "The Principle of Subsidiarity and Contemporary Natural Law." *Natural Law Forum*, 3 (1958).

Vanni, Rovighi S. *Uomo e natura: Appunti per una antropologia filosofica*. Milan: Vita e Pensiero, 1980.

Vazquez, G. *Commentarium* on the *Summa theologiae*. 1598–1615.

Veatch, H. B. "The Defense of Natural Law in the Context of Contemporary Analytic Philosophy." *The American Journal of Jurisprudence*, 14 (1969).

————. *For an Ontology of Morals*. Evanston, IL: Northwestern University Press, 1971.

————. *Swimming Against the Current in Contemporary Philosophy*. Washington, D.C.: The Catholic University of America Press, 1981.

————. "Natural Law and the 'Is'–'Ought' Question: Queries to Finnis and Grisez." In *Swimming Against the Current in Contemporary Philosophy*. Washington, D.C.: The Catholic University of America Press, 1981.

————. *Human Rights: Fact or Fancy?* Baton Rouge, L.: Louisiana State University Press, 1985.

————. Veatch and J. Rautenberg. "Does the Grisez-Finnis-Boyle Moral Philosophy Rest on a Mistake?" *Review of Metaphysics*, 44 (1991).

Villa, V. *Conoscenza giuridica e concetto di diritto positivo*. Turin: Giappichelli, 1993.

Villey, M. *La Formazione del pensiero giuridico moderno*. Trans. R. D'Ettore and F. D'Agostino. Milan: Jaca Book, 1986 [*La Formation de la Pensée Juridique Moderne*. Paris: Monchrestien, 1968].

Viola, F. and M. Urso. *Scienza giuridica e diritto codificato*. Turin: Giappichelli, 1989.

————. "La critica dell'ermeneutica alla filosofia analitica italiana del diritto." In M. Jori, ed., *Ermeneutica e filosofia analitica: Due concezioni del diritto a confronto*. Turin: Giappichelli, 1994.

————. *Dalla natura ai diritti: I luoghi dell'etica contemporanea*. Bari: Laterza, 1997.

Walter, J. J. "Response to John Finnis: A Theological Critique." In T. G. Fuechtmann, ed., *Consistent Ethic of Life*. Kansas City: Sheed & Ward, 1988.

Weinreb, L. L. *Natural Law and Justice*. Harvard: Harvard University Press, 1987.

————. "Natural Law and Rights." In R. P. George, ed., *Natural Law Theory: Contemporary Essays*. Oxford: Oxford University Press, 1992.

————. "The Moral Point of View." In R. P. George, ed., *Natural Law, Liberalism, and Morality: Contemporary Essays*. Oxford: Clarendon Press, 1996.

Wojtyla, K. *The Acting Person*. Boston: D. Reidel Pub. Co., 1979.

————. *Love and Responsibility*. Revised Edition. Trans. H. T. Willetts. New York: Farrar, Straus, Giroux, 1981.

Zaccaria, G. "Tra ermeneutica ed analitica: dal contrasto alla collaborazione." In M. Jori, ed., *Ermeneutica e filosofia analitica: Due concezioni del diritto a confronto*. Turin: Giappichelli, 1994.

Zanetti, G. "John M. Finnis e la nuova dottrina del diritto naturale" (1999). In G. Zanetti, ed., *Filosofi del diritto contemporanei*. Milan: Raffaello Cortina Editore, 1999.

Index